CONSUMING GRIEF

CONSUMING
GRIEF

COMPASSIONATE
CANNIBALISM
IN AN
AMAZONIAN
SOCIETY

UNIVERSITY OF TEXAS PRESS, AUSTIN

BETH A. CONKLIN

Twelfth paperback printing, 2019

Requests for permission to reproduce material from
this work should be sent to:
    Permissions
    University of Texas Press
    P.O. Box 7819
    Austin, TX 78713-7819
    utpress.utexas.edu/rp-form

♾ The paper used in this book meets the minimum
requirements of ANSI/NISO Z39.48-1992 (R1997)
(Permanence of Paper).

Library of Congress
Cataloging-in-Publication Data

Conklin, Beth A.
Consuming grief : compassionate cannibalism in an
Amazonian society / Beth A. Conklin.—1st ed.
    p. cm.
Includes bibliographical references and index.
ISBN 978-0-292-71236-2 (pbk. : alk. paper)
    1. Pakaasnovos Indians—Funeral customs and
rites. 2. Cannibalism—Brazil. I. Title.
F2520.1.P32 C56 2001
394.9'089'9839—dc21   00-047976

doi:10.7560/712324

*In memory of
my brother Jim (1961–1989),
and for our parents.*

CONTENTS

ACKNOWLEDGMENTS

My research among the Wari' of Rondônia, Brazil, has been supported by grants and fellowships from the Fulbright Commission, the Inter-American Foundation, the Wenner-Gren Foundation for Anthropological Research, the Tinker Foundation, and the Robert Penn Warren Center for the Humanities at Vanderbilt University. A Charlotte W. Newcombe Fellowship from the Woodrow Wilson Foundation supported dissertation writing, and a Vanderbilt University Research Council grant provided assistance while writing part of this book. I am grateful to all these institutions for their generosity in making this work possible.

The initial field research on which this study is based was carried out in 1985–1987, under the sponsorship of Julio César Melatti of the Universidade de Brasília, who provided invaluable assistance in facilitating authorization of my research by the Conselho Nacional de Desenvolvimento Científico e Tecnológico (CNPq) and the Fundação Nacional do Indio (FUNAI). Luis Carlos Pannunzio of CNPq and Ezequias Herrera Filho, Olga Novion, Delvair Melatti, and Luis Otávio of FUNAI, Brasília, helped get my research under way. Conceição Militão at FUNAI's Brasília archives and the staffs of the Conselho Indigenista Missionário (CIMI) and the Museu do Indio in Rio graciously facilitated access to archival materials.

Anthropology in Brazil flourishes in a dynamic community of scholars doing some of the most stimulating work in the discipline today. In the evolving conversations about native Amazonian ways of living and dying, my thinking owes special debts to the work of Bruce Albert, Manuela Carneiro da Cunha, Carlos Fausto, Philippe Descola, Peter Gow, Christine Hugh-Jones, Stephen Hugh-Jones, Joana Overing, Anne-Christine Taylor,

Terence Turner, and Eduardo Viveiros de Castro. I thank Carlos Coimbra Jr., the late Denise Maldi Meireles, Martin Ibañes-Novion, Carmen Junqueira, Betty Mindlin, Ari Teixeira Ott, Alcida Ramos, Aryon Rodrigues, and Ricardo Santos for the many forms of intellectual guidance, advice, and assistance they have shared with me during my work in Brazil. Márcio da Silva has my eternal gratitude for his suggestion to study the Wari', for the language materials he provided, and for a memorable *carnaval*.

In Rondônia, Dídimo Graciliano de Oliveira, the longtime director of FUNAI's regional administration based in Guajará-Mirim, has been unfailingly supportive and helpful. The success of my work and the ongoing efforts to ensure the well-being of the Wari' owe much to his dedication. My warm appreciation goes also to Aldo Pituaka and Lúcia Carneiro, directors of nursing and health services at the Casa do Indio clinic, for their insights, aid, and friendship, and for their many years of service to improve Wari' health conditions. Many others who have worked with the Wari' also provided invaluable assistance and companionship: Gilles de Catheu, the late Pascoal Ferreira Dias, Geniltan "Gaúcho" Pivoto, Francisca Fernandes, Francisco das Chagas Araújo, Maria D'Ouro, Edineia T. Mota, Edna da Silva Gonçalves, Valdir de Jesus Gonçalves, Anunciada Ferreira de Lima, Noemi Bormann, Maria Oro Nao', Francisco Peixoto da Silva, Juscileth (Preta) Pessoa, and Marivaldo Abreu. I am grateful to the New Tribes missionaries Barbara and Manfred Kern and Royal and Joan Taylor for sharing insights and recollections from their many years of work among the Wari', and for their many kindnesses in moments of need. I also thank Dona Seila, Basílio, Carmelita, Abílio, Ester, and Nidy; and Claudeliz, for the antibiotics that allowed me to stay in the field at a critical time in my research.

Many people have contributed to the development of the work on which this study is based. My interest in lowland South America's native peoples blossomed under the guidance of Brent Berlin at the University of California at Berkeley and Frederick Dunn at the University of California at San Francisco. Patricia Lyon has been a most faithful and attentive reader of my work. Together with her co-conspirator, Ken Kensinger, she has fostered an ethos of generosity and collegiality that has welcomed successive generations of ethnographers into the family of South Americanist scholars. For influential conversations and comments about ideas in this book and ethnographic writing, I thank Debbora Battaglia, William Crocker, Gertrude Dole, Laura Graham, Catherine Howard, Thomas Gregor, Waud Kracke, Lynn Morgan, Donald Pollock, Edward Schieffelin, Marilyn Strathern, and James Trostle. Any errors or omissions are, of course, my own.

A fortunate event during my second year among the Wari' was the arrival of Aparecida Vilaça, an ethnographer from the Museu Nacional who began a long-term study based in the Wari' community of Rio Negro-Ocaia. Her positive spirit and sense of irony sustained us through good times and difficulties. The questions and insights she has brought to studying the Wari' have enriched my understandings, and the many kindnesses she and her family have extended have made my time in Brazil more pleasant and meaningful. As *comadres,* godmothers to each other's sons, our lives have become linked in more than one way, and I am grateful for her company on the journeys that have unfolded since we met.

To the Wari' who have shared with me their knowledge, memories, and hospitality, I owe the greatest debt. I am especially appreciative to Pan' Kamerem, Duí, André, A'u, Nacom, Orowao Xiao, and Maxun Jam' of Ribeirão; Xowa, Timain, and Nawacan of Lage; Awo Pana, A'ain, and Jimain To of Tanajura; and Wan E', Paletó, Mamxun Wi', and Oron Cun of Rio Negro-Ocaia. My deepest thanks, affection, and *saudades* go to the people of Santo André, especially the older men and women who worked with me intensively on the issues addressed in this book: Maxun Kwarain, Manim, Oro Iram, Tocohwet Pijo', Tocorom Mip, Jimon Maram, Quimoin, Tocohwet, Nacom, Horcin Totoro', Torein, Diva, Rosa, Capitão, Horein Mowam, Jimain Wom, and Orowao Xok Waji. Jap and her husband, Pipira Suruí, shared their home with my husband and me, and the friendship of Maria, Elsa, Wem Xu, and Joana enlivened and enriched each day. In Jimon Maram and Quimoin, I found an elder brother and elder sister.

Most of the ethnographic information and ideas presented in this book have come from Wari' who saw themselves as my teachers and tried to enlighten me about their understandings. Wari' have expressed interest in being known as individuals and recognized for their knowledge. In deference to that desire, I have, like previous ethnographers who have written about the Wari', used some individual names when I was confident no harm would come to them from doing so. I hope Wari' will understand why I also have used pseudonyms and disguised identifying characteristics to protect identities in relation to more sensitive material. The individuals whose photographs appear here are among the most respected members of their communities; none were involved in any of the more controversial incidents described in the text. My hope is that, as outsiders learn more about the Wari' as individuals and as a society, this will contribute to greater public understanding of why it is so important to protect the future of the Wari' and other indigenous peoples, and what will be lost if we do not. To further that goal, any author's earnings from this book will go to the Wari' to further their goals for community development.

My parents, Dwight and Charlene Conklin, have contributed innumerable forms of help and encouragement for my work. My sister, Barbara, graciously managed my stateside affairs while I was in the field. Bob Pierson took a giant leap of faith in saying "yes" in a Portuguese-language wedding ceremony of which he understood not a word, and managed to maintain his good humor while starting married life under the curious eyes of an indigenous community. I thank him for his patience in enduring the insects, heat, illnesses, mounds of baggage, lack of privacy, and endless waiting, and for his companionship over the years.

* * *

Portions of Chapter 3 appeared in "Consuming Images: Representations of Cannibalism on the Amazonian Frontier," *Anthropological Quarterly* 70(2): 58–78 (1997), and part of Chapter 10 appeared in "Rainforest Magic," *The Colorado College Bulletin* December 1993: 22–25. The text also draws upon material from my articles "Thus Are Our Bodies, Thus Was Our Custom: Mortuary Cannibalism in an Amazonian Society," *American Ethnologist* 22 (1):75–101 (1995); "Babies, Bodies, and the Production of Personhood in North America and a Native Amazonian Society," *Ethos* 24(4):657–694 (1996), coauthored with Lynn M. Morgan; and "Visions of Death in Amazonian Lives" and "Hunting the Ancestors," *Latin American Anthropology Review* 5(2):55–56, 65–70 (1995). All are used with permission from the publisher and my coauthor.

All photographs are by the author. All translations from foreign language texts are by the author, unless otherwise noted.

About the Artist and Illustrations

The drawings reproduced in this book were made by Wem Quirió Oro Nao' of Posto Indígena Santo André, the eldest son of Jimon Maram Oro Nao' and Quimoin Oro Eo. Wem Quirió is one of the best-educated and most articulate younger Wari', and he increasingly is called upon to serve as a leader representing his community in dealings with the government and other outside agencies. In 1987, when Wem Quirió was twenty-two, he worked with me for a period of several weeks compiling a list of vocabulary items in the Wari' language. Toward the end of our work together, he asked whether I would like him to draw pictures of some things that were *iri' wari'*, "truly Wari'." I gave him the only drawing materials I had, typing paper and a set of felt-tipped pens in eight basic colors, and told him to draw whatever he chose. Among the sketches he produced were scenes of precontact funerals and the giving of gifts to a slain peccary, which appear in Chapters 4 and 10. In 1999, at my request, he redid some of his earlier pictures as line drawings in black ink to make them easier to reproduce in this book.

Wem Quirió was born in 1966 and never witnessed precontact funerals himself. He based his sketches on what he had heard older people describe. We showed his drawings to a number of older men and women who had participated in precontact funerals and asked for their feedback. Everyone who saw the sketches expressed enthusiastic approval, except for two details of body adornment that elders identified as inauthentic. Wari' had no clothing before the contact, but when Wem Quirió's mother saw his drawings, she told him she thought his drawings of male genitals were immodest. To please his mother, he added loincloths to some of the figures. Elders also criticized the fact that people in the scene with the slain peccary were shown wearing scarlet macaw feathers. Aside from this, everyone who saw the drawings agreed that they were good representations of scenes from the past. I thank Wem Quirió for his permission to reproduce his drawings here and hope that this will bring favorable recognition for his work and for the efforts he and others in the rising generation of younger Wari' have undertaken to look for new paths toward a future that will assure their people's well-being and cultural survival.

A Note on Orthography

The Wari' language has been studied by members of the New Tribes Mission (NTM) since the mid-1950s. The linguists Royal Taylor and Barbara Kern have done the most intensive work on the language and on translating books of the Bible and religious and educational materials. The first major study published on the Wari' language appeared in 1997, coauthored by Barbara Kern and Daniel Everett, a linguist and specialist in Amazonian language from the University of Pittsburgh and Summer Institute of Linguistics.

The orthography used in this book generally follows the NTM writing system, which some Wari' have learned to read and write. However, I deviate from the NTM orthography in representing the hard "k" sound. Whereas the NTM system uses "c" or "qu," I use "k." The exception is in individuals' proper names, for which I have retained the spellings with which Wari' themselves are familiar.

Pronunciation approximates the sounds of vowels in Spanish and consonants in Portuguese or Spanish, with the following exceptions:

c	Pronounced like the English *k* in *kit*.
h	Pronounced like the English *h* in *hot*.
j	Varies between a French *j* and the English *y* in *you*.
m	Varies between *b* and *m*.
qu	Pronounced like the English *k* in *kit*.
r	Pronounced as in English, with some variation toward *d*.
x	Varies between *ch* and *sh*.
w	Pronounced like the English *w* in *wind*.
'	Denotes a glottal stop, a quick cutoff of the preceding sound in the back of the throat.

All accents fall on the last syllable. There are dialectic variations in vocabulary and pronunciation among Wari' populations in various regions. In this book I generally follow the dialect that predominates in the community of Santo André.

INTRODUCTION

"I don't know if you can understand this, because you have never had a child die," Jimon Maram said quietly. "But for a parent, when your child dies, it's a sad thing to put his body in the earth."

His wife, Quimoin, turned away, bowing her head over the baby girl cuddled in her lap. Two years earlier, they had buried the child before this one, a two-year-old son.

"It's cold in the earth," Jimon continued, and Quimoin's shoulders trembled. "We keep remembering our child, lying there, cold. We remember, and we are sad." He leaned forward, searching my eyes as if to see whether I could comprehend what he was trying to explain. Then he concluded:

"It was better in the old days, when the others ate the body. Then we did not think about our child's body much. We did not remember our child as much, and we were not so sad."

Santo André village, 1987

"In the old days when the others ate the body . . ."

Jimon and Quimoin's people call themselves Wari' (pronounced wah-*REE*), though in western Brazil, where they live, most outsiders know them as the Pakaa Nova.[1] When Jimon and Quimoin were children in the 1950s and early 1960s, the Wari' still lived independent of Western civilization, and they disposed of the bodies of their dead as their ancestors had done, by eating the roasted flesh, certain internal organs, and sometimes the ground bones. This book examines how Wari' understood and experienced this kind of cannibalism and explores how this seemingly exotic practice reflects

1. Jimon Maram and Quimoin, with some of their grandchildren.

on broad human questions about love and loss, emotional attachments, and how people cope with death and bereavement.

Cannibalism used to be the normal treatment for all Wari' who died of any cause, except for a few circumstances in which bodies were cremated rather than eaten. In some funerals, especially funerals for children, all or most of the flesh was eaten. In funerals for adults and adolescents, often only part of the flesh was consumed (and the rest was burned), because the corpse was not roasted until two or three days of crying and eulogizing had passed, by which time it was nearly too decayed to stomach. Even then, Wari' still considered it important to consume at least some of the corpse. They did not eat their dead because they liked the taste of human flesh, nor because they needed the meat. Rather, they ate out of a sense of respect and compassion for the dead person and for the dead person's family.

The individuals who ate the corpse at a funeral—the "others" of whom Jimon Maram spoke—were mostly in-laws (affines) of the deceased. Except in certain exceptional cases, Wari' did not eat their own close blood relatives or spouses. The people they ate were individuals to whom they were not closely related by blood. The duty of eating the corpse at a funeral was a social obligation among affines, one of the reciprocal services owed to the families with whom one's own kin had intermarried.

At funerals, the people who ate the corpse did so at the insistence of the dead person's close relatives, who urged the others to eat. Wari' emphasize that they did not eat for self-gratification; indeed, the decayed state of many corpses could make cannibalism quite an unpleasant undertaking. Yet even when the flesh was so putrid that it made them nauseous, some individuals would still force themselves to swallow bits of it. To refuse to consume any of the corpse at all would have been seen as an insult to the dead person's family and to the memory of the deceased.

When Wari' talk about their former practice of funerary cannibalism, one of the recurring themes is that consuming the corpse pleased the dead person's spirit. Wari' wanted their own corpses to be eaten, or at least cremated.[2] For dying individuals, the idea of disappearing into fellow tribes-members' bodies apparently was considerably more appealing than the alternative of being left to rot in the ground. In the 1950s and '60s, when outsiders forced them to start burying their dead instead of eating them, Wari' were appalled.

* * *

The Wari' stopped practicing cannibalism after they were contacted by government-sponsored expeditions that set up base camps on the edges of Wari' territories with the goal of making contact with the Wari' and persuading them to accept peaceful relations with the national society. Various groups of Wari' entered contact in stages between 1956 and 1969, with the majority of the population entering contact in 1961–62. In each case, interactions with outsiders exposed Wari' to a devastating onslaught of infectious diseases against which they had acquired little or no immunological resistance. As one epidemic of malaria, influenza, measles, mumps, whooping cough, and other diseases followed another, hundreds of Wari' died. Within two or three years after the beginning of sustained contact, about 60 percent of the Wari' population—three out of every five people—were dead.

Constantly sick and traumatized by the sudden loss of so many of their relatives, those who survived the early postcontact epidemics were often too weak and demoralized to farm, hunt, fish, or care for their own sick family members. In order to get the food, antibiotics, and medical care they so desperately needed, they came to depend heavily on aid provided by Protestant missionaries, employees of the government Indian agency, and Catholic priests. Putting an end to cannibalism was a top priority for these outsiders, and they used a combination of persuasion and coercion to pressure Wari' to abandon the practice of eating their dead.

Many Wari' were deeply unhappy about being forced to give up cannibalism. Burial was a horrifying substitute, a practice they considered barbaric. Wari' think of the ground as cold, wet, and polluting. To leave a loved one's body to rot in the dirt was disrespectful and degrading to the dead and heart-wrenching for those who mourned them. Even today, decades after they stopped practicing cannibalism, many elderly Wari' (and even some middle-aged people like Jimon and Quimoin, who were too young to have taken part in eating the dead themselves) still find burial emotionally problematic. They look back upon the cannibalistic funeral practices of their past with a certain nostalgia for what they describe as a better, more loving and compassionate way to deal with death and bereavement.

The Question of Compassionate Cannibalism

Understanding this indigenous concept of compassionate cannibalism is the issue at the heart of this book. In focusing on it, I follow the themes that Wari' themselves emphasize when they explain why they used to eat their dead. Every Wari' elder living today took part in or witnessed cannibalistic funerals, not just once, but repeatedly. Even though they are aware that most outsiders see cannibalism as sin or savagery, most still speak openly about it.

When one asks older men and women, "Why did you eat the dead?" the answer they give most often is "*Je kwerexi'*" [Thus was our custom]. This statement deserves to be taken seriously. For Wari' before the contact, cannibalism was the norm. It was how their people had disposed of their dead for as long as anyone could remember, and it was considered the proper, most honorable way to treat a corpse. Most Wari' seem to have given no more thought to the question of why their society preferred cannibalism than most North Americans and Europeans give to the question of why our own societies permit only burial or cremation.

When Wari' elders do reflect on the deeper significance of what eating the dead meant to them personally, they tend to talk about this in a remarkably consistent way. In conversation after conversation, older women and men in various villages have independently offered explanations revolving around two related ideas: that cannibalism was done out of compassion for the person who was eaten, and that it also was done out of compassion for the bereaved relatives, as a way to help lessen their sorrow.

Wari' express the notion of compassion in the phrase *xiram pa'*, meaning to feel sorry for someone. *Xiram pa' wiriko ko mi' pin na, je para kao' inon* [I felt sorry for he who had died; that's why I ate him] Out of compassion for the deceased, one ate the corpse. Wari' also speak of eating the corpse as an act of compassion for the dead person's family. This was necessary, they say, because a corpse left intact is a painful reminder of the lost loved one, a focus for memories that prolong the grieving process. Making the corpse disappear by eating it was thought to help family members dwell less on memories of the person who had passed away, so they eventually might come to terms with their loss.

When Wari' talk about this felt need to alleviate sorrow by having the corpse eaten, they tend to speak, as Jimon Maram did in the passage at the beginning of this introduction, not from their perspective as eaters, but from their perspective as mourners who did not eat, as the dead person's close relatives who *wanted* their affines to eat the corpse. Again and again, older people echoed the idea that, "When the others ate the body, we did not think longingly about the ones who died; we were not so sad."

Today, Wari' speak from the perspective of people who have changed to a different way of disposing of their dead. Burial is now the universal practice, and the younger generation thinks of cannibalism as a curious custom that their grandparents tell about from the old days "when we used to live in the forest." Though Wari' of all ages still hold many of the values and ideas in which the practice of cannibalism was based, it is almost inconceivable that they would ever think of reviving cannibalism in the future. Young people have grown up with other ways of living and dying, and the practice of cannibalism has no part in their images of themselves. Wari' are keenly aware that people eating would brand them as savages in the eyes of the outsiders with whom their lives are now intertwined. Wari' depend on their relationships with non-Indians to obtain the goods and services (especially medicines, schools, ammunition, and metal tools) that they have come to need and want. At the same time, they want to be left alone to manage their own community affairs, and they know that the slightest rumor of cannibalism would unleash a barrage of prurient curiosity, criticism, and unwanted interference from outsiders.

Yet although no one advocates a return to cannibalism, older people's conversations about contrasts between the past and the present often express the feeling that something useful and meaningful has been lost. Some say that today, when corpses are buried rather than eaten, their thoughts return over and over to their loved one's body lying alone under its mound of dirt in the cemetery outside the village. In the past, when corpses were eaten or burned, one did not think so much about the dead, they say, because eradicating the body removed the most tangible focus for memories and grief.

* * *

My interpretation of Wari' mortuary cannibalism traces the conceptual framework behind this indigenous theory of body, memory, and emotion. The assertion that cannibalism made mourning easier reflects the distinctive ways Wari' think about the human body, ideas that make the fate of the corpse a matter of concern and a prime factor in how mourners think and feel about the dead. Like many other Amazonian Indians, Wari' see the human body as a social entity constituted through interactions with others. In the "anthropology of the body" in lowland South American societies, the physical body appears as a primary site where personhood, social identities, and relationships to others are created and perpetuated. Conversely, the body also is a prime site for enacting and marking changes of identity and for terminating or transforming relationships. When native South Americans dismembered and cooked, ate, or burned a corpse, they were acting to transform, not just a physical body, but other aspects of the dead person's identity or social connections as well.

Wari' see the body as something that connects the dead and the living through the ties of blood, flesh, and other elements that close family members share with each other, and through the emotional bonds of memory, especially memories of nurturance and support given and received. Physical bodies are a source of individuation: our bodies separate us from one another. But Wari' also recognize that, through our bodies, we are linked to each other, not just by ties of birth and blood, but also by the many forms of sociality and care giving—the feeding, holding, grooming, cuddling, love-making, healing, and work—exchanged in the course of daily life. Such life-supporting exchanges create bonds among individuals that are simultaneously and inseparably both physical and emotional. In the human body, Wari' read histories of social relationships, corporeal records of *caring* in both meanings of the word.

For Wari', the connections that develop between individuals in the give-and-take of social life are *embodied* connections in the fullest sense. From the way they talk about loved ones who have passed away recently, it seems apparent that this sense of embodied connectedness does not necessarily dissolve at the moment when a relative dies, but may persist even after the spirit and consciousness that made social interaction possible are recognized to be long gone. Given the body's salience in Wari' sociality, it is not surprising that (as described in Chapter 4), during funerals, expressions of grief and affection focus on the corpse itself.

This sense of the body as a place where relationships are formed and transformed is one key to understanding what eating their dead meant for Wari'. To act upon a corpse to alter or destroy it was to act upon the relationships of which it was comprised. The eradication of the corpse was intended to help loosen ties that bind the living and the dead too tightly. Wari' are keenly aware that prolonged grieving makes it hard for mourners to get on with their lives. Bereaved individuals, they say, must gradually disengage from dwelling on memories of the past. To accomplish this, it helps to eradicate reminders that bring the dead person to mind. The corpse itself is the single most powerful reminder. By removing that material focus for felt attachments, the ritual process of dismembering and eating or burning the dead person's body made it easier, elders say, to think less about the deceased and achieve some degree of detachment and tranquility.

Cannibalism was not just a destructive act; it also was a creative act. Besides eradicating the corpse, the ritual in which the eating of the dead occurred presented mourners with dramatically new images as they watched their loved one's body be cut up and roasted, much like game, divided into pieces that progressively became less and less identifiable, more and more similar in appearance to animal meat. This is another piece in the puzzle of Wari' funerary cannibalism: it made graphic statements about the loss of human identity and the destiny of the human spirit, and about meat-eating and the relations among people, and between humans and animals, through which food is produced and exchanged.

Wari' believe that the spirits of their dead join the realm of animal spirits, from which they return sometimes in the bodies of white-lipped peccaries (a piglike wild animal) that offer themselves to be hunted to feed their living loved ones. Thus, Wari' engaged in a kind of double cannibalism, consuming the flesh of their dead first as human corpses at funerals, and later as animal prey. The cannibalism that took place at the funeral was one step in a larger social process of mourning structured around ideas about transformations and exchanges between living Wari' and the spirits of animals and ancestors.

Relocating Cannibalism in the Context of Mourning

Although today they no longer destroy the corpse itself, Wari' continue to consider it important to remove from their environment everything that might evoke memories of individuals who have died. Just as they did in the past (and as many other South American Indians also do), they burn a dead person's house and all of his or her personal possessions. Wari' also change the appearance of neighboring houses, reroute paths, and burn places in the forest associated with the deceased. References to those who have recently died vanish from conversation as people stop using their names altogether or try to avoid speaking of them as much as possible.

Wari' emphasize that when they used to destroy corpses by eating or burning them, this had the same purpose as burning the house and other acts of destruction aimed at eliminating things that remind mourners of lost relatives. Elders have been bemused and at times rather irritated by anthropologists' apparent obsession with the subject of eating human flesh. "Why are you always asking about eating the ones who died?" one man complained to me. "You talk to me about eating; Denise [Meireles, a Brazilian ethnographer] came here and asked me about eating. The missionaries and the priests always used to say, 'Why did you eat people? Why did you eat?' Eating, eating, eating! Eating was not all that we did! We cried, we sang, we burned the house, we burned all their things." Pointing at the notebook in my lap, he directed, "Write about all of this, not just the eating!"

* * *

One of my hopes is that this case study of the Wari' will call attention to the fruitfulness of thinking about cannibalism in relation to questions about how cultural frameworks for mourning guide bereaved individuals or make certain social and symbolic resources available to them in their experiences of mourning. Funerary cannibalism is, by definition, a cultural response to the loss of a member of one's own group, part of how a certain community copes with a specific person's death. But although it would seem to be an obvious approach, scholars have paid little attention to the question of how the socially constituted symbols of cannibalism relate to bereavement and processes of coming to terms with the death of a relative or friend. Rather than focus on questions about mourning and individuals' emotions, most ethnographers who have written about funerary cannibalism have focused on the societal level, analyzing its cultural logic and symbolism, emphasizing how cannibalism fits into collective systems of thought and meaning. Symbolic analyses are essential to understanding cannibalism, and the rich symbolic resonances of Wari' thought will provide material for anthropologists and psychologists to analyze for years to come, especially as new details emerge that illuminate more aspects of precontact Wari' culture. But an approach that treats cannibalism merely as a symbol located in a system of cultural ideas cannot capture its whole significance. The problem with limiting analysis to the level of ideas and symbols, as many anthropological studies have tended to do, is that this leaves out the very aspects that Wari' themselves emphasize: cannibalism's relation to subjective experiences of grief and social processes of mourning.

My approach has been to begin by taking seriously what Wari' say about cannibalism's relation to experiences of bereavement. I treat the eating of the dead and the acts that surrounded it as pragmatic activities through which Wari' constructed and conveyed values, images, and relationships that individuals could draw upon in dealing with the death of someone close to them. Approaching cannibalism from this direction resonates with the more general anthropological trend toward studying ritual as "practice," trying to understand how people use rituals, symbols, and beliefs to cope with concrete problems in social life. From this perspective, the meaning of a cultural belief or ritual action is seen to be located "not in its pretension to mirror a so-called external world nor in the way it fits into some supposedly static 'system' of beliefs, but in how it carries people into relation with the world and with others, transforming their experience, helping them cope with existence" (Jackson and Karp 1990:20). As institutionalized cannibalism fades out of contemporary human experience, the Wari' offer one of the best, and probably one of the last, opportunities to understand how cannibalism may have served as a symbolic resource for coping with death and mourning.

Forms of Cannibalism

Before the contact, Wari' practiced two forms of cannibalism: they consumed the corpses of their fellow Wari' at funerals, and they ate the flesh of enemy outsiders whom Wari' warriors killed. Wari' saw these two forms of eating human flesh as quite distinct from each other, and they treated the corpses of enemies and the corpses of fellow tribesmembers very differently. The manner in which they roasted and consumed their own dead conveyed honor and respect for the person who was eaten. The way they handled and ate enemy corpses explicitly marked the enemy as a nonperson and expressed hostility and hatred.

Wari' emphasize that warfare cannibalism and funerary cannibalism conveyed and evoked very different meanings and emotions. They see about as much of a connection between eating their own dead and eating their enemies as we see between burying our dead and burying our garbage.

* * *

This contrast between the two forms of Wari' cannibalism corresponds to the distinction that anthropologists often make between *exocannibalism* and *endocannibalism*. Exocannibalism means eating outsiders—that is, enemies or other human beings who are not members of one's own social group. Endocannibalism means eating insiders, members of one's own social group. Since endocannibalism usually takes place during funerals or other mortuary rituals, it is commonly called mortuary cannibalism or funerary cannibalism. In this book, I use the terms endocannibalism, mortuary cannibalism, and funerary cannibalism interchangeably.

One reason it is worth listening to what Wari' can tell us about their experiences is that this is some of the most detailed information we have about endocannibalism. The ethnographic and historical literatures contain a lot more material on exocannibalism, such as the famous sixteenth-century accounts of the ritual execution and consumption of war captives among the Tupinambá of coastal Brazil and the Aztecs of central Mexico. It may be that exocannibalism was more common than endocannibalism, at least in the past few centuries. For whatever reasons, the information we have on mortuary cannibalism is quite limited, and we are unlikely to obtain much more, since almost all the peoples who used to practice it have stopped doing so, leaving few individuals able or willing to speak about their own experiences with people eating.

The Wari' case is unusual in that so many individuals who are still alive today participated in cannibalistic funerals and have been willing to talk about their experiences with me and other anthropologists, linguists, and missionaries. Wari' elders' testimonies provide one of the richest accounts of endocannibalism ever recorded, and they speak to some of the aspects of cannibalism about which we know least. Their perspectives suggest new insights that might be gained by taking a closer look at the distinctive forms and meanings of lowland South American cannibalism.

Funerary Cannibalism in Lowland South America

The German ethnographer Hans Becher (1968) once called South America "the continent of endocannibalism," for this type of cannibalism seems to have been more widely practiced in lowland South America than anywhere else in the world.[3] Cannibalism was by no means universal; most South American Indians probably never engaged in any form of people eating. Yet mortuary cannibalism has been reported at some time in the past in lowland regions ranging from coastal Venezuela and the Caribbean islands in the north to Paraguay in the south. In the early twentieth century, the greatest concentration of surviving endocannibalism practices seems to have been in western Amazonia among native groups located in a broad swath along both sides of Brazil's borders with Peru and Bolivia.[4]

Lowland South American mortuary cannibalism mainly occurred in one of two forms: people either consumed the ground, roasted bones or bone ash, or they consumed the cooked flesh. Bone-eating (osteophagy) seems to have been the more common practice. It was concentrated especially in northern Brazil, the Upper Orinoco region of southern Venezuela, and western and northwestern Amazonia. When only the bones were eaten, the preparation of the corpse would begin with the removal of the flesh. Usually this was accomplished by cremating the corpse or by burying it for a while and then exhuming the skeletal remains. Sometimes the corpse was left exposed to the elements until the flesh had rotted away.[5] Stripped of flesh, the bones would be roasted, ground into a powdery meal, and mixed into food or beverages, such as corn or manioc beer, plantain soup or honey.

Flesh-eating seems to have been less common than bone-eating in South America, but it has been reported in several areas. A number of Panoan groups in southeastern Peru reportedly ate the flesh of their dead (Dole 1974:305). In Paraguay, the French ethnographers Pierre and Hélène Clastres collected detailed accounts of flesh-eating at a Guayakí funeral in 1963, at which, the participants told them, almost the entire corpse was consumed (P. Clastres 1974, 1998). The Cashinahua consumed both flesh and bones (McCallum 1996b). The Wari' also practiced both variants of endocannibalism: they always ate the flesh, but sometimes they also consumed the bone meal mixed with honey.

The manner of cooking human flesh varied; some native South Americans roasted the corpse, others boiled it, and some used both methods. Arrangements concerning who ate whom also seem to have varied, though it is difficult to say much about this, because many accounts are not very clear about exactly who took part. Many writers simply noted that the corpse was eaten by relatives of the deceased, without specifying which relatives. Where more precise information is available, factors of age, gender, and kinship usually seem to have determined who did and did not eat. Commonly, corpse substances were eaten only by adults or the elderly, although children took part in the 1963 Guayakí funeral. In some societies, the dead were eaten mostly or exclusively by their immediate blood relatives (consanguines). In others, close kin did not eat, and the task was performed by affines (in-laws) and more distant consanguines. In both societies for which we have the most recent and detailed information on flesh endocannibalism, the Wari' and the Guayakí, close kin did not eat the dead.

Who was eaten and who was not also varied. In some lowland South American societies, such as the Cashinahua (aka Kaxinawá), the honor of having one's bones or flesh eaten was reserved for high-status individuals, such as chiefs and their wives, important religious specialists, or renowned warriors (Kensinger 1995, McCallum 1996b). In other societies, including the Wari', almost everyone who died was eaten, regardless of their age or status.

Although probably only a fraction of Amazonian Indians ever actually practiced cannibalism, it is a prominent theme for many other native South Americans who project images of cannibalism in their myths, cosmologies, and eschatologies (ideas about what happens to a human spirit after death) (see Basso 1995, Sullivan 1988). One common idea is that death itself is a form of cannibalism. Yanomami, for example, think of every death as an act of cannibalism in which the human soul is devoured by a spirit or an enemy (Clastres and Lizot 1978:114–116). The Araweté (Tupian speakers of Pará, Brazil) believe that, at death, human spirits are cannibalized by the gods, then rejuvenated and transformed into gods themselves (Viveiros de Castro 1992). The Kulina (Arawakan speakers of Acre, Brazil) believe that when a human spirit journeys to the underworld, it is ritually welcomed and devoured by the Kulina ancestors, who have become white-lipped peccaries (Pollock 1993). In these Amazonian cosmologies, cannibalism mediates the human spirit's transition from life to death, from mortal human to a new immortal identity in the afterlife.

The predatory imagery in these visions of ancestors attacking and eating human spirits resonates with the notion of the dead as enemies of the living, an idea expressed in a number of societies in the South American lowlands (Carneiro da Cunha 1978:143, H. Clastres 1968, Lévi-Strauss 1974:234, Sullivan 1988:517–519). Where the dead are symbolically equated with enemies or other outsiders, endocannibalism (eating members of one's own group) begins to resemble exocannibalism (eating social outsiders). As many South American scholars have noted, the customary anthropological distinction between endo- and exocannibalism blurs in the face of the complex ways in which native South Americans approach cannibalism in their cosmologies, mythologies, and rituals (P. Clastres 1974:320, Erikson 1986:198, Lévi-Strauss 1984:142, Overing 1986, Viveiros de Castro 1992).

Although Wari' drew sharp distinctions between eating enemies or animals and eating their own dead, these various forms of consumption nonetheless had certain elements in common.

One prerequisite to understanding South American endocannibalism is to recognize that eating is not just a process of incorporation (transferring substance into the consumer's stomach). It is also a process of destruction and transformation. The object that is eaten vanishes from sight and ceases to exist as a distinct entity; it becomes something else. Notions of eating as a mechanism of destruction, dissociation, and (meta-)physical transformation are salient themes in many native lowland South American cultures.

Contrasts to Endocannibalism in Melanesia

Aside from South America, the other part of the world where mortuary cannibalism has been widely reported and studied by anthropologists is Melanesia, the area north of Australia comprised of Papua New Guinea, Irian Jaya, and neighboring islands. Much of the information we have about endocannibalism comes from Melanesia, and anthropological interpretations have been heavily influenced by the distinctive features and cultural ideas associated with Melanesian brands of endocannibalism.[6]

In Melanesia mortuary cannibalism most often involved eating small bits from selected body parts, though some groups (such as the Gimi described in Gillison 1993) reportedly consumed larger amounts of flesh. The individuals who ate corpse substances typically included close relatives of the deceased, and endocannibalism generally was not an activity in which most of the members of a community participated. Usually only a relatively small number of people (sometimes only women) consumed corpse substances.

This contrasts markedly with Wari' practices. Whereas Melanesians commonly consumed only tidbits of fellow group members' flesh in mortuary rites, Wari' ate substantial amounts. And whereas the Melanesians who ate corpse substances were most often close blood relatives or spouses of the deceased, among the Wari' these were precisely the people who did *not* eat. In Amazonian endocannibalism, the consumption of corpse substances (whether flesh or bones) tended to be a public event and a focus of collective ritual activity that most of a community either performed or witnessed. In Melanesia, the eating seems often to have been done rapidly or in secret; when larger amounts were consumed (as among the Gimi), the flesh was cut up and distributed for people to cook and eat in their own homes. In South America, mortuary cannibalism's prominence as a public performance is consistent with the idea that eating the dead was a social obligation considered necessary to ensure or promote collective well-being, not just the well-being of the individuals who ate the flesh.

The ideas and motives associated with South American and Melanesian endocannibalism also differed. Although various Melanesian endocannibalism systems expressed a variety of local cultural meanings, they tended to share two main ideas: the belief that cannibalism primarily benefited the individuals who ate the corpse, and the belief that the corpse contained substances or vital energies that needed to be recaptured and recycled into the bodies of those who consumed it. By eating pieces of the corpse, the dead person's relatives kept these vital elements circulating in their own bodies and kin group, in a kind of closed economy of body elements.

North American and British scholars have tended to look to Melanesia for data on endocannibalism, and as a consequence, their general theories of endocannibalism have tended to emphasize Melanesian cultural themes. In particular, Anglo American theorists have tended to assume that incorporation—the idea of eating a corpse as a way for living people to absorb the dead person's vital energies or body substances—was always the motive behind mortuary cannibalism.[7] In South America, one can find echoes of Melanesian-type notions of incorporation in some writers' comments about endocannibalism in certain societies.[8] But in most native South American societies—notably including the three most recent and best-documented cases, the Wari', Yanomami, and Guayakí—endocannibalism seems to have had little or nothing to do with such ideas about incorporation.

Native South Americans think about persons, bodies, and spirits in distinctive ways that give South American endocannibalism its distinctive orientations. In contrast to endocannibalism in Melanesia, which aimed to preserve, perpetuate, and redistribute elements of the deceased, South American endocannibalism more often had the objective of *eradicating* the corpse in order to *sever* relations between the dead person's body and spirit, and between living people and the spirits of the dead.

For Wari', the imperative to distance, destroy, and transform relations to the dead was linked to concerns with memory, mourning, and the human body's role in composing persons and their relationships. Although Wari' ideas resonate with many general themes in lowland South American ethnology, they should not be taken as typical or representative of endocannibalism in South America or anywhere else. I know of no other case in which native people have spoken so directly about cannibalism's relation to memory and its effects on emotional ties between the living and the dead. Yet although one cannot generalize from the Wari' example, it points to issues that may be more widespread than has been previously recognized. Scattered throughout the ethnographic literature on endocannibalism in other societies in South America and elsewhere, one finds mention of native peoples who said that their practice of endocannibalism was motivated by compassion for the deceased, or the desire to save the corpse from decay, or the belief that the eating of the corpse lessened mourners' grief. Presented with such claims, scholars have seldom taken them seriously enough to explore what they meant, but instead have tended to look for other, more exotic psychological motives and symbolic schemes. Paying attention to what Wari' and other native South Americans have said about how their practices of cannibalism related to experiences of memory and mourning points to issues that are ripe for rethinking in the anthropology of cannibalism.

Conundrums of Culture and Experience

This book is about Wari' mortuary cannibalism, not about eating enemies. My choice to limit the scope of my analysis is partly an economy of focus; a comprehensive treatment of Wari' warfare and exocannibalism would require a book in itself. Mostly, it is a matter of intellectual and personal interest. The themes that emerge from Wari' enemy-eating—the notion that cannibalism expressed hostility and symbolically marked the enemy's "otherness," equating enemies with animal prey—are familiar ideas that have been widely recognized in cannibalism theory and in studies from other societies.

Yet if the meanings and sentiments associated with eating enemies appear fairly straightforward, the reasons why Wari' ate their own dead are more difficult to discern. There is no simple answer to this question, though missionaries, priests, and anthropologists have tried for decades to find one. As discussed in Chapter 5, most of the models that anthropologists and psychologists have used to explain cannibalism in other societies and in Westerners' dreams and fantasies do not apply very well to the Wari'. The Wari' did not eat their dead because they needed the protein. They were not trying to absorb the dead person's life force, courage, vital energies, or other substances or qualities. Nor did eating their dead have much to do with acting out anger, aggression, resentment, dominance, or desire to hold onto the deceased. The ideas and emotional and social dynamics associated with Wari' endocannibalism do not fit neatly into any of the major theories of cannibalism. Wari' mortuary cannibalism poses an anthropological conundrum.

There is another, more personal side to this sense of Wari' endocannibalism as something of a mystery. Quite simply, I find it harder to understand than the eating of enemies. While I recoil at the thought of eating human flesh myself, I do not find it difficult to imagine that in warfare people might be motivated to eat an enemy's corpse out of hatred or a desire for vengeance, especially if they regarded their enemies as radically different from themselves or even subhuman. I have more trouble imagining what it would be like to butcher, cook, and consume someone whom I had known intimately, someone with whom I shared a common identity and a history of social interactions.

Mortuary cannibalism brings us up against fundamental questions about human psychology and the way that culture shapes individual experiences and emotions. The sentiments of caring and attachment, and the feelings of loss and insecurity, that Wari' express when they talk about their experiences of bereavement are among the most nearly universal human emotions. Yet Wari' interpret and deal with these emotions through practices grounded in a worldview quite different from our own, in which cultural ideas about bodies, spirits, memories, and the human spirit's post-mortem existence formerly made cannibalism seem to them the most honorable and helpful way to deal with death and mourning. The radical "otherness" of Wari' views of cannibalism challenges us to examine some of our deepest notions about our relations to those with whom we live, the role that our bodies play in these relationships, and how we cope with the ruptures death forces into our lives and emotions.

* * *

"I don't know if you can understand this . . ." Jimon Maram said in the conversation that opened this introduction. He was referring not just to the distance between his cultural perspective and my own, but also to the differences in our life experiences. Jimon Maram spoke as a husband and the father of eight living children and as someone who, as a child, had lived through the mass epidemics that took the lives of his mother and many other relatives. He spoke also, and perhaps most poignantly, as a man who recently had buried a young son and a beloved adult brother.

As I talked with Jimon Maram, Quimoin, and the other Wari' whom I interviewed during my first two years of fieldwork, when I collected most of the data for this study, I could interpret what they said only through the narrow lenses of my own limited life experiences. When I first went to live with the Wari', I was newly wed and childless, and, like many young North

Americans, I had had little personal experience with serious sickness and death. The only funerals I had attended were for grandparents and great-aunts who had died, peacefully and not unexpectedly, in old age. I had never dealt with the chaotic emotions aroused by the untimely death of a younger relative or friend, nor had I nursed anyone through a life-threatening illness. This began to change a few weeks after I left the Wari' to return to the United States in July of 1987, when my sister was in a near-fatal car accident. Today, I write from the perspective of deeper experiences with family life and family crises: as one who spent weeks at my sister's bedside confronting in the most pragmatic way the question of what links spirit to body as we tried to bring her out of a coma; as a daughter who is watching her parents' bodies and lives change as they age; as a mother who gave birth to a son and has seen him grow strong and vibrant from the milk of her body and the food and loving care given by his father and others; and as a sister who lost a cherished brother. There is nothing unusual in these experiences; most Wari' have lived some or all of them by the time they are half my age. But these personal events have influenced my interpretation of their ideas and practices, in that they made me listen more closely and take more seriously what Wari' say about their own experiences with illness and death and the part that bodies and caring for bodies and emotions play in family relations.

The way in which personal experiences converge with academic understandings became clearest when I returned to Brazil in 1991, after the death of my youngest brother. I arrived at Santo André to find the Wari' also in mourning for two recent deaths in their community. Wari' friends responded to my grief and drew me into theirs in ways that revealed fundamental differences in how our respective societies treat the dead and those who mourn for them. But we also discovered how much we shared in struggling with our private sorrows.

This is a book about cannibalism. It is also a book about issues that confront us all: our attachments to others and how we deal with our experiences of loss and our memories of those we have loved. The ways in which Wari' have dealt with the problem of bereavement and mourning, which used to involve consuming the corpses of their dead, may appear extreme to outsiders. Yet by looking at cannibalism from Wari' points of view, we are reminded that sometimes it is in the extremes of cultural practices that we most clearly see the dilemmas of social life, and the ways of caring and coping, that unite us as human beings.

PART I

CONTEXTS

CHAPTER ONE

CANNIBAL
EPISTEMOLOGIES

Cannibalism is a difficult topic for an anthropologist to write about, for it pushes the limits of cultural relativism, challenging one to define what is or is not beyond the pale of acceptable human behavior. As one of the last real taboos in contemporary cosmopolitan society, cannibalism evokes a mixture of revulsion and fascination that guarantees any account of it will be read against a host of preconceptions.

Beyond the emotional reactions the subject of cannibalism provokes, there is the issue of its political implications. Cannibalism is a staple of racist stereotypes, and one of the oldest smear tactics in the game of ethnic politics is to accuse one's enemies, or people one wishes to degrade or dominate, of eating human flesh, whether or not there is any truth to the accusation. In South America and elsewhere, rumors and false and distorted reports of cannibalistic native peoples have been manipulated for centuries, used as propaganda to serve certain political and economic agendas.[1] Recognizing that many historical allegations of people eating probably were false, some scholars have suggested that we should not trust any of the information we have about situations in which cannibalism supposedly was a socially accepted practice. In the face of such skepticism, the Wari' case is significant, for it presents some of the most authoritative data on cannibalism ever recorded. How do we know what we think we know about Wari' cannibalism, and how reliable is this knowledge? This chapter addresses these questions. But before examining the Wari' evidence, it is useful to take a brief look at the relations among colonialism, interethnic politics, and representations of cannibalism in South American history in order to understand the kinds of documentary problems and distortions that have plagued the study of cannibalism.

Uses and Abuses of Images of New World Cannibalism

From the earliest years of the European invasion of the New World, reports that native people ate human flesh provided the conquerors with easy justifications for their brutal takeover of native lands and lives. European colonizers saw New World cannibalism as the quintessential expression of savagery and evil. Clearly, any way of putting an end to such depravity could be considered legitimate. The imperative to stamp out cannibalism could counter any criticisms about the morality of colonial projects and the brutalities of death, disease, misery, violence, and slavery that Europeans inflicted on native peoples.

People with the reputation of being cannibals were fair game for exploitation. In 1503, Queen Isabella of Spain decreed that Spaniards could legally enslave *only* those American Indians who were cannibals (Whitehead 1984:70).[2] Spanish colonists thus had a vested economic interest in representing many New World natives as people eaters. Political expediency clearly motivated a number of early chroniclers who wrote about cannibalism, particularly among the Carib (Caniba) Indians who lived in parts of Venezuela, the Guianas, and the Caribbean islands. (Columbus's accounts of the supposedly ferocious man-eating Caniba gave us the word *cannibal*, which has come to be used more widely than the older term *anthropophagy*.)

The Portuguese who invaded Brazil likewise found that representing the natives as cannibals provided a powerful rhetoric to assert European superiority and justify their violent conquest of the New World. The Catholic Church buttressed this position in 1510, when Pope Innocent IV declared cannibalism to be a sin deserving to be punished by Christians through force of arms.[3]

Where people-eating savages did not exist, they could be fabricated. There is little doubt that in the sixteenth and seventeenth centuries, some Spanish writers spread unsubstantiated reports of cannibalism in certain native populations (especially those that resisted European domination) as a pretext to justify slave-raiding and as a device to head off interference from Catholic clergy or government officials in Madrid. Many other colonial-era writings also are of dubious veracity, being secondhand accounts based on rumor and innuendo, not the writer's own observations. Even when there was no supporting evidence, historical documents tended to treat such allegations as facts.

In the nineteenth century, another genre of accounts of South American cannibalism emerged in the writings of naturalists, explorers, and adventurers who journeyed into remote areas of the Amazon basin and wrote about their travels for an international audience. Russel Wallace (1889) and Henry W. Bates (1864), two of the most respected nineteenth-century naturalists, both mentioned cannibalism (endo- and exo-) among Indians with whom they came in contact or about whom they heard while conducting field research along northern tributaries of the Amazon River. Less scientific writers penned melodramatic tales of encounters with bloodthirsty people eaters. These tended to portray the Amazonian rainforest as a dark and terrifying place with, as one twentieth-century author described it, "an aura of mystery and cruelty that hangs, like a miasma or an exhalation from the swamps and foetid undergrowth itself, over the limitless square miles of these regions" (Hogg 1958:70). This literary tradition continues in popular writings in which an encounter with cannibals serves as the ultimate mark of the intrepid explorer's machismo, an affirmation that he has indeed traveled into the wildest, most dangerous and exotic realms of human existence.

*　*　*

Accounts of cannibalism in South America have a long history of being used and abused to serve the interests of those who promulgated them. Recognizing this, some South American scholars began to voice doubts about the reality of cannibalism decades ago. Julio Salas (1920) suggested that the Caribs did not really practice cannibalism. J. Fernando Carneiro found the documentary evidence for Brazil's native peoples so fragmentary and contradictory that he concluded that "this [alleged] habit of our Indians to eat human flesh was a dubious thing, maybe inexistent or in any event much less general than it has been said to be" (1947:159). The French ethnographer Pierre Clastres came to a similar conclusion after an extensive review of South American historical and ethnographic literature. "[A]mong the numerous Indian tribes accused of cannibalism in the 16th and 17th centuries," he observed, "doubtless many of them did no such thing" (1974:309–310).

Clastres cautioned, however, against the opposite tendency of scholars to go too far and dismiss all evidence of cannibalism out of hand. He noted that "the 'mania' of the soldiers, missionaries, explorers and adventurers of past centuries to see a cannibal in every Indian, was answered by a reverse exaggeration on the part of some scholars that drove them consistently to doubt all statements of anthropophagy [people eating] and thus to reject some reports, extremely valuable due to the personal character of their authors."

The most recent outbreak of this impulse to "reverse exaggeration" began in 1979, when an American anthropologist named William Arens published a book called *The Man-Eating Myth,* in which he argued that cannibalism was just that: a myth without a clear basis in fact. After reviewing a selection of writings on cannibalism in various times and places, Arens concluded that "Rumours, suspicions, fears and accusations abound, but no satisfactory first hand accounts" (1979:21). Historians and anthropologists had long recognized the need to treat specific allegations of cannibalism with skepticism, and the documentary deficiencies that Arens pointed out reinforced that caution.

Arens went further, however, and suggested that cannibalism may have never existed anywhere as an institutionalized, socially accepted practice.[4] While he acknowledged that some starving individuals have been driven to eat human flesh in order to survive, he pointed out that "whenever it occurs this is considered a regrettable act rather than custom" (1979:9). Arens asserted that, throughout the world, people see cannibalism as a symbol of inhumanity, barbarism, and evil; "cannibal" is a derogatory label projected onto enemies, neighbors, and uncivilized "others." Emphasizing the self-serving purposes to which European colonizers have put such accusations, he suggested that reports of cannibalistic native peoples were no more than products of European prejudice and figments of European imaginations.

Ironically, although this argument that cannibalism never existed is based in a critique of colonialist mentalities, it seems to reflect some of the same ethnocentrism that lay behind European colonizers' horrified reactions to cannibalism (Gardner 1999). Like the many priests, missionaries, colonial officers, and others who considered cannibalism antithetical to what it means to be human, scholars who insist that all accounts of cannibalism must be false seem to assume that cannibalism is by definition a terrible act—so terrible, in fact, that it could only have been invented by those with damaging ulterior motives. They appear blind to the possibility that people different from themselves might have other ways of being human, other understandings of the body, or other ways of coping with death that might make cannibalism seem a good thing to do.

Both colonial discourses and much contemporary scholarship have tended to treat cannibalism as a one-way sign pointing toward the savagery of the native "other," the mark of negative difference in a symbolic construct that highlights the contrast between cannibalistic natives and civilized Europeans, to whom people eating is anathema. Scholars have criticized one side of this symbolic construct by questioning the claim that native peoples were cannibals. But almost no one has questioned the other side of this symbolic construct, the assumption that cannibalism was not part of European culture. As the literary critic Claude Rawson (1997:3) pointed out, "the common factor in the long history of cannibal imputations is the combination of denial of it in ourselves and attribution of it to 'others', whom 'we' wish to defame, conquer, appropriate, or 'civilize'." The impulse toward denial took a new twist in the efforts by Arens and others to deny cannibalism on behalf of all humanity. Rawson comments that "in the present atmosphere of post-colonial guilt and imperial self-inculpation the culture of denial has turned outward to those once accused of 'unspeakable rites'. Our time is perhaps the first in which denial about ourselves has been extended to denial on behalf of 'others', and in which the 'other' has been systematically rehabilitated into an equality with 'us' " (1997:3).

The problem with asserting the moral equality of all humanity by denying that any society ever accepted cannibalism as a routine practice is that there is substantial evidence that some people really did consume human flesh or bones in the past. Arguments over the evidence have received considerable attention.[5] Arens himself recently modified his earlier position of absolute denial to admit that ethnographer Gertrude Dole's report of bone-ash cannibalism in South America probably was true, though he suggests (without explaining why) that this should not be called cannibalism (Arens 1998:46–47).[6]

While most South American ethnographers accept the idea that some peoples did consider cannibalism socially acceptable, they are also acutely aware of the damaging effects of negative stereotypes. Allegations of cannibalism—even acts of cannibalism that purportedly took place long ago—continue to be feared for the stigma they carry and used as political propaganda against native peoples and their supporters. Two recent examples are the controversy over archaeological evidence of cannibalism among the ancient Anasazi in the southwestern United States and the controversy that arose in Australia when leaders of the country's right-wing political party, One Nation, used the claim that Australian Aborigines used to practice cannibalism (a claim most anthropologists consider unfounded) as rhetoric to support their opposition to Aboriginal rights.[7]

Recognizing how often representations of native cannibalism have been used and abused, the dilemma for ethnographers is how to write about cannibalism without contributing to the exoticizing and "othering" of the people we write about. Anthropologists have tended to deal with this by producing rather sanitized accounts that mute or erase the violent or apparently unsavory aspects of cannibalism by emphasizing its ritual context and religious and symbolic meanings. As Lestringant (1997:12) noted, "culturalist" interpretations of cannibalism tend "to idealize the violent act of eating, to shift the noise of teeth and lips towards the domain of language." The desire to erase the stigma of cannibalism and assert the equality of "them" and "us" culminates in the academic proposal to erase cannibalism itself from the record of human behavior by claiming that no one ever really did it.

Rawson, however, suggests another possibility: "An alternative 'equality', which says not that nobody does it, but that 'we' do (or did, or might do) it too." He notes that this possibility has "always exercised an uneasy pressure on our cultural psyche, in anxieties (and condemnations) of barbaric reversion which haunt our literature from Homer and Plato to Conrad's *Heart of Darkness* and after" (1997:4). In the sixteenth century, this uneasy pressure clearly was on the minds of some French writers, including the explorer Jean de Léry and the philosopher Michel de Montaigne. Both wrote about cannibalism among the Tupinambá of Brazil and compared it to acts of cannibalism in France. Léry (1990:212), who was a Protestant pastor, described incidents in which French Catholics ate human flesh during the rancorous sixteenth-century religious wars between Catholics and Protestants (Lestringant 1997:74–80, Whatley 1984). Whether or not this actually happened is unclear. But in any event, even if some Europeans did eat human flesh when facing starvation or in the passion of war and religious strife, these were not normative cultural practices but aberrant events, condemned in the society in which they supposedly occurred.

More intriguing is the socially accepted form of European cannibalistic practices to which Montaigne referred in his essay "On the Cannibals" when he wrote, "And our medical men do not flinch from using corpses in many ways, both internally and externally, to cure us" (1991:236). The practice of consuming human body parts for medicinal purposes was part of a long tradition that flourished in western Europe until just two centuries ago.

Cannibalism in Europe

Medicinal cannibalism has been documented in European medical literature since at least the first century A.D., when the Roman writer Pliny the Elder (23–79 A.D.) wrote that drinking human blood was a cure for epilepsy

(Temkin 1971:23). Besides blood, Europeans consumed human flesh, heart, bones (skull, burned bones, and bone marrow), and other body parts and body products (Gordon-Grube 1988:406, 1993:192–194). Physicians and pharmacists prescribed substances from human corpses to treat a variety of diseases, including arthritis, reproductive difficulties, sciatica, warts, and skin blemishes.

Blood was considered most effective when drunk immediately after the death of the person from whose body it was taken, and the blood of those who died violently in their prime was thought to be especially potent. Executed criminals were one of the main sources of body substances. In Denmark, epileptics were reported to "stand around the scaffold in crowds, cup in hand, ready to quaff the red blood as it flows from the still quavering body" (Peacock 1896:270–271). Until the nineteenth century, public executioners earned part of their living by selling criminals' body parts, especially the skulls and hands and fingers. (The touch of a dead man's hand was thought to cure goiter and warts, and thieves carried a dead man's hand to avoid detection when robbing a house; see Hand 1980:69–80.)

Therapies based on ingesting corpse substances were popular in Europe among both elites and lower classes. In the sixteenth and seventeenth centuries, medicinal uses of human corpses moved from folk medicine into the ranks of standard medical practice with the rise of the Paracelsian school of medical philosophy, which promoted the use of a variety of human body substances. Paracelsian physicians competed with physicians who followed the Galenist tradition. The Galenists eventually came to dominate, the medicinal use of animal products (including human substances) fell out of favor, and by the nineteenth century, the practice of medicinal cannibalism seems to have more or less faded out in Europe.

In the heyday of European medicinal cannibalism, dried and powdered human body products were regular items on the shelves of any well-stocked pharmacy. In the London apothecaries, one of the most popular remedies was "mummy," "a medicinal preparation of the remains of an embalmed, dried, or otherwise 'prepared' human body that had ideally met with sudden, preferably violent death" (Gordon-Grube 1988:406, 1993:193–195). Pieces of preserved human flesh and liquid *mumie* (known as "menstruation of the dead") were a universal panacea recommended by Paracelsian physicians, and the use of these escalated in England, France, Germany, and other parts of western Europe in the sixteenth and seventeenth centuries (Gordon-Grube 1988:407, Pouchelle 1990:74). One famous recipe for preparing mummy gave the following directions:

Take the fresh, unspotted cadaver of a redheaded man (because in them the blood is thinner and the flesh hence more excellent) aged about twenty-four, who has been executed and died a violent death. Let the corpse lie one day and night in the sun and moon—but the weather must be good. Cut the flesh into pieces and sprinkle it with myrrh and just a little aloe. Then soak it in spirits of wine for several days, hang it up for 6 or 10 hours, soak it again in spirits of wine, then let the pieces dry in dry air in a shady spot. Thus they will be similar to smoked meat, and will not stink (Schroeder 1963:1302, cited and translated in Gordon-Grube 1993:195).

Besides executed prisoners, the other major source of human corpses was Egypt. The famous sixteenth-century French surgeon Ambroise Paré clearly recognized the cannibalistic implications of the extensive European traffic in Egyptian corpses in his essay "Discours de la mumie," in which he wrote about the history of medicinal uses of substances from embalmed corpses. Kenneth Himmelman (1997:197) noted, "Paré's shame at the inclination of Europeans to travel to Egypt in search of corpses was evident in his description of a Jew in Alexandria who 'marveled greatly at how the Christians were so fond of eating the bodies of the dead' " (see Paré 1841:482). In view of the vogue for consuming human body parts in western Europe in the sixteenth and seventeenth centuries, it is ironic that during the same period, the European colonizers who were invading the New World reacted so vehemently against cannibalism in native American societies.

* * *

Did Europeans bring their practice of medicinal cannibalism to the New World? Karen Gordon-Grube (1993) found recipes using human corpse substances in the records of a Paracelsian-trained pharmacist in New England, but no evidence that he actually concocted such remedies. One practice that does seem to have made it to the New World is the use of human fat to dress wounds. The Spanish chronicler Bernal Diaz del Castillo, who accompanied Cortés in the conquest of Mexico, wrote that, after several battles, he and other Spaniards cut up the corpses of Indians and used their fat to sear the wounds of Spanish soldiers and their horses (Diaz del Castillo 1956:59, 127, 132).

In parts of Central and South America (especially Guatemala, Mexico, Peru, and Bolivia) indigenous peoples have believed for centuries that Europeans and their descendants consume Indian fat, flesh, or blood. Perhaps the best-known of these legendary "white cannibal" figures is the *pishtaco* or *nakaq* of the central and southern Andes (see Weismantel 1997). Just a few decades after Pizarro invaded the Inca empire, the Spanish chronicler Cristóbal de Molina reported the existence of this belief in his *Relación de las fábulas y ritos de los incas.* Historian Steve J. Stern notes that, in the region around Ayacucho, Peru, "As early as the sixteenth century, the region's Indians expressed fear that Spaniards sought their body fat for medicinal purposes. . . . The oral tradition which associated body fat, medicinal functions, and Spaniards was not invented out of thin air, but probably based on battle experiences in the sixteenth century" (Stern 1987:170–171n).

Might the pishtaco and other European or mestizo cannibal figures have been based on European colonizers' actual practices of using Indians' body substances as medicines? If so, were these uses limited to the external dressing of wounds with human fat, or did the European invaders also use Indian body substances as orally ingested medicines? I do not yet know. But we do know that many of their compatriots back in Europe were swallowing bits of their fellow Europeans, as well as the more exotic corpse substances imported from Egypt.

It is striking how thoroughly these practices of consuming human body substances have been erased from Europeans' collective self-images. Medical historians are well aware of these practices but have rarely labeled them "cannibalism." Perhaps this is because these medicinal usages of human body parts (which often were processed and packaged as commercial pharmaceuticals) seem so distant from popular images of "real" cannibalism (read: flesh-eating by primitives). Some readers may, like Arens (1998:47), suggest that these European medical practices should not be labeled anthropophagy. If not, why not? Where should we draw the line defining what is and is not cannibalism?

Europeans undoubtedly found it easy to see drinking "mummy" purchased from an apothecary as very different from the savagery they imagined among the Tupinambá, whom European artists always portrayed eating human flesh in the form of big hunks of recognizably human body parts (cf. Staden 1928). But when European citizens lined up at a scaffold to drink a prisoner's fresh blood, could it really have been easy to deny the humanity of what they were consuming? Gordon-Grube (1993:199) rejects the idea that Europeans did not recognize the ingestion of mummy and human blood as cannibalism. She notes that as early as 1582, Ambroise Paré "spoke out against these remedies precisely on the grounds of cannibalism," and she quotes Paré's statement (in reference to Egyptian mummies) that "the ancients were very eager to embalm the bodies of their dead, but not with the intention that they should serve as food and drink for the living as is the case at the present time." In New England, the Puritan preacher Cotton Mather expressed similar reservations about the cannibalistic implications of ingesting human skull, saying:

> I declare, I abominate it. For I take Mans Skull to be not only a meer dry Bone, void of all Vertue, but also a nasty, mortified, putrid, carrionish piece of our own species; and to take it Inwardly, seems an Execrable Fact that even the Anthropophagi [cannibals] would shiver at. And therefore, in my Opinion, it would be decent; and almost pious, to carry them all out of the Shops, and heap up a sepulchral mound for the reception of the bones (Mather 1972:145, cited in Gordon-Grube 1993:199).

Sixteenth-century intellectuals clearly saw elements of cannibalism in their own people's medicinal practices, and Montaigne pointed to the hypocrisy of condemning cannibalism abroad while prescribing it at home.

* * *

The tradition of medicinal cannibalism that flourished in Europe for nearly two thousand years was, like all institutionalized forms of cannibalism, the product of specific cultural ideas and social arrangements. Beyond its distinctive assumptions about the curative properties of human body substances, perhaps the most unusual feature of European medicinal cannibalism was its impersonality, the attitude of treating human body parts as commercial commodities. Outside Europe, institutionalized cannibalism almost always seems to have been based on a social relationship between the person who ate and the person who was eaten, be it a relationship between members of a family, between in-laws, between men and women, between nobles and commoners, between witches and those who executed them, or between enemies from warring groups. Regardless of whether it was performed with honorable or hostile intent, most non-European cannibalism was socially embedded cannibalism. In non-European cannibalism, the identities of and relationship between the human being who was eaten and the one who did the eating mattered a great deal, and the cultural significance of the act almost always related to domains of collective life and group welfare, such as kinship, marriage, leadership, religion, or war.

Europeans, in contrast, engaged in a profoundly asocial cannibalism, in which the eater and the eaten often had no relationship to each other at all and the social identity of the one whose body was eaten mattered little. What counted were issues of quality control: was the source of the corpse substances healthy, and had the corpse substances been treated properly to preserve their potency? European medicinal cannibalism depersonalized and objectified the human being whose body parts were eaten. Along with this went the desocialization and individualization of the meaning of eating human substance. This kind of cannibalism served no larger communal or religious purposes; its sole objective was to enhance the well-being of the individual eater. Human body parts were commercial commodities, bought and sold for profit.

The Old World tradition of medicinal cannibalism clearly was based on ideas and social arrangements quite different from the forms of ritual cannibalism practiced by New World natives. But the historical coexistence of institutionalized people eating on both sides of the Atlantic Ocean reminds us that cannibalism has appeared in a variety of forms, some of which Europeans have considered socially acceptable and even health-enhancing.

Cannibalism in South America

I think it is safe to say that, today, the vast majority of cultural anthropologists who study native lowland South America agree that some indigenous peoples probably did practice cannibalism in the past. In response to those who have suggested that cannibalism never existed, some scholars have taken a closer look at the evidence from South America and the Caribbean. Neil Whitehead (1984) looked at historical materials on the Carib and concluded that, while certain allegations of cannibalism are indeed suspect, others cannot be easily dismissed. D. W. Forsyth (1983) reached a similar conclusion about the Tupinambá, who lived on Brazil's northeast coast in the sixteenth century and were famous for their ritual consumption of enemies taken prisoner in wars against neighboring tribes.[8]

In addition to historical accounts, there is ethnographic and ethnohistorical evidence that cannibalism (of both the exo- and endo- varieties) continued into the twentieth century in a number of lowland South American communities. In the late 1950s, Gertrude Dole, an American anthropologist, observed osteophagy (bone-eating) among the Amahuaca Indians of southeastern Peru. Dole (1974) wrote of witnessing funeral rites for a baby that culminated with the grieving mother consuming her child's bones, which had been roasted and ground into meal. Anthropologists and other outsiders also have observed the consumption of bone ashes among the Yanomami Indians of northern Brazil and southern Venezuela, a practice that continues in some of the more isolated communities, as shown in a recent U.S. public television documentary (NOVA 1996).

Eyewitness accounts of cannibalism by anthropologists are, however, undeniably rare. One reason may be that cannibalism—especially the flesh-eating variety—always has been one of the first practices to disappear or go underground when native peoples begin to interact with powerful outsiders who abhor it. Anthropologists are seldom the first outsiders to set foot in a newly contacted society; they almost always follow in the footsteps of others, such as missionaries, government agents, frontiersmen, or traders, who as a rule see cannibalism as something to terminate immediately. Cannibalism does not survive long after the arrival of the "agents of civilization" who inevitably precede the anthropologist.

Most of the reliable ethnographic information we have about the practice of cannibalism is consequently based—like this study of the Wari'—not on an ethnographer's own observations, but on retrospective accounts collected from native informants who, though they no longer practiced cannibalism, could still remember and describe their experiences. Assessing the facts behind any informant's statements is an issue with which every ethnographer contends. Statements about the past must be treated especially cautiously, with constant attention to the need to confirm, cross-check, and probe for inconsistencies and misrepresentations. To emphasize that retrospective data must be used carefully, however, is not to say they can never be trusted at all. A large amount of the information that cultural anthropologists collect and accept as valid is based on what informants have said rather than what the researcher witnessed. Provided that the ethnographer is careful to assess the data's reliability and identify potential weaknesses, anthropologists generally accept the validity of retrospective data. In the Wari' case, most of what we have to work with is what people have said about what they did in the past.

* * *

I have never witnessed an act of cannibalism among the Wari'. Neither has any other anthropologist reported witnessing Wari' eat anyone. Nonetheless, as far as I know, every ethnographer, linguist, missionary, and priest who has worked with the Wari' has been convinced that they really did eat their dead. This conviction is based on two sources of information. First, there are accounts from North American missionaries and Brazilian government workers who said they witnessed cannibalism at Wari' funerals in the late 1950s and early 1960s. If these were the only evidence for Wari' cannibalism, the claim would have little credibility, for outsiders often have reasons to promulgate tales of cannibalistic natives. What lends most weight to the case for the reality of Wari' cannibalism is the testimony of Wari' themselves.

Since the 1950s, scores of older Wari' who remember life before the contact have talked about how they themselves participated in or witnessed cannibalism. Their accounts have been highly consistent, with individuals in different subgroups and different communities repeatedly describing the same events and similar practices. Younger Wari' have grown up hearing their elders talk about eating human flesh, and they regard it as a historical fact with the same degree of reality as other precontact practices they have heard about but never seen, such as the use of slanted beds and the ritual seclusion of warriors. If we cannot believe Wari' when they say they used to eat human flesh, then we ought to dismiss everything else they have said about their lives before the contact.

Studying the Wari'

The primary sources of information for this study are the dozens of older Wari' men and women who have talked with me about their experiences with cannibalism and mourning. I collected most of this information during nineteen months of fieldwork in Wari' communities between June 1985 and June 1987, using four main research strategies: intensive work with knowledgeable elders in one village (Santo André) over the course of a year and a half; similar but less intensive work with older Wari' (especially shamans) in four other villages; a semi-structured survey interview with one or more of the adult heads of the 198 households in these five villages; and my own observations and experiences of community life.

My fieldwork among the Wari' began in June 1985, a month after I had gotten married, when my husband, Bob Pierson, and I arrived in Guajará-Mirim, the town that is nearest to the Wari' reservations and is the commercial center for western Rondônia. My project was designed as a medical anthropological study of Wari' experiences of illness and death before, during, and after the contact. Between June and September, I visited the Wari' communities of Ribeirão, Lage, Tanajura, Santo André and Rio Negro-Ocaia, spending a week or two in each village getting to know people and collecting preliminary data on population and health conditions. In October of 1985, Bob and I moved into a house at Santo André, where I lived for most of the next year and a half. Bob left in April of 1986 to travel in the Andes before returning to the United States, while I continued to live primarily at Santo André until June 1987. Return visits in the summers of

Map A. Location of the study area in South America.

1991 and 1999 allowed me to confirm and cross-check some of my data and interpretations.

॥ ॥ ॥

The village of Santo André is situated on the left bank of the Rio Pacaas Novos, a compellingly beautiful blackwater tributary that flows from the highlands of the Serra dos Pacaas Novos to join the Mamoré River, the broad river that forms the border between Brazil and Bolivia. With its source in the Serra's ancient, weathered rocks, the Pacaas Novos River carries little sediment, and its clear waters are stained dark brown, the color of tea, by decomposing leaves and other organic material whose tannic acid offers welcome relief from the itch of insect bites.

One travels to Santo André by boat; there are no roads, nor footpaths from other villages. In good weather, the trip is easy and pleasant, and the river is like a smooth, dark mirror reflecting the dense tropical forests that line its banks. During storms, the point where the Pacaas Novos meets the Mamoré can be treacherous when protruding rocks and the force of the Mamoré's current create a navigational hazard. The sixty-kilometer trip upriver from the town of Guajará-Mirim takes four or five hours when travelling in one of FUNAI's lightweight aluminum boats filled to capacity with passengers and baggage and powered by a twenty-five-horsepower motor. Travel downriver is faster, especially when the water is high and the current strong. The trip is much slower in the larger barges that carry more people and cargo, and in boats or canoes powered by the small eight-horsepower *rabeta* motors used to navigate shallow water during the dry season.

One reason I had chosen to work among the Wari' was that I was interested in how they were being affected by a huge regional development program that was implemented in the early 1980s. The Polonoroeste project was funded by the World Bank and the Brazilian government. Its centerpieces were the establishment of new agricultural colonies in eastern Rondônia and the paving of a road (BR-364) linking Cuiabá and Porto Velho, the capitals of Mato Grosso and Rondônia, respectively. Tens of thousands of migrants—poor families in search of land, single men lured by the promise of the frontier, middle-class professionals, and entrepreneurs—poured into the region in search of economic opportunities. In the economic boom of the mid-to-late 1980s, Rondônia gained the dubious distinction of having one of the world's most rapid rates of deforestation. Many Indian communities saw their lands illegally occupied by farmers, ranchers, and timber and mining companies. Violence, disease, and social ills proliferated in the boom towns that sprang up in the dusty, denuded landscape where verdant rainforest had stood just a few years before.

The era brought many changes to Guajará-Mirim and the surrounding countryside, but the most intense road building, deforestation, and colonization took place on the other side of Serra dos Pacaas Novos, in the eastern part of the state. Wari' were lucky to be somewhat distanced from the areas that experienced the most rapid changes, but they were officially within the Polonoroeste's scope and were included in some of its projects. In response to critics who decried the project's negative social and environmental impacts, including threats to indigenous peoples and their lands, the World Bank stipulated that funds be devoted to protecting Indian lands and improving health and education in native communities. Although indigenous communities were supposed to be involved in the planning process, in practice the plans were controlled by government administrators and technicians. FUNAI received a considerable amount of Polonoroeste funding and used most of this money to hire more employees and build up the agency's infrastructure. New buildings were constructed in each major Wari' village, including a school, health clinic, and residences for FUNAI workers. Each village received one or more new boats and motors or trucks. In 1986, FUNAI's district office acquired a forty-horsepower motor that could make the trip from Guajará-Mirim to Santo André in less than two hours, cutting travel time for administrators and medical personnel and making it easier to evacuate sick or injured Wari' to Guajará-Mirim. Two-way radios were installed in each post in 1985–86, though Santo André's radio was broken during most of my stay. By the beginning of the '90s, broken equipment was the norm, for when Polonoroeste funding came to an end, FUNAI reverted to its chronically underfunded situation, with little money to repair or replace broken motors, boats, and radios.

In March 1987, Santo André had a population of 190 people living in 29 houses. By 1999, the population had grown to over 300. Santo André's thatched-roof houses are scattered around an open space in the center of the village, where young men play soccer almost every day before dusk. On one side of the clearing are three white-washed FUNAI buildings with aluminum roofs and concrete floors, which house the school, health clinic, administrator's office, and staff residences. In 1985–87, the FUNAI staff included two teachers, a nurse who doubled as post administrator, and sometimes one or two men contracted to do construction work and dig a well. In the 1980s, Royal and Joan Taylor, New Tribes missionaries who have worked with Wari' since before the first contact in the mid-1950s, lived in a house at the upstream edge of the village. After they retired in the early 1990s, Joan's nephew and his wife built a house in the center of the village.

Wari' from Santo André are the source of my most detailed information and understandings about Wari' society. Most of the people at Santo André are descended from the precontact subpopulation that lived in the Dois Irmãos River area, between the Pacaas Novos and Mamoré Rivers. For several decades before they were contacted in 1956, this group was isolated from the rest of the Wari', cut off by the presence of Brazilian rubber tappers who settled along the Pacaas Novos River. Although Wari' never bothered nor were bothered by certain rubber-tapper families, many Brazilians tended to shoot Indians on sight. To avoid hostilities, Wari' withdrew from the larger rivers and made their homes and fields only in the interior, along tributaries of the Dois Irmãos River. Since this river was the central artery around which their precontact settlements were oriented, I refer to the precontact inhabitants of this region as the people of the Dois Irmãos.

Isolated from contact with the rest of the Wari', the Dois Irmãos subgroup lived in a sort of self-contained social universe until 1956, when they became the first Wari' to accept sustained contact with one of the pacification teams composed of government workers and New Tribes missionaries. Most of the rest of the Wari' (in the Negro-Ocaia and Lage/Ribeirão areas) entered contact five years later, beginning in 1961.

In the Dois Irmãos region, Wari' who survived the first devastating epidemics relocated to live closer to the pacification team's base camp at Tanajura, on the left bank of the Pacaas Novos River. Eventually they built a big new village at a site called Pitop. Then in the early 1970s, they moved back into the interior to farm the rich soils near the Dois Irmãos River and its tributaries. In 1981, FUNAI officials declared that everyone had to move out of the interior and relocate at sites on the Pacaas Novos River. The Dois Irmãos population split into two groups that formed the villages of Tanajura and Santo André. This move out of the Dois Irmãos was a move that many Santo André residents resented and regretted, for the site FUNAI chose for Santo André is a long way from soil suitable for farming.

When I began my research in the late 1980s, Santo André was the most demographically and culturally homogeneous of the Wari' villages, with the least mixing of descendants of different precontact subgroups. The great majority of its residents were descended from the precontact Dois Irmãos subpopulation. Since the 1960s, there have been a number of marriages to Wari' from the nearby Negro-Ocaia area, but not until 1991 did a Santo André resident marry someone from the Lage/Ribeirão area.

The description and interpretation of cannibalism presented in this book is based mostly on the beliefs, practices, and recollections of Wari' who lived in the area around the Dois Irmãos River before the contact and who subsequently formed the core of the village at Santo André. My interviews with Wari' in other areas and Vilaça's work at Rio Negro-Ocaia have identified some minor variations in the regional subpopulations' precontact mortuary practices. I try to indicate these in the text, but the culture and history of the Dois Irmãos people are my primary concern. My understandings have been shaped by their ideas, practices, and experiences and by the particular emphases and inflections that the Wari' of Santo André give to their recollections and interpretations of the past. At Santo André, I discussed the issues at the heart of this book—cannibalism, cremation, burial, grief and mourning, and ideas about bodies, spirits, ancestors, animals, health, disease, and death—with all the older people on various occasions, and with many middle-aged individuals as well. The most detailed information and insights came from certain knowledgeable individuals with whom I worked over an extended period: three men and two women between ages sixty and seventy-five, two men in their fifties, and a man and woman in their early forties. The interpretation presented in this book is theirs as much as it is my own.

* * *

While I was living at Santo André in 1985–87, I did several short stints of research with Wari' at Ribeirão, Lage, Tanajura, and Rio Negro-Ocaia, where I worked with elders and shamans and interviewed one or both adults in each household. The 198 families in the five communities I studied comprised 85 percent of the total Wari' population. (The rest of the Wari' live in three villages located near the Mamoré River, which I have not visited: Sagarana, Rio Sotério, and Deolinda.) The main objective of my household interviews was to collect genealogies and information about family members' deaths and illnesses before and after the contact. I particularly wanted to document precontact illness symptoms, collect descriptions of deaths before and after Wari' encountered the diseases that followed contact with outsiders, and learn how people coped with these experiences of illness and death. I cross-checked these data to identify gaps and inconsistencies, to see how different individuals remembered the same events, and to see how Wari' memories of specific deaths and illnesses compared to records kept by health workers, administrators, and missionaries.

Almost everyone readily agreed to provide the family history information

I requested. This was surprising because, as mentioned earlier, Wari' used to strictly avoid speaking the names of the dead. When Alan Mason, the first ethnographer to study the Wari', arrived in the late 1960s, this cultural rule was still very much in place. Since then, however, name avoidances have relaxed somewhat, and by the time I arrived in the mid-1980s, people seldom hesitated to name long-dead ancestors when talking to outsiders like me, although in conversations among themselves Wari' still avoided referring directly to specific dead individuals. The emphasis on setting aside memories and erasing the individuality of the dead is still strong today, but it seems to be in tension with a contradictory desire to remember and talk about close loved ones. This came out in the way people responded to my requests for genealogical information when I was doing my household survey interviews, which often involved walking up to a home and introducing myself to people who had never laid eyes on me before. The cordiality with which most responded to my questions seemed partly a matter of hospitality and partly a function of curiosity and boredom. In a small community where everyone knows everything about everyone else, the entertainment value of the anthropologist with her naïve questions cannot be underestimated. (For some reason, my survey question, "Has anyone in your family been bitten by a dog?" invariably provoked peals of laughter.) Mostly, it seemed that many Wari' were happy to have an opportunity to talk about themselves and to tell a receptive listener about their families and their knowledge of the past. Especially with elderly women and men, these interviews often turned into conversations that wandered far beyond my standard inquiries about births, deaths, and illnesses. Discussions of relatives' deaths sometimes led to reminiscences about their funerals, which was how I first began to learn how Wari' felt about burial and cannibalism.

Systematically interviewing every family in five communities proved invaluable for piecing together a picture of the three major regional subpopulations' histories in the twentieth century. It also uncovered new information about some unusual events and practices, including things Wari' otherwise had avoided talking about, either because they regard them as immoral or aberrant, or because they know how strongly outsiders disapprove. For example, when I had asked directly about suicide and infanticide (the practice of killing unwanted babies at birth), everyone denied that such things ever happened in their society. But when I asked individuals to explain how their own relatives had died, several described cases of infanticide and suicide, and even an alleged murder and hunger cannibalism (discussed in note 2 to Chapter 5). Once they found that I knew about specific events, Wari' proved more open to talking about such sensitive topics, and this ended up revealing a great deal about where they draw the line between moral and immoral, loving and hostile ways to treat human bodies.

* * *

One of the arguments Arens (1979) used in suggesting that institutionalized cannibalism never existed was that people who are alleged to be cannibals almost always deny it. Cannibalism, in his view, is a slanderous accusation that serves the interests of the accuser, not a custom anyone admits as part of his or her own identity.

This is not true of the Wari', however. They freely affirm that they used to eat human flesh, and they talk about it in detail. This is not to say that they go around broadcasting the fact. Wari' want to be respected by outsiders, especially the rubber tappers, merchants, teachers, nurses, administrators, and others with whom they now interact. They are highly sensitive to criticism and accusations of being "uncivilized," and they know that their Brazilian neighbors consider people eating barbaric. When talking to strangers or outsiders who are likely to criticize them, Wari' tend to clam up or deflect questions about cannibalism. Among themselves and with outsiders with whom they are comfortable, they talk about it openly.

The openness with which Wari' admit to being former eaters of human flesh contrasts markedly with the way they hide or deny current practices that they know outsiders disparage. Acute sensitivity to criticism is a Wari' trait that outsiders have commented upon since the first decade after the contact, and it makes them careful about managing the image they present (von Graeve 1989:130). Not only do Wari' tend to deny shameful events like infanticide; they also go to considerable lengths to hide even relatively innocuous practices that Brazilians deem uncivilized.

Insect-eating is one example. There are about twenty species of insects (including beetle larvae, caterpillars, beetles, and ants) that Wari' consider edible, and many families eat insects once or twice a week. Yet I met Brazilian nurses and teachers who had lived in Wari' villages for years and knew nothing about insect-eating, so tightly had Wari' (literally) kept a lid on evidence of it. When I started to collect specimens of edible insects, Wari' were greatly amused, and friends of all ages would drop by my house to examine the creatures floating in jars of rubbing alcohol. Several men and women went out of their way to make sure I got specimens of all the edible species. In return, they made me promise not to let any Brazilians know about the insects, because the FUNAI nurse had announced that he would not give medicine to anyone who ate insects. My neighbor's children appointed themselves as lookouts to safeguard the secret. I always knew when one of the FUNAI employees was headed toward my house because a passel of giggling children would burst through the door, grab the jars off the shelf, and stuff them into a box under my bed. Then the kids and I would sit there trying our best to look innocent when my visitor arrived.

To avoid criticism, Wari' hide their insect-eating, and they initially denied that things like suicide and infanticide ever happened. If the allegation that they used to practice cannibalism were untrue, is it not reasonable to expect that at least one person would have said so in the past forty-five years? Yet I have never met nor heard of any Wari' who denied that eating corpses used to be the norm, nor have the other anthropologists, missionaries, priests, and others who have worked with the Wari' reported such a denial. On the contrary, numerous Wari' have told me and others about their personal experiences of eating human flesh. Over and over, unrelated individuals from different communities have described similar practices, ideas, and ritual details.

The information about Wari' cannibalism that I collected corresponds closely to the findings of other researchers who have worked with the Wari', though the depth of information we have collected has varied. The first anthropologists to study the Wari' were Alan Mason and Bernard von Graeve, North Americans who worked in the Tanajura/Pitop and Sagarana communities, respectively, in the late 1960s and early 1970s. They arrived only a few years after cannibalism had ended but found the Wari' (many of whom had recently converted to Christianity) reluctant to talk much about their traditional religious beliefs and rituals, including cannibalism. By the mid-1980s, Wari' were more open about such topics. In 1986, Denise Meireles, an anthropologist and ethnohistorian from the University of Brasília, published the first detailed analysis of Wari' cannibalism, based on interviews she conducted in short visits to various villages. The same year, Aparecida Vilaça, an ethnographer from the National Museum in Rio de Janeiro, began a study based at Rio Negro-Ocaia. Although we worked independently with different informants and have questioned each other's interpretations on certain points, the retrospective picture of precontact Wari' mortuary practices that has emerged from my work and that of of Vilaça and Meireles is coherent and consistent. By any reasonable standards for documenting past practices that can no longer be observed, there is no question that the Wari' ate their dead.

CHAPTER TWO

WARI' WORLDS

Wari' cannibalism developed and was practiced in the context of the way of life that Wari' experienced before they were brought under Brazilian governmental authority. In their precontact social universe, the distinction between *wari'* (we, persons) and *wijam* (enemies, outsiders) was fundamental. The line between endocannibalism (eating fellow Wari') and exocannibalism (eating outsiders) was drawn at the boundary between *wari'* and *wijam* and reflected the spatial and social separation that existed between the Wari' and other human beings.

For many decades before the contact, the network of groups that spoke the Wari' language constituted the totality of their social universe. Wari' knew of the existence of other Indians and non-Indians and periodically exchanged hostilities with them, but they seem to have no trade, intermarriage, or peaceful relations with other humans. An indication of their social isolation is the fact that, before the contact, Wari' were unfamiliar with a number of crops and technologies used by most other native peoples of the Brazilian rainforest. In contrast to their neighbors the Tuparí and Makurape, the Wari' had no canoes, did not sleep in hammocks, did not use poisoned arrows, did not use tobaccos or hallucinogens, did not grow bitter manioc (*Manihot esculenta*), and had less exposure to smallpox and other epidemic infectious diseases.

Today the Wari' number more than 2,000 people. They are the largest surviving indigenous population in the state of Rondônia and the only major group of Chapakuran speakers. Chapakuran is generally classified as an isolated language family, and its relation to other South American languages has yet to be decided. In the eighteenth and nineteenth centuries, a number of Chapakuran-speaking peoples lived in the floodplains and forests of eastern Bolivia and in Brazil, in upland forest areas along tributaries of the Guaporé, Mamoré, Madeira, and Machado Rivers in what is now the state of Rondônia.[1] By the mid-twentieth century, most other Chapakuran groups had died out or disappeared as a result of the diseases, massacres, enslavement, and assimilationist pressures that traders, settlers, and Jesuit missionaries brought to eastern Bolivia and western Brazil. The Wari' were the major exception. A combination of geographic, historical, cultural, and epidemiological factors made possible their remarkable survival into the second half of the twentieth century as an autonomous society.

In the early 1950s, Wari' territories extended from the lower elevations of the long mountainous ridge called the Serra dos Pacaas Novos to the Mamoré and Madeira Rivers that form the border between Bolivia and Brazil, and from the Ribeirão River and the headwaters of the Mutum Paraná River in the north to the middle Pacaas Novos and Novo Rivers in the south. Lying at an altitude of 115–200 meters, the terrain is mostly flat or gently rolling, covered with high, dense tropical forest growing on well-drained ground (*terra firme*). Lower-lying areas flood during the rainy season, which lasts from about November to April.[2]

Wari' tell a story from the time "of the ancient ones" (*pain hwanana*) about a huge rainstorm that made the rivers rise in a flood that drowned most of their people.[3] The only ones who escaped were a man and his daughters who fled to the Serra dos Pacaas Novos. There they met a group of strangers who lived in caves. The daughters married these cave dwellers' sons, and from their union came the ancestors of the Wari'. According to this story, as children and grandchildren were born, the families moved down from the mountains to grow corn and hunt and fish in the lowland forests around the Negro, Ocaia, and Ouro Preto Rivers, eventually spreading north toward the Lage and Ribeirão Rivers. Although archaeological evidence shows that humans have lived in western Amazonia for thousands of years, with pottery-making groups occupying sites on the middle Madeira River (northeast of Wari' territory) between 5400 and 3200 B.C. (Meggers 1985:310), the lands into which the Wari' moved seem to have been more or less uninhabited.

The population coalesced into territorial groups, which changed over time as new groups developed and others disappeared. In the 1950s, there were six named Wari' subgroups occupying distinct territories: the Oro Nao' (Bat People), Oro Eo (People Who Burp), Oro At (Bone People), Oro Waram (Spider Monkey People), Oro Waram Xijein (Other Spider Monkey

People), and Oro Mon (Feces People). (The prefix *oro-* designates a group of people, animals, or things.) Two smaller subgroups, the Oro Jowin (Capuchin Monkey People) and Oro Kao' Oro Waji (People Who Eat Unripe Things), had their own territories in the early twentieth century, but by the 1950s, they had begun to blend into other subgroups. Oro Kao' Oro Waji affiliated mostly with northern Wari' subgroups, especially the Oro Waram Xijein, while Oro Jowin individuals joined various northern and southern subgroups.

In the north around the Ribeirão and Lage Rivers lived the Oro Mon, Oro Waram, and Oro Waram Xijein. Farther south, around the Negro, Ocaia, and Ouro Preto Rivers, lived the Oro Nao', Oro Eo, and Oro At. Sometime around the beginning of the twentieth century, a third major regional subpopulation developed, when families from the Ouro Preto/Negro-Ocaia area migrated southwest across the Pacaas Novos River to settle in the fertile lands drained by the Dois Irmãos and Novo Rivers. These were the ancestors of the people who are the focus of this book. The original migrants were a mixed group of Oro Nao', Oro Eo, Oro At, and Oro Jowin, but their descendants eventually came to identify themselves as Oro Nao' in certain contexts, such as when they collectively hosted or performed at inter-group parties and later for government records and censuses. Privately, many still identify themselves as Oro Jowin or Oro Eo, reflecting the special pride attached to these two subgroups' precontact reputations for valor and musical accomplishment, respectively.

The story of the flood conveys the Wari' sense of themselves as people related to one another by a common origin and history. Wari' traditionally applied the term *wari'* only to members of the groups that trace their descent from events in that myth and share a common language, mythology, subsistence pattern, and set of ritual traditions. It is these cultural features, rather than any unifying political structure, that distinguish the Wari' as an ethnic group, for in the past they had no tribal-level organizations and little concept of ethnic unity. Before the contact, the largest social unit with which an individual identified was not the Wari' "tribe" but one of the named subgroups (Oro Nao', Oro Eo, Oro Mon, and so on).

Wari' subgroups differ from one another in nuances of cultural styles, including differences in food habits, artisanship, musical repertoires, death and illness keening, and details of myths and other oral traditions. Individuals identify with their own subgroup and are prone to make fun of the speech and supposed peculiarities of people from other subgroups. Dialects vary at both the subgroup and the regional subpopulation levels.

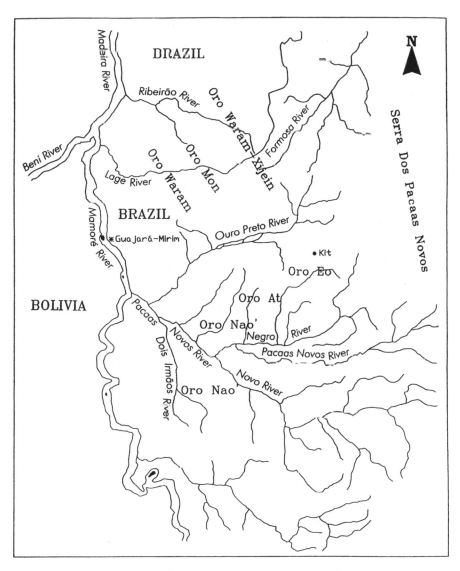

Map B. Precontact Wari' subgroups.

Aside from these stylistic distinctions, the question of the subgroups' social function is a puzzle. Wari' subgroups were neither clans nor lineages. They had no formal leadership nor political structure. Most Wari' married within their own subgroup, but there was no rule of endogamy, and many people married members of other subgroups. In the genealogies I collected from five communities, a third of all individuals had parents from two different subgroups, and the majority identified themselves as members of their mother's subgroup. According to my informants at Santo André, when children were born to parents with different subgroup affiliations, the child's place of birth generally determined his or her subgroup affiliation. As evidence, they pointed to examples of siblings who were born in different subgroup territories and have different subgroup affiliations. Vilaça's informants have suggested other bases for determining subgroup affiliation. For Wari', the question is of little concern, for subgroup identities are flexible and individuals may identify with different subgroups in different contexts and at different times in their lives. Today as in the past, married couples may live in any community where they have kin who will accept them, and they tend to take on the identity of the subgroup that dominates the community where they live. Immigrants often continue to self-identify privately with the subgroup affiliation of their birth, but adopt the dialect and comportment of those among whom they live, and affiliate with the dominant group in collective activities such as inter-group parties.

Relations among families in a precontact subgroup tended to be cordial, with much intermarriage and cooperation in parties, ritual activities, and warfare. Members of different subgroups also married and exchanged parties, but the more distant the relationship, the more likely it was to involve mistrust and wariness. Precontact Wari' subgroups were not always on good terms with one another, and some conflicts flared into open hostilities and even lethal attacks. For the most part, however, Wari' tried to live in peace with one another. They considered their real foes to be non-Wari' outsiders—Brazilians, Bolivians, and other Indians—all of whom they considered potential enemies.

Isolation and Survival in a World of Enemies

The Serra dos Pacaas Novos (where the mythic Wari' ancestors found refuge from the flood) historically has protected the Wari' by forming a natural barrier that discouraged non-Indians from settling east of their territory. The long ridge of the Serra runs from Mato Grosso (where it is called the Serra dos Parecis) through the center of the state of Rondônia. Rising to an elevation of about six hundred meters, its eroded sandstone and strange mushroom-shaped formations are some of the oldest rocks on the planet. As one approaches the Serra, the terrain becomes hilly and streams cascade over rapids and waterfalls, making it impossible to travel by water

These low mountains have served as a refuge where Indians from many different groups have managed to avoid or escape contact with Brazilian national society. Even today, the Serra is home to an unknown number of uncontacted native peoples. A few Wari' hunters have made the long journey to the Serra's lower elevations, but the presence of these "wild," potentially hostile Indians deters them from venturing far in that direction. Among the recently contacted peoples of this region, the most famous are the Uru-Eu-Wau-Wau, a group of several hundred individuals whom Brazilian government teams contacted in the early 1980s. Several other small groups were contacted in the 1990s. For Wari', the Serra's relative isolation has been a blessing, for it has shielded them from attacks and invasions by non-Indians coming from that direction.

Before the contact, Wari' generally tried to avoid face-to-face encounters with other human beings unless they had reason to attack or retaliate against certain enemies. One factor that helped them avoid contact with outsiders was a subsistence pattern oriented to exploiting the resources of the interior forest (terra firme), away from the larger rivers. Wari' had no canoes before the contact and did not fish much in deep water. Their fishing methods were limited to bow and arrow, poison, and catching fish by hand, all techniques that work better in shallow water. Their farming pattern also oriented them away from the bigger rivers, for their principal staple crop is corn (Zea mays), which grows on upland terra firme. Wari' say that corn grows well only in certain dark, friable soils they call 'iri makan, "real earth," and in the Dois Irmãos area, these fertile soils are found only near the smaller rivers and streams, not near the larger Pacaas Novos River. Historically, non-Indians tended to travel and settle along bigger rivers, so the farming and fishing practices that focused Wari' on the soils and shallow streams of the interior forest may have helped reduce encounters with outsiders. This spatial and social distance amounted to a sort of de facto epidemiological buffer zone that probably protected Wari' from some of the infectious diseases that wiped out so many other native populations in the region.

Invasions and Violence

Although Wari' still lived independently in the 1950s, they had been under attack by their neighbors for generations. In the nineteenth century, their enemies were mainly other Indians such as the Karipuna and Uru-Eu-Wau-

Wau, but in the twentieth century, the non-Indian Brazilians and Bolivians who invaded their lands in search of rubber, Brazil nuts, medicinal plants, and minerals came to be their main enemies. Few outsiders settled in the countryside until the late nineteenth century, when the invention of the vulcanization of rubber sparked a commercial boom that sent swarms of rubber tappers up the Ouro Preto and Pacaas Novos Rivers, where rubber (*Hevea brasiliensis*) trees were abundant.[4] To transport latex and other goods out of the region, the Madeira-Mamoré railroad was constructed between the towns of Porto Velho and Guajará-Mirim in 1905–1911, by a U.S. company that had just finished building the Panama Canal. Immortalized as "Mad Maria" and "the Devil's Railroad," the Madeira-Mamoré was built at a staggering cost of over 6,000 workers' lives (about 20% of the work force) lost to malaria, yellow fever, dysentery, beriberi, and other diseases. The tracks ran along the western edge of the territory of the northern Wari' subgroups (the Oro Mon, Oro Waram, and Oro Waram Xijein), and railroad workers killed and kidnapped some Wari'. Wari' warriors retaliated by harassing the train crews and passengers. Older men at Lage chuckled with a tinge of self-mockery as they reminisced about how, in their youth, they used to shoot arrows in vain at the huge black locomotive. Brazilian settlers built homesteads along the rail line, and in 1949, the government established an agricultural colony at a site called Iata on the Madeira River north of Guajará-Mirim. With the permanent presence of more outsiders, the northern Wari' communities increasingly suffered from yellow fever and malaria.

South and east of the town of Guajará-Mirim, rubber tappers settled along the Ouro Preto River, not far from Oro Eo, Oro At, and Oro Nao' villages. This region had been the geographic and economic center of Wari' society, for the stone used for axes and knives came from a site called Kit (which means "knife") on a left-bank tributary of the Ouro Preto. Kit was an Oro Eo village, and Wari' from elsewhere journeyed there to obtain stones, which their Oro Eo hosts gave as gifts to visitors at the end of parties. When rubber tappers took over the Ouro Preto area, Wari' lost control of Kit and lost their source for stone tools, intensifying their need to get metal tools by raiding Brazilian homesteads.

After the world market for Amazonian rubber collapsed in 1912, many rubber tappers left. This decline in the non-Indian populace helped Wari' maintain their autonomy for almost another half century. World War II sparked a second rubber boom when the Japanese blockade of Pacific sea routes cut off Allied supplies of Malaysian rubber, and the Brazilian government offered incentives to boost Amazonian rubber production. Hundreds of poor Brazilians once again poured into the forests of western Rondônia. By the 1950s, 789 rubber tappers were working in the region around the Pacaas Novos River (von Graeve 1989:29, 50). Many of these newcomers were Nordestinos, migrants from northeastern Brazil who had little experience with Indians and tended to shoot on sight if they saw one. Their presence made it more and more dangerous for Wari' to travel between the northern communities in the Lage/Ribeirão area and the southern communities around the Ouro Preto and Negro-Ocaia Rivers. Although they still maintained some contacts through visiting and intermarriage, these two Wari' regional populations became increasingly separated.

The third regional population, the Wari' who had settled in the Dois Irmãos area around the turn of the century and who are the focus of this book, stayed in touch with their relatives on the other side of the Pacaas Novos River for a while, but the growing non-Indian presence made travel increasingly dangerous. By the 1930s, the Dois Irmãos people were cut off entirely from the rest of the Wari'. Surrounded by enemies, Wari' felt more and more threatened. In this context of interethnic hostilities, killing an enemy outsider was the most highly valued act a Wari' man could perform.

Warfare and Exocannibalism

Wari' defended themselves and scared off intruders by shooting those who invaded their territory. They also retaliated for attacks against their people by organizing groups of warriors who walked long distances through the forest to attack Brazilians on the outskirts of Wari' territory. In many ways, Wari' equated killing enemies with hunting animals, and their preparations for warfare reflected this. When a group of men decided to form a war party, they honed their skills and built up their esprit de corps by hunting together day after day in an animated spirit of raucous exuberance celebrated with whoops and calls back and forth among the group. The warriors and the older boys who would accompany them separated themselves from women and children and slept together in the men's house, where they cooked their own food, made new arrows, and prepared for the war expedition.

To reduce the risk of retaliation, Wari' war parties usually walked for several days to attack enemies who lived at a distance. Their journey was surrounded with rituals to ensure the success of the attack, and these were the special obligation of a man chosen to serve as the expedition's ritual leader. His primary duty was to carry a special bundle of firebrands (made from slow-burning palm petioles called *muruhut*), which was treated as sacred and held carefully in the arms, "like a baby," Wari' say. These firebrands were tied together with the same kind of liana (*makuri xe'*, "fire vine") that Wari' used in funerals to tie the firewood for roasting a corpse in preparation for endocannibalism. On war expeditions, the firebrands tied with this liana were used to roast the enemy's body parts in preparation for exocannibalism.

When the warriors reached the place chosen for the attack, the ritual leader untied the bundle and gave each man one of the firebrands to carry. Wari' say this allowed him to make fire if he became separated from the others after the attack. The ritual fire bearer was supposed to shoot the first arrow, which was followed by a volley of arrows from his companions. Although everyone who participated in the attack was considered to have killed the enemy, the fire bearer was said to be the "true" killer.

After shooting an enemy, Wari' usually took body parts. If the attack occurred far from home, the warriors commonly took only the head and limbs and left the heavy body trunk behind.[5] They then scattered in various directions to make it more difficult for pursuers to follow. After regrouping in the forest, they put their firebrands together again and kindled a fire to roast the enemy's flesh. The warriors did not eat any of this themselves but carried it home to be eaten by people who had not taken part in the kill. When killings took place closer to home, so that spoilage of the flesh was not an issue, warriors left the body parts raw and carried them home to be roasted by those who had stayed behind (Vilaça 2000:90).

When they arrived home, the warriors received a joyous ritual welcome. The women picked up the men and carried them in their arms to the men's house (*kaxa'*), where they bathed them with warm water and rubbed their bodies with fresh oil. The enemy body parts received less ceremonious treatment. Villagers, especially young boys, gathered around the body parts to heap them with abuse and ridicule, beating them with sticks and shooting them full of arrows. Afterward, the flesh was divided among various individuals, who carried it home to eat.

My informants insist that in the Dois Irmãos area, enemy flesh was eaten only by men, especially the elderly men who had stayed at home and had not taken part in the kill.[6] No one who shot the enemy or witnessed the killing could eat it, for a basic principle of Wari' cannibalism is that one does not eat one's own blood relative, and Wari' believe that the victim's blood enters the bodies of everyone who sees the killing, whether or not they actually shoot an arrow. Absorbed into the killer's body, this enemy blood creates a relationship analogous to consanguinity between the killer and his victim's spirit. Wari' say the enemy spirit becomes the "child" of the killer in whose body it resides and calls the killer "father." Just as a father does not eat his own dead children, Wari' warriors did not eat their victims.

The spirit-blood that entered the warriors' bodies was thought to be a powerful vitalizing, health- and growth-enhancing substance, and the members of a war party cultivated its positive effects by observing several weeks of ritual seclusion. Individual Wari' placed far more value on incorporating this invisible enemy spirit-blood than on eating enemy flesh. They did not believe that those who ate enemy flesh acquired the victim's courage, life force, personality, identity, or anything else. The flesh was just dead meat, inert substance devoid of any special properties. It was the enemy's spirit-blood, not the flesh, that had transformative powers.

Westerners tend to think of cannibalism only in terms of oral ingestion, but for Wari' and many other native South Americans, eating or drinking flesh or bones is just one mode of consuming and incorporating the bodies of others. Although pursuing this would lead far beyond the scope of this study, it is worth noting that in lowland South America, flesh eating is part of a broad range of incorporative acts that may include taking trophy heads; conquering, taming, or seducing enemy spirits; and absorbing and transforming enemy blood.

Though the Wari' who ate roasted enemy flesh gained no particular material or spiritual benefit from doing so, they savored the act of eating as the most tangible embodiment of their collective triumph over the enemy. The way they handled and ate enemy body parts expressed hatred and disdain and marked enemies as non-persons equated with animal prey. Although Wari' cooked and ate enemy flesh in much the same way as they cooked and ate animal meat, they never treated animals quite so rudely. Elders say that when they ate enemy flesh they grunted, joked, and made rude comments about the victim. In marked contrast to the respectful "table manners" of funerary cannibalism, in which bits of flesh were held delicately on wooden picks and eaten slowly and carefully, Wari' grasped big chunks of enemy flesh in their hands and ate it directly off the bone. Their practice of exocannibalism was a classic example of the use of cannibalism to express antagonism and dominance—in this case, dominance over the hostile enemies who lurked beyond the bounds of Wari' society. Closer to home, very different relationships and modes of consuming human bodies prevailed.

Precontact Communities

At the center of Wari' life before the contact was the intimate world of households, villages, and social networks organized around ties of kinship and marriage. In the mid-1950s, there were several dozen Wari' settlements that varied in size but most typically consisted of about twenty to thirty individuals living in three to seven family dwellings. Unlike many other Brazilian Indians, Wari' did not build large multi-family dwellings (called *malocas* in Portuguese). Nuclear family households were and still are the norm. Two families with children rarely live together on a permanent basis, although elderly parents, childless newlyweds, and divorced or widowed adults often live with relatives.[7]

Before the contact, all but the smallest settlements had a men's house, called the *kaxa'*.[8] Boys moved into the kaxa' when they were about eight to ten years old and slept and ate there until they married. The kaxa' was a center of activity for married men also, a place where they socialized in the evening and slept at times that required separation from women and children, such as before and after an enemy-killing expedition.

Precontact dwellings were tall lean-to structures, open on three sides, with a thick palm thatch roof that rose four to five meters in front and slanted down to within half a meter of the ground at the rear. Under the high roof in the front of the house, the family had its cooking hearths on the dirt floor and stored ears of corn in tall cylindrical stacks as much as two meters in diameter. Most of the rest of the space inside the house was taken up by a long, slanted bed called a *tapit*, made of a log frame covered with slats of *paxiuba* bark (*Iriartea* sp.).[9] Five meters or more wide and about 140 centimeters deep, the bed tilted markedly from head to foot. At the top, a long, thin log served as a pillow; at the foot, a thicker log supported sleepers' knees and legs. Wari' kept small fires burning on the ground underneath to provide warmth and repel insects. This space beneath the tapit was also where they buried placentas, stillbirths, and the pulverized remnants of burned bones, ceramic pots, firewood, and ashes left after a funeral.

Before the contact, Wari' built their houses next to their corn fields. Each household cleared and planted its own field, but all the fields in a settlement usually were adjacent to one another, so that homes were scattered around a single large clearing. In the Dois Irmãos area, families usually cleared a new field and built a new house every year. A settlement ideally remained in the same general area until fertile soil or other resources started to run out (usually after about three to five years) or other events (such as the death of an adult) made the group decide to move to another site, which usually was on a different stream in the same general region. In the Negro-Ocaia/Ouro Preto region, some villages seem to have remained longer in the same place, a circumstance that my Dois Irmãos informants attributed to laziness. In 1961, when Oro Nao' from the Dois Irmãos area renewed relations with

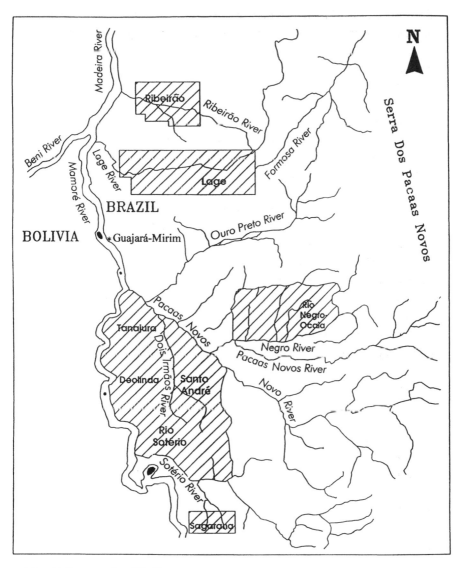

Map C. *Present-day Wari' reserves.*

Oro Nao' in the Negro-Ocaia region, they nicknamed the Negro-Ocaia people "Bat People of the Feces" because their villages stank. In general, however, periodic mobility was and is a principle of Wari' adaptation to the local environment.

Contemporary Communities

Settlement patterns changed markedly after the contact, and this affected Wari' subsistence and social life in many ways. Today they live in eight major villages and several smaller hamlets in legally recognized indigenous reserves located within an eighty-kilometer radius of the town of Guajará-Mirim. The Brazilian government's Indian agency, FUNAI, administers seven major communities in these reserves: Ribeirão, Lage, Tanajura, Deolinda, Rio Sotério, Santo André, and Rio Negro-Ocaia. The Catholic diocese of Guajará-Mirim administers an eighth community, Sagarana. Descendants of the northern Wari' subgroups—the Oro Mon, Oro Waram, and Oro Waram Xijein—are the core members of Lage and Ribeirão. To the south, most people who live at Rio Negro-Ocaia are descended from the Oro Nao', Oro At, and Oro Eo subgroups. Descendants of Dois Irmãos area inhabitants are the core of Santo André, Tanajura, Deolinda, and Rio Sotério. Sagarana was established by Catholic priests in 1965, at a site near the confluence of the Guaporé and Mamoré Rivers that was not within precontact Wari' territory, and its residents include descendants from all three precontact subpopulations, especially the Lage/Ribeirão and Negro-Ocaia groups.

One of the biggest changes after the contact was the abandonment of the institution of the men's house (*kaxa'*). Most bachelors now live with their families, and men no longer have a gathering place of their own. Wari' also stopped building tall lean-to-style houses and sleeping on slanted beds. Today their houses are similar to those built by their Brazilian neighbors: rectangular structures of hardwood beams covered with a peaked thatch roof and one or two rooms enclosed by four walls. Many are raised on stilts, with a *paxiuba* bark floor that often extends past one wall to make a porch where much domestic activity and socializing takes place. Other houses sit on the ground and have dirt floors, with walls of palm bark slats, woven mats, or sometimes mud bricks or boards. A few families never get around to erecting walls and simply live in the open on a raised platform under a thatched roof. For funerals and parties, Wari' remove the house floor and three walls, thereby approximating the spatial arrangement of precontact dwellings.

Most households have little or no furniture, though a few families have made or bought stools, a shelf, or a table and bench. Families sleep together under mosquito nets on mats on the raised floor or on a flat sleeping platform, often using a long, thin log as a pillow. Cooking hearths are on the ground or on clay-covered wooden tables under an extension of the thatched roof. As they did in the past, Wari' light small fires beneath the house floor to ward off the cold and the mosquitoes, and they continue to bury placentas and miscarried fetuses under the sleeping platform or floor.

* * *

The policy of Brazil's government Indian agency has been to concentrate Wari' into a few administrative villages and to provide medical care and schools only at the larger villages, and most Wari' families now have a house in one of them. Each village has a school and a small medical clinic, staffed by one or more teachers and a nursing aide who live in the village. The larger villages also have a resident administrator, the *chefe de posto* (post chief). Until recently, FUNAI employees and their families were all non-Indian, except for one nursing aide, who is a Wari' woman who was orphaned and raised by a Brazilian family. In the past few years, some young Wari' men and women have begun to work as teachers and health aides (*monitores de saúde*).

Six villages are accessible only by boat, and two are accessible by road. Most are located at sites where Wari' did not live before the contact, since administrators chose these sites to mark reserve boundaries or for their easy access to boat or truck transportation, not for their abundance of subsistence resources. Santo André's location is particularly unfortunate, because people have to walk over ten kilometers (almost seven miles) or canoe for many hours to reach the nearest place with soil suitable for planting corn. Consequently, they increasingly eat less nutrient-rich corn and more starchy manioc and expend a lot of energy carrying food from the fields to the village. Family life is disrupted when adults have to live at their gardens while their children attend school in the village.

All the present FUNAI villages except Deolinda are much larger than precontact settlements were, ranging from about one hundred to four hundred or more inhabitants. This has had negative effects on subsistence, for game, fish, fertile soils, and other resources are quickly depleted in the vicinity of large, sedentary settlements. Subsistence resources are dispersed in the rainforest, and exploiting them requires mobility so that plants and insects can be gathered and game and fish killed when and where they are available. FUNAI's policy of pouring its limited resources into building up large, permanent village infrastructures conflicts with Wari' ecological priorities. Among inhabitants at Santo André, administrators' refusal to let them relocate to a more fertile site has been the single biggest grievance against the government.

Social Relations

Wari' society is highly egalitarian, and differences in personal wealth are minimal. They have no chiefs, headmen, or permanent positions of leadership, although in the 1990s, in response to pressure from outsiders, Santo André villagers began to elect four or five men to serve simultaneously as "chiefs" for a while. At the community level, major decisions are made by consensus, and both women and men take part in public discussions. Wari' tend to respect the opinions of certain individuals more than others, and men and women gain status when they organize festivals, lead musical performances, know a great deal about oral traditions and precontact culture, or (for men in the past) serve as ritual leader of a war expedition. Leadership tends to be ephemeral, and someone who leads in one activity will not necessarily lead other activities. No one has power to coerce others; even within a household, parents have only limited authority over their children, and a husband has little power to force his wife to do something against her will. The biggest control on individual behavior is acute sensitivity to public opinion and criticism.

Wari' have no lineages, formal descent groups, or ritual organizations. Kinship is the glue that holds their society together,[10] for individuals have a highly developed sense of responsibilities to their relatives by blood and by marriage. These include expectations about how game and fish should be shared and help provided, ideas about who should support whom in a conflict, and definitions of the proper roles of consanguines and affines in funerals. Most marriages are arranged by the parents or other senior kin of the bride and groom. There are no rules to specify who should marry whom, but there are extensive incest rules specifying which relatives should not marry. Marriage is forbidden within the nuclear family and to first cousins (both cross-cousins and parallel cousins) and their offspring; parents' siblings; and grandparents, grandparents' siblings, and their respective offspring (Meireles 1986:273, Vilaça 1992). This forces individuals to seek spouses from outside their own close kin groups and promotes ties to other families. At the same time, families tend to encourage young people to look for spouses in the families that already have intermarried with their own (Mason 1977:122–124). For example, if a woman from Family A marries a man from Family B, her younger siblings (in Family A) are likely to consider marrying someone from Family B, such as a sibling or cousin of their sister's husband. This preference for repeating pre-established marital alliances means that each extended family tends to recognize certain other extended families as their primary affines. When someone dies, it is these close relatives by marriage whom the dead person's family calls on to perform the tasks necessary for the funeral, which used to include eating the corpse.

The Wari' practiced polygyny before the contact, but only a few men actually had more than one wife. Among those who did, the preference was for the second wife to be a sister or classificatory sister of the first wife. The sense of marriage as a relationship between two families, not just two individuals, is evident in the practices of levirate and sororate. When a married man dies, his brother or other close male relative is expected to marry the dead man's widow and raise his children. When a married woman dies, her sister or other close female relative is expected to marry the widower. After the contact, outsiders discouraged polygyny, and since men no longer have second wives, more widows and widowers never remarry, though Wari' still recognize their duty to take care of a deceased sibling's spouse and children.

A newly married husband owes an informal period of bride service to his wife's family, which he typically fulfills by living with her parents for a year or so, during which time the son-in-law is expected to hunt for his wife's family and help his father-in-law clear fields. This is a kind of trial marriage period; if the couple does not get along, they can separate with little fuss or stigma, as long as the woman is not yet pregnant. With the birth of their first baby, the marriage is considered permanent and indissoluble. Couples with children rarely divorce, and the few men who abandon their children suffer irredeemable loss of status. With the birth of their first child, young couples usually build a house of their own. They are free to live near either spouse's family, and Wari' families commonly live in several places over the course of their lives—sometimes near the husband's relatives, and other times near the wife's.

Before the contact, there was no rule of village exogamy, but in practice, most Wari' married someone from another village. This happened because settlements were smaller than they are now and tended to be composed of closely related families among whom (because of the extensive incest rules) young people could find few potential marriage partners. Thus, Wari' tend to think of their affines as outsiders, as people who come from elsewhere

(Vilaça 1996:75). Since the contact, the population's concentration into a few large villages has permitted more marriages between men and women from the same community. Although big villages create social and ecological problems, Wari' say that one of the few good things about today's bigger villages is the greater possibility that both husband and wife can live near their own kin.

Sibling relations are among the most important in Wari' lives, and both women and men consider it ideal to live near their own sisters and brothers. Relations between same-sex siblings are intimate, and siblings of the same sex work together a great deal. Relations between sisters and brothers also are close. Elder brothers ideally have a role in arranging their sisters' marriages, and brothers defend their sisters in disputes. In funerals, the dead person's adult siblings act as a group and take an active role in making decisions about funeral arrangements.[11]

* * *

The tenor of everyday life in Wari' communities is generally calm. People treat each other politely; they seldom scream or shout at one another except in jest, and they avoid overt confrontations. When disagreements do arise, most are resolved quickly, but serious internal conflicts may be dealt with through ritualized fights called *ka mixita wa*. (*Mixita* is a verb meaning "to strike on the head.") The most common offenses that spark such fights are adultery or a man's threat to beat his wife; thus, mixita fights typically pit groups of affines against one another. Each adult man has a long fighting stick (*temem*) about a meter and a half in length, made of the hard, smooth wood of the *pupunha* palm. Men keep these sticks in the rafters of their houses, and when a fight breaks out, they grab them and rush to aid the participants to whom they are most closely related. Although theoretically only men fight, women (especially older women) have been known to do their part in defense of their kin, though women do not use temem.

Mixita fights follow strict rules. Blows can be struck only with temem, and opponents are supposed to hit each other only on the head and shoulders; no other weapons or physical contact are allowed. In one fight at Santo André in 1986, a man grabbed a machete and cut off the tip of his father-in-law's finger. He was widely criticized, not because he struck his wife's father, but because he used a nontraditional weapon and cut him on the hand. Wari' say the objective of mixita fights is never to kill, but only to hurt and punish. The fighting continues until blood is flowing from the heads of people on both sides, and then it stops. In the cases I observed, the outburst of violence seemed cathartic. Afterwards, the aggrieved parties either sat down to talk through the problem, or one family left the village for a while, returning later after passions had cooled. After such confrontations, those involved usually maintain carefully reserved behavior toward one another.

On the surface, minor grievances are quickly forgiven if not forgotten, but serious conflicts can poison interpersonal relations for years or even generations. When relations between two families that have intermarried are irreparably strained, senior kin may declare that there will be no more marriages between them. Affines who are on bad terms with each other will not be asked to serve as helpers at funerals.

Beneath the surface of civility, Wari' communities (like small communities everywhere) are a tangle of factions, feuds, and long-running resentments. As is common among native Amazonians, one frequent response to social tension is to move away. Extended kinship networks composed of relatives by blood and marriage expand individuals' options to relocate elsewhere and thus provide a kind of social safety valve. Kin ties are also invaluable in times of crisis. During the precontact massacres and contact-era epidemics, Wari' fled to their relatives' villages. Today, as in the past, after someone dies, his or her immediate family often goes to stay with relatives elsewhere for months or even years.

Intergroup Festivals: Models of Death as Predatory Exchange

In addition to ties of kinship and marriage, amicable relations among members of different communities and subgroups are created and maintained through various types of parties or festivals, including *tamara, hütop,* and *hüroroin.* Understanding these parties is central to understanding how Wari' think about death, because Wari' see their relations to the spirits of their dead and other members of the underworld as analogous to relations between groups that host parties for each other. In the underwater world of the ancestors, a hüroroin festival is constantly underway, and when someone is dying, his or her spirit journeys there and becomes a guest at that party. When the ancestors come to earth as a group, they act like guests who sing and dance for their hosts, the living Wari'.

These Wari' parties are structured around ritualized oppositions between a group of hosts and a group of guests. In parties attended by people from different villages or subgroups, the guests travel to the host village and sing and dance for their hosts. The hosts feed their guests and (in hüroroin and hütop) symbolically kill, then later revive, some of the male guests.

The most elaborate festival is hüroroin, which goes on day and night for

2. Shielded behind a screen of palm fronds, male visitors emerge from the forest making a cacophony of sounds on hüroroin, "trumpets" made of long reeds with duck eggs and gourds mounted on the end. When they reached the center of Santo André's village space, the men summoned the hosts' unmarried daughters and engaged them in teasing banter with sexual innuendoes. (Hüroroin party, 1986)

3. Smeared with black resin, male guests become wind spirits (jami hotowa), who storm out of the forest to vandalize the hosts' houses. On the left, Quimoin tries to protect her house. (Hüroroin party, 1986)

4. The shaman, Maxun Kwarain (in the center, wearing a hat), helps a guest who is feeling unsteady during the beer drinking and vomiting. Two other hosts, Tito (left) and Jimon O' (right), look on. (Hüroroin party, 1986)

5. As a senior host, Oro Iram (in the center) sits watching over the male guests who passed out after drinking and vomiting. The men are in the state of unconsciousness that leads to itam, but Wari' said no one at this party went into complete itam, which is indicated by bleeding from the mouth. The hosts carried the unconscious guests to the forest, where female guests sat in a line (behind Oro Iram), singing nonstop throughout the festival. Periodically, rowdy groups of male hosts swooped into the clearing and moved single file down the line of singing women, pantomiming sexual intercourse with each one. The men competed to come up with outrageous erotic gestures, much to the amusement of their wives and children, who stood watching. The singing women totally ignored the men's antics. (Hüroroin party, 1986)

several days against a backdrop of complex syncopated rhythms from two suspended log drums played by two men simultaneously. In hüroroin, male guests act out various forms of transgression against their hosts. Shielded behind a wall of palm fronds, they emerge from the forest to invade the host village, blowing a cacophony of sounds on long, trumpet-like instruments called *hüroroin*. Male guests engage in lewd sexually-charged banter with host women, and (in the guise of wind spirits, *jami hotowa*) they vandalize houses. Their hosts punish these offenses by making the adult male visitors drink great quantities of strongly fermented corn beer brewed in a vat made of a huge hollowed-out log. It is a point of honor for male guests to demonstrate their fortitude by consuming all the beer, and since it is impossible to drink so much, they make themselves vomit in order to be able to drink more. There is an art to vomiting elegantly, and some men practice (by tickling the throat with a feather) for weeks before a party.

With repeated drinking and vomiting, some male guests pass out in a state of unconsciousness (called *itam*), which Wari' consider a kind of death. This is explicitly analogous to hunting animals and killing human enemies: when a guest falls into itam and bleeds from the mouth, the male host who organized the party exults, "I've killed my prey [*watamata*]!" or something similar. Thus, hüroroin casts hosts and guests in the roles of predator and prey.

Wari' see this as the model for human death. When a dying person's spirit arrives at the hüroroin party in the underworld, the master of the underworld offers corn beer. If the person's spirit drinks it, the spirit passes out in itam underwater, while on earth his or her physical body dies. Thus, human death is directly equated with the rites of symbolic predation at intergroup parties.

It would be easy to interpret the dynamics of these parties only in terms of oppositions and hostility, but anyone who has stayed until the end of a hüroroin party knows that is not the whole story. While guests lie unconscious, senior male hosts sit nearby watching over them as the female guests sing. Then at dawn on the final day, the hosts revive the male guests with a warm water bath, which Wari' associate with birth and rebirth. The ritualized interactions between hosts and guests immediately change from opposition to solidarity. All the senior men from both groups form a long line, arms around one another's shoulders, and together they perform a long, raucous song and dance in an exuberant celebration of the spirit of temporary unity that anthropologists call *communitas*. Several people at Santo André told me that smoothing relations between hosts and visitors is one of the purposes of such parties. For several months after the hüroroin at Santo André in 1986, the good feelings toward Rio Negro-Ocaia were palpable and most evident in the fact that Wari' travelling downriver from Rio Negro-Ocaia stopped to visit, whereas before they usually passed by with just a wave.

Consistent with the balanced reciprocity that pervades Wari' social arrangements, intergroup parties ideally are loosely reciprocal: sometime later, the people who were guests at the first party ought to throw a party in return. Roles reverse, and the former hosts become the guests who sing, dance, commit ritualized transgressions, drink beer, vomit, and are "killed" and revived. A parallel role reversal in relations between the living and the dead occurs when the spirits of Wari' ancestors and their underworld companions periodically emerge from the water in animal bodies to sing, dance, and let themselves be killed by living Wari'.

* * *

The precontact Wari' universe was organized like a series of concentric spheres distinguished by different degrees of trust and intimacy and different dynamics of exchange, predation, and bodily consumption. At the center was the intimate world of domestic life and the network of neighboring communities, a world in which mutual obligations and responsibilities to one's kin by blood and by marriage were paramount. Among affines, these responsibilities included commitments to share meat and fish and to perform funeral services for one another, including the duty to consume one another's corpses in the respectful rituals of endocannibalism.

Moving outward through increasing degrees of spatial and social distance was the network of Wari' regional subgroups that interacted through visits, intermarriage, and exchanges of parties. Similar relations extended to the underworld society of ancestors and animal spirits. Within this sphere, one killed and consumed others symbolically in the ritual predation enacted at parties that framed interactions between social groups in an idiom of voluntary mutual predation. The world of *wari'*, persons, revolved around arrangements in which partners repeatedly traded positions as predators and prey, eaters and eaten, willingly letting themselves or their relatives be symbolically "killed" at parties or literally eaten at funerals.

Outside this social sphere organized by reciprocity lay the dangerous realms of *wijam*, enemies with whom relations were unmitigatedly hostile. Lacking any positive relationships of social exchange with non-Wari' human beings, Wari' viewed them as nonpersons and killed and ate them in ways that expressed this. The distinction between *wari'* (persons) and *wijam* (nonpersons, outsiders) was vividly enacted in the contrasting modes of endo- and exocannibalism. In the 1950s and '60s, the separation between the worlds of *wari'* and *wijam* ended when wijam invaded Wari' lives in ways that changed them forever.

CHAPTER THREE

CULTURAL COLLISIONS

The end of Wari' autonomy came in stages between 1956 and 1969, when expeditions sponsored by the SPI (Indian Protection Service, the Brazilian government Indian agency at that time) persuaded various groups of Wari' to break their isolation and enter into peaceful relations with outsiders. Wari' in the Dois Irmãos area were the first to be contacted, in 1956, by a team composed of Brazilian SPI employees and missionaries from the United States and Canada affiliated with the New Tribes Mission (NTM), an evangelical Protestant organization devoted to bringing Christianity to native peoples, especially those with little prior contact with Western civilization. Most of the rest of the Wari' population entered contact in 1961–62, as a result of government expeditions into the Lage, Negro-Ocaia, and Ribeirão areas. NTM missionaries took part in the Lage expedition, a Catholic priest accompanied the Negro-Ocaia expedition, and the SPI handled the contact at Ribeirão on its own.

Contact with members of these expeditions introduced infectious diseases to which the previously semi-isolated Wari' population had acquired little or no immunological resistance. These diseases — and the medicines the outsiders could give to treat them — were the key factor that undermined Wari' autonomy. As sickness spread and deaths mounted, they began to allow the outsiders to bring medicines into their villages or moved closer to the outsiders' camps. However, some families, including most of the Oro Eo subgroup in the Negro-Ocaia area, rejected contact and moved away deeper into the forest. Some managed to live independently for a year or more, but malaria and other diseases still reached them, undermining even the most determined survivors' ability and will to live on their own. By 1962 or early

1963, nearly all Wari' had given up resistance and moved to live in or near the government-administered settlements.

The exception was a group of about thirty Oro Mon, who fled the Lage epidemics in 1961 and took refuge in the lower Serra dos Pacaas Novos near the headwaters of the Mutum Paraná River. They lived independently until 1969, when Brazilians shot some of their people and Oro Mon retaliated by attacking a Brazilian family. This prompted the SPI to send pacified Oro Mon men to track down the "wild" Oro Mon and persuade them to come out of the forest. "Just come visit us; your relatives miss you a lot," they pleaded. A few days after arriving at the SPI post, the newly contacted Oro Mon were shipped off to the distant Catholic-run settlement at Sagarana. Two weeks later, a measles epidemic at Sagarana killed fifteen of the thirty newly contacted Oro Mon. To this day, survivors nurse bitter memories of what they regard as a betrayal of their trust.

* * *

The pressure to pacify the Wari' came from businessmen and politicians eager to exploit the rubber, Brazil nuts, cassiterite (tin ore), and other commercial resources in the lands that Wari' controlled. From World War II onwards, hostilities had been mounting. Rubber entrepreneurs in Guajará-Mirim hired men to attack Wari' villages and equipped them with machine guns, shotguns, rifles, and revolvers. These assassins' attacks usually came at dawn, when sleepy Wari' women and children offered easy targets. In the two decades or so before the contact, attacks by Brazilians caused a quarter of all Wari' deaths (Conklin 1989:529–530). A local newspaper reported that hired gunmen sometimes took Indian body parts as trophies to prove they had fulfilled their contracts. The assassins would cut off an ear or gouge out Wari' children's eyes and display these body parts in town (*Alto do Madeira* 1957).

Wari' retaliated with what amounted to a kind of guerrilla warfare of sudden attacks at unpredictable locations. Though the number of Brazilians killed by Wari' was relatively small, gruesome tales of mutilated corpses and missing body parts terrified Brazilians living at isolated farms and rubber-collecting sites. Panic swept the countryside, and settlers abandoned their rural homesteads in droves to seek safety in town.

In counterpoint to this guerrilla warfare, one Wari' man invented a sort of guerrilla theater. As a youth, he had been shot, wounded, and kidnapped by Brazilians, who took him to live in a town to the north, where he learned to speak Portuguese. Several years later, SPI agents took him back to the

Lage-Ribeirão area in hopes that he would help them contact the Wari'. Instead, the young man escaped and found his way back to his relatives. For years afterwards, he delighted in using his knowledge of Portuguese to taunt Brazilian settlers and play off their fears of savagery, sex, and cannibalism. Decked out in bright red body paint and feathers, he would suddenly materialize at the edge of a clearing near a settler's house. Shaking his penis in one hand and brandishing a bow and arrow in the other, this "wild" Indian would unnerve the settlers by crying out in Portuguese, "*Traz uma mulher bonita pra mim! Quero comer!*" [Bring me a pretty woman! I want to eat!]. ("Eating" is a euphemism for sexual intercourse in Brazil.)

Rumors of cannibalism were prominent in the incendiary mix of images that swirled through western Rondônia in the 1950s and early 1960s, feeding the public outcry for the government to bring the Wari' under control. Journalists reported grisly details of how the corpses of victims of Indian attacks had been dismembered and mutilated. A photograph in the Guajará-Mirim newspaper showed a man's corpse studded with arrows and thirty-six arrow wounds. Although outsiders seem to have had little or no direct evidence of cannibalism, the missing body parts were widely believed to have ended up in Wari' stomachs. One particularly inflammatory incident was the case of a Catholic priest from São Paulo who disappeared in 1950 while attempting to make contact on his own with Wari' in the Lage area. Like others who disappeared in the region, the priest was rumored to have been killed and eaten.

The rumors of cannibalistic Indians that circulated in Rondônia in the 1950s played much the same role that sixteenth-century accounts of cannibalism had played in the European conquest of coastal South America: they provided moral justification for taking control of Indians and their land. Under pressure from politicians, businessmen, and the public, employees of the SPI (which was chronically short of funds and personnel) joined forces with the New Tribes missionaries, who had a long-term commitment to the work of bringing God's Word to the Wari'.

First Contacts

In 1954, a joint SPI/NTM team established a base camp at an abandoned rubber-collecting site called Tanajura on the left bank of the lower Pacaas Novos River. Following the standard "attraction" procedures that Brazilian government agents have used for decades, the SPI/NTM men left knives, machetes, clothing, food, mirrors, and other presents along trails in the forest where Wari' might find them, hoping these gifts would convince them of the outsiders' peaceful intentions and entice them to come closer. In 1956, small groups of Wari' men and boys began to come out of the forest and receive presents directly from the men of the SPI and the NTM.

This was the beginning of the end of Wari' independence, for after the presents came the diseases. By all accounts, NTM missionaries tried hard to prevent disease from spreading to the Wari'. They required all missionaries to be quarantined from any contact with Indians for two weeks after each trip to town. But the SPI agents were less careful about sanitary precautions. Small groups of Wari' men and boys began to spend the night at the expedition's base camp, sleeping under mosquito nets with the SPI workers. Soon Wari' were coming out of the forest with reports of people dying from strange sicknesses. Mumps, influenza, and malaria seem to have spread in quick succession.

The New Tribes missionaries gave anti-malarials and penicillin to sick Indians who arrived at Tanajura. The penicillin's rapid, seemingly miraculous effects convinced Wari' to let members of the contact team bring medicines to sick people in the villages. Although epidemics killed many in the Dois Irmãos population, the New Tribes missionaries' diligence in providing medical care in those early years kept the death rate considerably lower than in the other, less well managed contacts that followed in 1961–62 and 1969.

On one of their early visits to Wari' villages in 1957, members of the contact team arrived during the funeral for a respected middle-aged Wari' man. Among the visitors were a Canadian missionary, two U.S. missionaries, and a Brazilian SPI employee. In 1985, one of these missionaries described to me the funeral scene he had witnessed in 1957. He recalled that Wari' crowded together around the corpse, keening endlessly for days. Three decades after the event, he still cringed as he recalled how the putrid stench of the decaying corpse forced him to crouch upwind from the funeral gathering. The New Tribes missionaries stayed through the funeral, but having so recently gained the Indians' trust, they did not feel themselves to be in a position to interfere. They watched in horror as Wari' dismembered the corpse and began to cook it. In this man's words, the body parts were "roasted on a rack like *carne assada* [grilled meat]." He observed that close family members did not eat the body and that the people who did eat it ate slowly in small bits. The eating and crying went on through the night. After the flesh was gone, the bones were roasted and ground and eaten.

After this missionary first told me about his experience of observing cannibalism at the first Wari' funeral he witnessed, I mentioned that some schol-

ars have suggested that cannibalism has never existed as a customary practice in any society. He looked incredulous, then shook his head and said,
"No, it was real, all right. I saw them do it; they really did eat the body."

* * *

For those who participated in the early contact and pacification efforts,
the reality of Wari' cannibalism reinforced their sense of purpose and their
belief in the righteousness of their mission. They dedicated themselves to
putting an end to it. However, contrary to what one might assume about
Westerners' tendencies to exploit images of native savagery, the NTM missionaries and SPI officials who worked on the 1956 contact did not publi-
cize their observations of Wari' cannibalism in the first five years after the
contact. This was a period of growing political pressures to quickly pacify
the rest of the Wari' in the Lage/Ribeirão and Negro-Ocaia areas. Aware
that a too-hasty contact would likely lead to out-of-control violence and
disease, the SPI and NTM tried to buy time to pursue a slower, more carefully planned, and better financed contact effort. SPI officials mounted a
sort of public relations campaign in the local media and initiated legal proceedings against businessmen whose hired gunmen were massacring Wari'
and fueling the explosion of interethnic violence. SPI agents' reports and
the letters they sent to government officials during these years are full of
complaints about abuses and atrocities by Guajará-Mirim entrepreneurs
and their henchmen. Local newspaper stories increasingly incorporated this
critical perspective, pointing out that Wari' attacks on Brazilians were understandable responses to the brutal killings of their own people by Brazilians. Aware that news of cannibalism would inflame public opinion, SPI and
NTM personnel kept their knowledge of this practice to themselves. In the
first five years after the contact at Tanajura, the public seems to have heard
little more than the same vague rumors that had circulated for years.

Wari' Cannibalism in the News

It was in 1961 that evidence of the reality of Wari' cannibalism became public knowledge. By 1960, banks and businesses were seeing their fortunes
held hostage by the Wari' "savages", as regional rubber production plum-
meted because so many rubber tappers abandoned their homesteads. Public outrage rose to a fever pitch in 1960, when a ten-year-old boy riding a
bicycle on the outskirts of Guajará-Mirim was shot with arrows and his
corpse was found missing the legs. Local banks advanced loans to finance
two SPI pacification teams. With the help of Wari' from the already-

contacted Dois Irmãos group, these 1961 expeditions succeeded in making contact with most of the rest of the Wari' population. In April, a small SPI/NTM team contacted the northern Wari' around the Lage and Ribeirão Rivers. In June, a larger SPI expedition contacted the southern Wari' groups in the Negro-Ocaia area. The leaders of that expedition took the news about Wari' endocannibalism to the national media, where the story got mixed up in a tangle of accusations of deceit and corruption.

The expedition to the Negro-Ocaia area was a hastily organized affair sponsored by the army and headed by two special agents, José Fernando da Cruz and his second-in-command, Gilberto Gama, both of whom had been appointed by the territorial governor. From the start, the expedition was embroiled in conflicts between Fernando da Cruz and Gama, and between the SPI and the New Tribes Mission. SPI officials barred the missionaries from taking part and instead took along a Catholic priest, Father Roberto Gomez de Arruda.

As manpower for this venture, Fernando da Cruz recruited forty men off the streets of Guajará-Mirim. By all accounts, the kind of individuals willing to enlist in what locals dubbed the "Suicide Expedition" were mostly poor, illiterate frontiersmen with little preparation for dealing with uncontacted Indians. Many were sick, coughing and wheezing as their boats traveled up the Pacaas Novos River. With the help of Wari' from the Dois Irmãos area who had accepted contact five years earlier, the expeditionaries soon contacted a group of 164 Indians.

Fernando da Cruz, the expedition's leader, took photographs and returned to town, where he sold these pictures to the newspaper and announced that he had discovered over one thousand Indians. Among them, he claimed, were a white woman and a six-year-old white boy—a message certain to inflame townspeople's passions. Later, Gilberto Gama, the expedition's second-in-command, said that this white woman "captive" was a Bolivian whom Fernando da Cruz had persuaded to take off her clothes, pluck out her body hair, and pose for a picture with newly contacted Wari' women.

Back at the Negro-Ocaia contact site, the SPI workers had already infected the Indians with influenza. Shortly after a group of sick Indians arrived at the SPI team's base camp, a baby girl died. Gama, who was in charge of the expedition in Fernando da Cruz's absence, gave the following account of what happened next. Communicating through Wari' interpreters, Gama told the baby's family that the SPI workers would take care of the burial. He reported that, "At that moment, the place became empty. I asked the reason for the Indians' leaving. Tiam [a Wari' man] replied, with the greatest naturalness, 'They are going to eat the child.' Horrified, I called the interpreter and ran to stop the act" (*Folha de São Paulo* 1962).

Unable to persuade the baby's relatives to desist, Gama said he stood by and watched while the infant was eaten. Afterwards, he reported, "Upon returning to the old maloca [where the SPI team was camped], I told the story of this occurrence to the priest [Father Gomez de Arruda]. He grew pale, I believe that his eyes flowed with tears. . . . That day, we resolved to dissuade the Indians from such a primitive practice" (*Folha de São Paulo* 1962).

Sometime between June and November of 1961, Fernando da Cruz went to the Lage area and photographed the dismemberment and roasting of a Wari' girl who had died of disease. He then resigned from the SPI and traveled to São Paulo, where he sold these photographs to a weekly newsmagazine, *Os Cruzeiros*, for CR$250,000. These pictures never appeared in print, however, for anthropologists, Catholic clergy, and SPI officials intervened to stop them from being published.

Anthropologists got involved when the publisher of *Os Cruzeiros* convened a meeting of some of Brazil's most prominent scholars—including Egon Schaden, Roberto Cardoso de Oliveira, Roberto da Matta, and others —to evaluate the authenticity of Fernando da Cruz's photographs (*Cruzeiros* 1961). The anthropologists acknowledged that the pictures seemed to be authentic, but argued that publishing them would do irreparable harm to Brazilian Indians by branding them as savages in the public's mind. Top officials from the SPI were also at this meeting and voiced similar concerns. In late December 1961, Dom Francisco Xavier Rey, the respected bishop of Guajará-Mirim, brought the weight of the church's authority to bear on the controversy. The bishop told reporters that Fernando da Cruz was an opportunist who had persuaded the Wari' to revive a practice they had already abandoned so he could photograph it.

The accusation that Fernando da Cruz's pictures were staged rings true. The photos are a series of black-and-white pictures showing the corpse of a pretty but painfully emaciated Wari' girl who appears to be (as the newspaper story said) about nine years old. With her are two middle-aged men. One man holds the girl's corpse in his arms. The other man squats nearby, his head bowed in the conventional posture for crying at funerals. They are the only people in the pictures, and the scene is a clearing rimmed by trees. Clearly this was not a normal funeral, for Wari' funerals take place in a house, and many people would attend the funeral of a girl this age.

The progression of scenes shows the second man dismembering the corpse on a mat woven of palm fronds while the first man cries. The dismemberment occurs in the sequence Wari' describe, with the head cut off first. Perhaps because the little girl looked so much like other Wari' girls I have played with and hugged, the visual shock of the picture of her decapitated head was intense. In one photo, her body was intact. In the next, her severed head sat alone, squarely facing the camera. My visceral recoil at that first image of dismemberment brought home a point that Wari' have emphasized to me many times: for the dead person's close relatives, the most emotionally traumatic event in precontact funerals was not watching the flesh be eaten; rather, it was the moment when the corpse was taken from their arms and dismembered.

The photographs showed the sequential removal of innards, the severing of arms and legs at the joints, and the placement of body parts on a roasting rack like those on which Wari' roast game. What this set of pictures did *not* show is any *eating* of the body parts; the sequence of images ended with the roasting. It is unclear why this is so, or whether other photographs originally did show eating. If the bishop's accusation was true and the scene was staged at the photographer's request, the girl's corpse may not have been eaten at all. The recently contacted Wari' were under intense pressure from the SPI and the NTM to stop practicing cannibalism, and it seems unlikely that individuals would have done so at the urging of an SPI agent. Certainly it would have been highly unusual for a corpse to have been eaten by only one or two people.

Regardless of the truth about the circumstances under which the photographs were produced, the bishop's denunciation undermined their credibility to the point that *Os Cruzeiros* could no longer represent them as legitimate. Paradoxically, the bishop's denunciation also intensified media interest in Wari' cannibalism, for in denouncing Fernando da Cruz, the bishop also verified the fact that Wari' really did practice cannibalism, though he claimed they had stopped doing so (*Ultima Hora* 1961).

At this point, the magazine publishers found themselves in a tricky position. They had bought rights to some of the most sensational photographs of the century, but their authenticity was in doubt, and members of Brazil's scientific community, Catholic clergy, and government officials stood poised to denounce publication of the pictures as profiteering at Indians' expense. How could the magazine take advantage of this fantastic opportunity without appearing to stoop to tabloid sensationalism? The editors solved the dilemma by presenting the story of Wari' people eating as an anthropological investigation into the question of whether cannibalism really existed in Amazonia. Amid great fanfare, they dispatched a reporter and a photographer to seek the truth in the wilds of Rondônia.

Os Cruzeiros then published a dramatic story based on Fernando da Cruz's account of the Negro-Ocaia expedition. In this retelling, the disorganized expedition with its motley crew of men coughing and wheezing their way upriver was transformed into a "group of men who disregarded their own lives for the benefit of science" (*Cruzeiros* 1961). Their objective? Not pacification for economic or political motives alone, but a quest for ethnographic truth. Under this guise, the writer was able spice the tale with gory imagery without directly accusing the Wari' of actually engaging in such barbaric practices:

> They [the government team] were going to prove or disprove a myth: were the stories true that the [Brazilian] natives told about the cannibal Indians . . . ? The stories told in the capital and in the neighboring cities were astounding: rites of cannibalism and necrophagia; children murdered, shot with arrows, to serve as the meal at diabolical dinners. The expedition had one goal only: to discover the Pakaa-Novas and, upon confirming the feasts on human flesh, to pacify them (*Cruzeiros* 1961:195).

After *Os Cruzeiros* broke the news, a host of other Brazilian newspapers jumped in to report their own angles on the Wari' cannibalism story (*Correio da Manhã* 1962a-g, *Diário de Noticias* 1962, *Ultima Hora* 1961). The nation's most respected daily paper, the *Folha de São Paulo*, scored a major coup by publishing an eyewitness account of the baby girl's funeral provided by Gilberto Gama, who had been the second-in-command on the Negro-Ocaia expedition. In that article, Gama tried to establish his credibility by distancing himself from the accusations of opportunism that had sullied Fernando da Cruz's reputation. Expanding upon the bishop's accusations, he alleged that Fernando da Cruz had staged the scenes of cannibalism just as he had faked the pictures of the white woman and boy captives. Gama said that by persuading Wari' to dismember and roast the little girl's corpse, Fernando da Cruz had "revived in the Indians' spirit the habit of cannibalism, [which had been] neutralized by the efforts of Father Roberto [Gomez de Arruda]." For this deed, Gama characterized Fernando da Cruz as "the most repellent individual who has stepped on the virgin soil of Amazonia" (*Folha de São Paulo* 1962).

The *Folha de São Paulo* story ran under the headline "Sertanista Did Not Succeed in Stopping the Indians from Eating the Dead Girl." (A "sertanista" is a backwoodsman—in this case, an SPI agent who works with uncontacted Indians.) The headline's message and its moral claim were clear: where the unprincipled Fernando da Cruz had encouraged an act of cannibalism, Gama had tried to stop it. The article based on Gama's account was a straightforward narrative written in a tone sympathetic to the Indians' situation and motives. Gama stated that the baby girl was eaten, but the article presented only a few details about how her corpse was cut up, cooked, and handled. Aside from referring to cannibalism as "this most barbarous of rituals," there was no overt condemnation of the Indians. Instead, most of the article focused on trying to explain why Wari' ate their dead.

After the story of Wari' cannibalism hit the newsstands of urban Brazil, anthropologists and Catholic clergy mounted a concerted effort to dissociate public images of Indians from the practice of cannibalism. Both groups tried to use the media publicity to focus public attention on the desperate plight of the newly contacted Wari', who were dying by the hundreds. Media images of the fierce warriors who had terrorized Rondônia's citizenry soon were replaced by images of Wari' as the hapless victims of outsiders' brutality, incompetence, and indifference.

The *Os Cruzeiros* journalists returned to São Paulo from their trip to Rondônia in February 1962, apparently without having seen any people eating. Nonetheless, their story was headlined "Pakaanovas: Cannibals of Amazônia" (de Carvalho 1962). In addition to describing Wari' funeral customs, the reporter wrote at length about the sickness and hunger ravaging the recently contacted Wari', a point illustrated all too vividly by a photograph of emaciated men and boys.

The Change from Cannibalism to Burial

Epidemic after epidemic of influenza, measles, mumps, tuberculosis, dysentery, and respiratory infections swept through the Wari' population in the first years after contact. From a population conservatively estimated at 1,000 or more in 1955, 399 individuals survived in 1962. The epidemics gave outsiders powerful ammunition for their battle to put an end to cannibalism: they told Wari' that the new diseases were spread by eating people who had died from those sicknesses.

Wari' were receptive to this argument, for they were understandably terrified of the unfamiliar diseases and anxious to learn how to avoid them. This idea also made sense to them because it fit their own beliefs about corpses and contamination. Before the contact, Wari' did not eat corpses whose lungs contained pus, for they see respiratory congestion as a sign of systemic blood contamination. They thought that people would get sick, and even die, if they ate the flesh or breathed the fumes from roasting body parts of a corpse whose lungs were full of pus. After the contact, respiratory infections and respiratory congestion were common secondary complications of many of the diseases killing the Wari'. According to the criteria Wari' traditionally used to decide which corpses could not be eaten and had to be cremated instead, most of the individuals who died in the early postcontact period would not have been eaten anyway.

Some deaths, however, resulted from accidents or illnesses that did not involve respiratory congestion or other symptoms that would have ruled out cannibalism. These corpses normally would have been eaten, but when Wari' tried to do so, SPI agents and missionaries forced them to bury them instead. Outsiders also tried to persuade Wari' of the immorality of cannibalism. One man from Rio Negro-Ocaia remembered being lectured by a missionary who told him, "Eating is for animals. People are not animals; people are not meat to be eaten." Wari' quickly learned that cannibalism revolted and alienated the outsiders. Older people at Santo André described a funeral at which a certain SPI agent "went crazy" (*tamanain*) at the sight of the corpse being eaten and ran, screaming, into the forest. The poor fellow, they said, was never quite right in the head after that.

Another strategy some members of the contact teams used to stamp out cannibalism was to threaten to withhold food and medicine from individuals who took part in eating corpses. An elderly Wari' man recalled how an SPI employee told him, "If you eat bodies, you don't need to eat my medicines."

Wari' were not easily persuaded to change their funeral practices and resisted efforts to make them switch to burial. Families carried corpses into the forest to be roasted away from outsiders' eyes, but the smoke and keening were hard to hide and were inevitably discovered. A missionary who lived at Lage in the early 1960s described how, one night after a man had died, she was inside her house when she heard the sound of a canoe passing by. "I knew they were trying to take his corpse away to eat it," she recalled. "I ran outside and yelled to them to come back with the body and bury it."

Why did Wari' cling so hard to the practice of eating the dead? Part of the reason was the intensely negative feelings they had about burial, which violated some of their most fundamental values. Wari' consider the ground "dirty" (*mixem*) and "polluting" (*homirixi*). Adults who take pride in their bodies do not sit directly in the dirt, but squat or sit on a mat or a log. Discarding things on or in the ground is disrespectful, and special ritual objects should not touch the earth. Wari' are careful to avoid spilling food on the ground, especially food that has a human-form spirit, such as corn or certain animals' meat.

These negative associations shaped attitudes towards burial. Respectful treatment for human remains involves keeping them dry and warm. Before the contact, the only honorable place to bury human remains was beneath the household sleeping platform, where small fires burned constantly, keeping the ground both warm and dry. This is where funeral ashes, placentas, miscarried fetuses, and stillbirths were buried. In contrast, burying something outside the village connoted dishonor. Before the contact, Wari' normally buried human remains in the forest only when they wanted to make an explicit statement about social rejection of the dead individual. When a woman had given birth to several stillborn infants in succession, or had had several babies die very young, her family sometimes decided that her most recently deceased infant should be buried in the forest in an unpleasant spot, such as an anthill (*mujik karan*) or the wet earth beside a stream. I never got a coherent explanation of why this was done, but it seems to have been partly intended to discourage the spirit of the woman's next baby from dying by demonstrating the repulsive treatment it could expect if it did.

For Wari', burial was not something that decent people would do to someone they cared about or respected. The negative values associated with burial—dirtiness, pollution, cold, wetness, and abandonment—made it hard to accept the switch to burial that outsiders forced upon them. One man told me about how, when his father was dying, he was so unhappy at the prospect of having his corpse buried in the earth that he asked to be dismembered and have his body parts placed in a large ceramic cooking pot. His family did as he asked, and a female affine carried the big, heavy pot on her back to the forest, where they buried it.

If Wari' considered burial horrible but outsiders insisted that cannibalism had to stop, why didn't they switch to cremation instead? Cremation destroys a body just as effectively as cannibalism does, and it would have been an easier alternative, for Wari' already cremated corpses that they thought could not be eaten (because of the risk of infection, for example). A change from cannibalism to cremation would have been far less disruptive than the change to burial. Cremation, however, was apparently never an option in the minds of the outsiders who contacted the Wari'. Both the Brazilians and the North Americans seem to have considered burial in a cemetery the only proper or feasible way to dispose of the dead. In addition, cremation was unacceptable and almost unknown to the larger Brazilian public. Brazil is the world's largest Catholic country, and the Catholic Church has long opposed cremation (Irion 1968:74–85). Some Protestant missionaries also have opposed the practice of cremation in other native Amazonian groups. After the contact, if Wari' had tried to burn their dead rather than bury them, they would have run into a great deal of opposition and criticism. As it was, cremation was never presented as an option.

Ultimately, all Wari' gave in to the pressures to bury their dead in the outsiders' fashion, as intact corpses wrapped in a hammock or blanket or enclosed in a homemade coffin. This did not happen all at once. Throughout 1962 and into 1963, families who had been living independently in the forest continued to arrive in the villages administered by the SPI. These newcomers inevitably got sick and just as inevitably had to be discouraged from disposing of their dead in the customary manner. The eradication of cannibalism was an uneven process.

When an incident of endocannibalism among the Wari' was reported in 1963, some time after they supposedly had stopped practicing it, a Catholic priest used this report to denounce the SPI for mishandling the Wari' situation. The priests had had a falling-out with local SPI officials, who had barred them from working in Wari' communities. In their battle to regain a foothold for work among the Wari', the claim of cannibalism offered fresh ammunition. Father Gomez de Arruda wrote that the starvation imposed on the Wari' by the government Indian agency's mishandling of the situation had driven them to eat human flesh.[1] The trajectory of public images of the Wari' had reached complete reversal: from fiercely independent cannibal warriors, they had come to be represented as wretched dependents, so miserably hungry that they were forced—reluctantly—to eat one another.

Cultural Changes

The 1960s and early '70s were a period of intense culture shock and adjustment for the recently contacted Wari'. The death of over half their population brought profound social disruption and a loss of faith in many tribal traditions. In the 1960s, many grief-stricken or curious men and women went off to work for Brazilian rubber gatherers or as laborers in Guajará-Mirim and elsewhere. By the early 1970s, most had returned to the Wari' reserves, and there has been little out-migration since. Though young people may rebel against their parents in many ways, almost everyone still marries within the group.

In the decades since the contact, Wari' have worked to fashion new identities as "civilized" Indians. They want to be respected and treated as competent, rational individuals by the government personnel, missionaries,

Catholic clergy, and others on whom they have come to depend for medicine, nursing care, metal tools, clothing, and help in dealing with the outside world. Beginning in 1969, many Wari' converted to Christianity, initially under the influence of the Protestant missionaries. They gave up or hid many aspects of their indigenous culture that outsiders found objectionable or that attracted unwanted attention. Their desire to ward off criticism and win respect was one reason why, in the 1950s and '60s, they chose to abandon the most flagrantly exotic markers of cultural difference, including nudity and the daily use of body paint (Conklin 1997a). Wari' have strong norms of modesty and propriety, and non-Indians' negative reactions to their nudity were a strong motivation to use clothing. Today, all but the youngest children wear clothes all the time, including on ritual occasions.

Cannibalism died out among the Wari', and the exoticism formerly attached to their public images died out as well. When I began my fieldwork in the mid-1980s, I often heard them referred to (by anthropologists and others) as "the poor Pakaas Novas." The Wari' had a reputation for being uninteresting (*chato*, "boring") Indians who had lost most of their distinctive culture under the domination of NTM missionaries. The reality, as I hope this book shows, turned out to be more complex and far from boring.

One of the biggest problems Wari' face today is the question of how to earn money to buy the things they now need and want. For decades before the contact, Wari' used metal tools obtained by raiding Brazilian homesteads. Since the contact, they have adopted the use of canoes, shotguns, fish hooks and fishing line, flashlights, metal pots, soap, matches, blankets, and mosquito nets, as well as new crops and domestic animals. Although the bulk of their diet still comes from foods they produce themselves, Wari' use some commercial foods, especially sugar, salt, and cooking oil. Everyone wants to have decent clothing and sandals in order to present a respectable appearance, especially when they go to town. Adolescents covet soccer shoes, t-shirts, radios, and boom boxes. Even more than material goods, younger Wari' want to have enough knowledge of Brazilian culture and enough competence in dealing with it to be treated with respect and not be cheated or denigrated.

Involvement in the market economy has been marginal and sporadic for Wari'. The ups and downs of the national economy result in fluctuating prices for latex, Brazil nuts, and garden produce, and most Wari' have learned the hard way not to depend on cash for basic subsistence needs. When market prices are high enough, families collect and sell forest products, grow cash crops, and sell manioc flour, baskets, and other handiwork to non-Indians. Elderly people receive a small government old-age pension, and some men find temporary low-paying employment working or piloting boats for FUNAI or working for cattle ranchers or rubber tappers. Until recently, no Wari' made most of their living from wage work or depended on money for food. This began to change in the late 1990s, when a few of the better-educated young men and women began to work as teachers and health monitors, for which they receive a small salary.

Despite the many changes in their way of life, Wari' maintain a high degree of social and cultural integrity. Although children learn Portuguese in school and some adults and adolescents are fairly fluent in the dialect of rural Rondônia, the native language is the only language normally spoken in Wari' homes, except in the few households in which one spouse is from another tribe and in the Catholic community at Sagarana, where many Wari' speak mostly Portuguese. Though it is impossible to know what the future will bring, Wari' have been relatively fortunate in some respects so far. Most importantly, they have not suffered the invasions and assaults on their land rights and resources experienced by many other native peoples in Rondônia and elsewhere.[2] So far, they have not had to deal with the problems of alcoholism, idleness, domestic violence, suicide, and other self-destructive behaviors that plague many native communities, though this could change as young men and women spend more and more time in town. Since the mid-1980s, an exceptionally dedicated medical staff at the regional Casa do Indio clinic has done a great deal to improve health care for the Wari', despite years of scanty government funding and persistent problems in the organization and delivery of health services.

Over the past three decades, the Wari' population has made a remarkable recovery. Births now greatly outnumber deaths, and in the 1980s, the population surpassed its estimated precontact size. Along with this demographic recovery and the return to near self-sufficiency in food production came renewed confidence in their own distinctive traditions and values. By the mid-1980s, a kind of low-key cultural revival was under way. There was a surge of participation in shamanism and traditional music, and festivals came back into vogue for a while, though interest in these has waned in the 1990s, as more and more of the elders with the most knowledge of these ritual traditions have passed away.

Cannibalism plays little part in how Wari' think of themselves today. For young people, it is little more than an interesting story from a way of life that seems distant from their present reality. For their elders, cannibalism is now a memory bound up with that lost way of life. These memories surface most poignantly when older people talk about their sorrow over the deaths of family members and the lingering dissatisfaction some feel with burying their loved ones' bodies, rather than eating them.

PART II

MOTIFS
AND
MOTIVES

CHAPTER FOUR

FUNERALS

Since the 1960s, Wari' have buried corpses instead of eating or burning them. Although the way they dispose of bodies has changed, many other precontact funeral practices have continued through to the present. In the following description of Wari' funerals, I try to make clear which practices have been modified or abandoned since the contact.

Much of this account is based on interviews rather than observations, for fortunately no one has died in a village while I was present, and consequently I have never seen a whole Wari' funeral. The closest I have come was witnessing a truncated version of a funeral that took place when a boat carrying a baby boy who had died at the hospital in Guajará-Mirim stopped at Santo André on the way upriver to the baby's parents' home at Rio Negro-Ocaia. The family had relatives at Santo André, and when the boat stopped, the community immediately organized an impromptu wake. All the adults and older adolescents gathered to cry and keen around the corpse and the grieving parents. The dead baby was inside a little Styrofoam coffin provided by the hospital. As the crying intensified, his parents took his tiny body out of the coffin, and the close relatives embraced it and gently passed it around to hold. After about two and a half hours of keening and crying, the boat departed, carrying the baby's corpse, his parents, and a few of their relatives from Santo André who went to represent their families at the funeral. Aside from this scene of funeral behavior, I have observed death keening and the comportment of mourners on a number of occasions in four Wari' villages; but the rest of the information that follows comes from conversations with Wari' in the five communities I studied, with corroboration from non-Indians who have witnessed Wari' funerals and from Vilaça's work at Rio Negro-Ocaia.

Responses to Illness

Most Wari' die at home, for although, these days, seriously sick individuals are often taken to the hospital or FUNAI's clinic in Guajará-Mirim, most Wari' still strongly prefer to be cared for by their families. Wari' react with alarm when anyone is seriously ill or injured. Close family members drop whatever they are doing and rush to the sick person's bedside, where they remain almost continuously until the crisis passes. The closer the individual seems to death, the greater the number of relatives and neighbors who crowd into the house to see what is happening and offer their support.

The events that take place around the sickbed and deathbed set the stage for what happens at the funeral, for the ways in which Wari' respond to illness and manage the process of dying are continuous with certain aspects of their behavior at funerals, especially the emphasis on holding the body, keening, and affirming the dead or dying person's social connections and belonging. Expectations for how one should act when a close family member is sick or dying mirror expectations for how one should act in mourning.

Consanguines are the primary care givers for patients of all ages;[1] even when a married person is sick, his or her natal family usually takes charge and makes decisions about how to treat the illness. Affines, and sometimes even the sick person's husband or wife, play secondary roles or may be excluded altogether from therapeutic activities, for Wari' see illness and death as events that affect close blood kin most strongly.

Much care giving focuses on trying to ensure that patients know the strength of their family's affection and appreciation for them. This is conveyed in multiple ways: communicated through physical touch (a primary manifestation of caring) and verbalized in the laments sung around the sickbed. Seriously ill people are held constantly in their relatives' arms and almost never left lying alone, even for a few minutes.[2] Usually someone sits cradling the sick person's head and shoulders in his or her lap, in the conventional posture that Wari' use to comfort close relatives or friends when they are sick or tired, or when removing lice. Other kin, especially older relatives such as grandparents, aunts, and uncles, gather close about the sickbed, sitting or lying quietly on mats and surrounding the sick person from head to toe. Frequently someone will run his or her hands along the patient's arms and legs several times in rapid succession, moving from the body trunk outward toward the fingers or toes. The touch is very light, for unlike a European-style massage, the objective is not to relax muscles, but to move blood into the extremities and keep it circulating.

In conditions perceived as life threatening, the sick person's close kin begin to keen in a high-pitched, mournful tone. Some illness keening is wordless crying. Other times, people sing conventional laments that repeatedly affirm their ties to the sick person. Some lyrics promise a joyful reunion if he or she returns to health, invoking images of pleasant social activities like fishing, gathering fruit, or eating together. "*Mo xi 'e' ma, mija xira ka kerek te' xim kakam xerem*," goes one common lament [If you return to life, there will be great happiness for your siblings].

Symbolic oppositions between sadness and oral activities are a theme that runs through Wari' behavior in illness, funerals, and mourning. In the conventional behavior of the Wari' sick role, those who are seriously ill typically speak and move very little, even when racked by the shifting fevers and chills of malaria. This is a striking contrast to the behavior of the non-Indian Brazilians with whom I have sat through bouts of malaria, who communicated their discomfort in a near-constant stream of words expressing sensations of heat, cold, and body pains and their desires for water, air, blankets, a doctor, their mother, or evacuation to the hospital.

Wari' see eating, speaking, and singing as expressions of happiness, sociality, and engagement with communal life; conversely, such oral activities are antithetical to states of sorrow and disengagement. Giving and receiving food is one of the most direct affirmations of positive relations with others. When Wari' are very ill, they typically eat and drink little or nothing (which exacerbates the risk of dehydration in a hot, humid climate). They say that sick people simply do not feel like consuming anything, but this behavior also communicates social messages. Relatives become especially alarmed when a sick person refuses to drink sweet (i.e., unfermented) *tokwa* (corn *chicha*), the nourishing staple of household diets. Giving and accepting tokwa express kinship, amity, and social engagement, while refusing it can imply distancing or a negation of social ties. Family life revolves around orally oriented activities: engaging in conversation, producing and sharing food, and eating together. A sick person's withdrawal from such interactions dramatizes the seriousness of the illness and its threat to rend the kin group. To Wari', it also translates as evidence of a lack of the will to live. Conversely, accepting chicha indicates a return of vitality and a reintegration into family life. One day in 1986, when Torein Oro Nao' had been very ill for several days from a poisonous insect bite, his daughter, Maria, burst through my door with a radiant smile on her face. "My father drank tokwa!" she announced. "He's going to be all right!"

When an individual is suffering from a condition deemed life threatening, his or her close relatives stop performing most of their normal household duties and focus their energies on the patient. Close kin behave in ways that express strong identification with the sick person's physical state. They subdue their own oral and verbally expressive activities, eating little and speaking quietly. They do not sing, shout, run, dance, or go to parties. Individuals who violate these norms are roundly criticized and are liable to be accused of not loving the one who is ill. These expectations for the behavior of close relatives of the sick are virtually identical to the behavioral expectations for bereaved relatives in the months following a death in the family.

Serious illness affects not just the immediate family but the entire local group. The opposition between sadness and oral activity extends to the community level, for people in a community where someone has recently died or is very sick are not supposed to sing, dance, or attend parties. When a community does attend or sponsor a party, this is an affirmation of their group's well-being.

Acute illness episodes become public dramas in which nearly everyone in the village crowds into the sick person's house or watches from outside. One or more family members, often a senior kinswoman of the patient, typically deliver a long monologue in a high-pitched, rapid, forceful tone. This narrative details events that led up to the illness episode and often affixes blame or suspicion about culpability. If death seems near, messengers are dispatched to summon relatives who live elsewhere. As each group of newcomers arrives, they are greeted with a repeat rendition of this narrative.

The more respected and socially influential the sick person, the larger the number of people who will gather at the bedside to cry/sing their concern and sense of impending loss. In 1991, Santo André's elderly shaman, Maxun Kwarain, came close to dying of bronchial pneumonia. In response to the threat of his imminent demise, many people traveled from other villages to gather around his sickbed. When I arrived a couple of months later, this was the first thing he told me:

"I was sick, really sick, like I was going to die," Maxun Kwarain said. "And *everybody* came—from here, from the other villages! All the Wari' were crying, crying, crying. Men, women, children! My house was completely full; the people couldn't fit inside," he reported, with obvious pride. Gesturing around the house, he pointed, "They were here, and here, and here. There were so many people crying here [he indicated the porch where we were sitting] that the floor started to break! One day, another day, and another day, all the Wari' cried and cried. The sound was huge! But," the old shaman chuckled, "I didn't die. I'm still here!"

Responses to Death

Wari' see death not just as a biological occurrence that happens at one particular moment, but as one event in a continuum of interlinked social and physical processes. They treat any loss of consciousness as a kind of dying (*mi' pin*) in which cardiac functions and blood circulation diminish and the spirit is at risk of separating from its body. This presages what happens at the moment of final (physical, biological) death. Although they do not distinguish it with a special linguistic term, Wari' recognize final death as a distinctive event in which the heart stops functioning. They take cessation of the pulse and breathing to be key indicators of death and emphasize that the blood stops circulating and collects in the chest cavity and joints, where it coagulates into dark clumps.

Corpses are never left to lie alone. From the moment of death until the body is disposed of, grieving kin constantly cradle the corpse in their arms, hugging it, pressing their own bodies against it.

When someone dies, the keening intensifies and shifts to a slightly different melody, cadence, and lyrics. This death keening is a high-pitched, nasalized, repetitive wail—part singing, part crying—and it goes on nonstop until the end of the funeral. The distinctive sound announces the death to everyone within earshot, and any adults and older adolescents in the community who are not already at the sickbed hasten to join in crying around the corpse. Death keening follows a simple melodic pattern that varies slightly among Wari' subgroups. The same melody is repeated over and over, but several forms of verbal expression may accompany it. Some keening is simply wordless crying or the singing of kinship terms for the deceased, such as, "My father, my father, my father . . ."

In a multitude of ways, Wari' funeral practices highlight the dead person's social connections, the bonds of kinship and affection that link mourners to the deceased. Consanguinity (being related by blood) is a primary metaphor for many kinds of social relatedness, and in daily life, Wari' often call affines by consanguineal kin terms. In funerals, people express their affection and their sense of loss by emphasizing consanguineal ties to the dead person. When Wari' mourn the death of an affine, they often project a fictitious blood relationship by calling the dead affine by consanguineal kin terms. Alternatively, affines may use compound phrases that emphasize that the singer and the dead affine have consanguines in common. When a married man dies, for example, his father-in-law may cry for him either as "my son-in-law" or as "father of my grandchildren." Similarly, a man may cry for his dead mother-in-law as "maternal grandmother of my children." A husband may sing of his wife as "mother of my children," while a wife may sing of her husband as "body/flesh of my children" (*kwerekekem homajü*) (Vilaça 1989:287, 1992:209).

When Wari' cry at funerals and elsewhere, their bodies move into a conventional posture that conveys sorrow and empathy for those who suffer: one places a hand on the shoulder of the next person, bowing one's head and leaning toward the other while crying. Wari' see crying as more than an expression of individual emotion or an outlet for private grief. Crying is, they say, also a kind of service that must be done to honor the dead individual, and they speak of the need to "help" the dead person's family by crying and thus contributing to the expression of collective sorrow.

The dead person's close kin remain near the corpse through the days and nights of mourning. Affines and other less closely related individuals typically cry a while, then leave to care for their children or attend to personal needs, returning later for more stints of "helping" with the communal mourning. At any given moment, most of the adults in a village will be gathered around the corpse, keening.

It is difficult to convey the intensity of feeling generated by this ceaseless collective keening. Throbbing through the nights and days of mourning, the repetitive rise and fall of the death cadence becomes a hypnotic counterpoint to the funeral events. At times the sound seems to be an almost tangible force filling the air, reverberating off the surrounding forest in a haunting mantra of collective sorrow.

After the funeral, when the keening suddenly stops, there is an abrupt emptiness, an unnerving silence in which the cadence of grief seems to pulse, echoing in the air, unheard but still present.

Roles of Affines and Consanguines

After someone dies, his or her corpse is usually carried to the house of a senior kinsman, where it is laid on mats in the center of the house. Ideally, this is someone whom the dead person addressed as "elder brother" (*aji,* a term applied to a number of male relatives on both the mother's and the father's side) or "father" (*te,* a term used for father, father's brother, and certain other male relatives on the father's side). The household's sleeping platform or raised floor and three walls are removed to allow mourners to crowd in under the thatched roof, leaving a space that approximates the arrangement of precontact Wari' homes, which were open on three sides.

The dead person's close kin (especially parents and adult siblings) make decisions about funeral arrangements by a process of consensus. Usually one man (typically an older brother, father, or uncle of the dead person) serves as family spokesman and takes the leading role in moving events from one phase to another.

The division of activities in funerals revolves around two loosely defined groups of people. One is the *'iri nari,* "true kin." These are the dead person's close consanguines and spouse. The other group is the *nari paxi,* which translates as "those who are like kin but are not truly related." Most properly, the nari paxi are affines, individuals related by marriage to the dead person or to one of the dead person's own close relatives. However, Wari' extend the term *nari paxi* to include all non-consanguines or distant relatives present at the funeral. In the past, the nari paxi had the duty of eating the corpse, and Wari' often refer to them as *ko kao',* "those who ate." Besides consuming the corpse, they were responsible for most of the other tasks involved in carrying out a funeral. This pattern of assigning to affines the duty of disposing of the corpse is common in other native lowland South American societies, as well as other parts of the Americas.[3]

As the first step in organizing a Wari' funeral, the dead person's close consanguines choose individual affines to serve as the primary helpers. The male helpers ideally will be two or three strong young men who are the brothers-in-law or sons-in-law of the deceased. To be chosen as a funeral assistant is an honor of which Wari' men speak proudly, and they take their duties seriously. In contrast to the ironic attitude and joking demeanor with which Wari' approach many other kinds of work and social activities, they behave with utter solemnity when performing tasks related to a funeral. Anything less would open the offender to accusations of disrespect for the dead person, with the implication of disrespect for the dead person's family as well. The affines who help at funerals comport themselves with dignity and put themselves entirely at the disposal of the grieving consanguines, whom they treat with the utmost deference.

The Gathering of Kin

The male helpers' first task is to carry news of the death to the dead person's relatives in other villages. Strong young men usually are designated to be the messengers, because speed is essential. Wari' believe that close kin should arrive as soon as possible after a death, and they enjoin the messengers to "Run! Don't walk! Don't sit down along the path!" in order to get word to the relatives as quickly as possible.

Upon learning of a relative's death elsewhere, a Wari' adult immediately goes inside his or her house to cry. I once was at Tanajura when the local FUNAI administrator received a radio message that someone had died at Lage. He told one of the dead person's relatives at Tanajura, but no one else knew about the death until we suddenly heard the distinctive death keening melody coming from the house. Everyone stopped and stood stock-still for a moment, visibly sobered. Even when few or none of the people in a village are directly related to someone who dies in another community, news of a death casts a sobering shadow. At least two distinct emotions seem to be involved. One is anxiety, for Wari' know that if the dead person's family blames the death on sorcery (as they often do), their suspicions often focus on some man in another village. Wari' seldom confront those whom they suspect of sorcery, but kinsmen of the deceased might retaliate with their own sorcery aimed at harming a vulnerable person (especially a child) related to the sorcerer who supposedly caused the death. People are acutely aware of how a death may destabilize the always tenuous harmony among families and communities.

News of a death also evokes profound sadness, even for some who did not personally know the individual who has just died. Several times I have seen people turn away and begin to cry upon hearing of the demise of someone whom they had never met, for each death tends to remind people of their own dead loved ones, especially those who have passed away recently. The sound of the death keening is another powerful stimulus to memory, evoking other times when one has keened one's own sorrow. The conventionality of the keening—the fact that it is done the same way every time—connects each new episode of keening to each one that has gone before. It is both a response to the immediacy of a present reality (the death that has just occurred) and an evocative embodiment of a series of similar acts in the past. Death and mourning take a community out of normal time, and the sense of this as a liminal moment is most palpable in the haunting melody whose high, sorrowful tone links generations of Wari' in their sorrow.

Upon being informed of a death, close relatives are expected to drop everything and, after crying a little while, leave immediately for the funeral. As an expression of their complete absorption in sorrow, they are not supposed to carry any possessions or food with them. As they journey to the funeral, they continue to cry along the way. More distantly related individuals may not leave right away, but may linger a bit in order to listen to the messengers' narrative of the events that led up to the death. In the past, when Wari' traveled only on foot, it often took several days for all the relatives to be notified and get to the funeral. Today, with the use of canoes and FUNAI's motorboats and trucks, people can assemble more quickly. Understanding how important it is to Wari' to attend funerals, FUNAI staff go to great lengths to help people get to their relatives' funerals, even in the face of difficulties such as the near impossibility of scraping together enough gasoline during the frequent fuel shortages that plagued Guajará-Mirim in the 1980s.

Approaching a village where a wake is in progress, one hears the collective keening long before the houses come into sight. Wari' believe that close consanguines (*'iri nari*), especially the dead person's siblings (*'iri kwaji'*), should be the first to arrive at the funeral, so more distant relatives and affines sometimes wait in the forest outside the village so that the close kin may arrive first. Upon entering the house where mourners are gathered around the corpse, new arrivals hear the story of the events that led up to the death, told in a high-pitched, singsong voice by an adult relative. This narrative frames the individual's death as a social drama: it typically establishes the circumstances that contributed to the death and positions the survivors in relation to these events, affirming that they did all they could to save their loved one. These narratives also offer an opportunity to verbalize resentment against those held to blame for the death.

All the mourners press around the family members who are holding the corpse and lean on each others' shoulders, squatting and crying. The first phase of Wari' funerals revolves around evoking and dramatizing the dead person's identity, life history, and relationships to others. Before the corpse is taken from its relatives' arms to be disposed of, mourners surround the corpse with affirmations of the bonds of kinship and affection that connect them to the deceased. Some Wari' call this phase of funeral activities *ka mam pe' wa,* which translates loosely as "making them [the deceased] be here." They consider it imperative that all relatives take part in honoring the deceased. When asked why they considered it important to wait until the third day to cut the corpse, people at Santo André emphasized the importance of honoring the deceased with ka mam pe' wa.

At times during funerals, mourners perform a type of keening eulogy called *aka pijim,* literally "to cry to speak." In this song-recitation, an individual creates lyrics describing his or her personal memories and relationships to the deceased. People sing of the dead person's life and what he or she meant to them; they sing of the person's deeds and kindnesses and things they did together. In particular, they often emphasize events revolving around the giving and receiving of nurturance, especially food: "My grandfather, who used to fish with me . . ."; "My sister, who brought me honey to eat . . ."; "Our daughter, who used to grind corn for us . . .". To Wari', tangible exchanges of food and work are at the core of what family life is about, and this comes out clearly in the keening eulogies of aka pijim. After a funeral, mourners remember the words they sang and may repeat them to those who were not at the funeral.

Holding the Corpse

In this first phase of the wake, the corpse is treated as if its kin have not yet completely given their loved one over to death. This perspective was most explicit in a brief ceremony that used to be performed at some funerals, in which the family momentarily treated the corpse as if it were alive. This was a special honor for the deceased, reserved mostly for warriors who had killed many enemies and for girls who had served a great deal of chicha to their brothers during the warriors' ritual reclusion. In this brief ceremony, close kin stood the corpse up on its feet and placed its arms around theirs or around the neck of a strong young man who supported it on his back. They formed a dance line on each side of the corpse and sang the *tamara* songs that had belonged to the dead person.[4] The intent was to evoke a sense of joy and celebration, and the funeral crowd would laugh and cheer as the corpse swayed to the music, its head swinging loosely. As in tamara parties, the singers stopped once in a while to let the corpse "drink" sweet chicha poured into its mouth. When this little celebration was over, the family spokesman announced, "Happiness has ended; now the sadness begins."

As far as I know, Wari' have not performed this ceremony for some time. The last time people at Santo André remember a celebration of this sort was in the mid-1960s, at the funeral of a respected middle-aged warrior. Jimon Maram and his brother, Torein, talked about performing the ceremony in 1984 at the funeral for their younger brother, who (though he never killed an enemy) was famous for his love of music and parties. Ultimately, they decided not to do so because, they said, they simply felt too sad to delay crying.

The corpse remains in its relatives' embrace until the moment when it must be prepared for disposal. To an outsider, the atmosphere may seem semihysterical, as distraught relatives reach for the corpse and throw themselves upon it, pressing their bodies against it. At one man's funeral several years ago, the dramatic expressions of grief reportedly got so out of hand that the corpse was in danger of being pulled apart by people struggling to embrace it. A senior kinsman finally enforced order by declaring that only one relative at a time could hold the body.

As part of their expression of self-identification with the deceased, close relatives frequently express desires to join their loved one in death. Since Wari' equate any loss of consciousness with death, fainting is a form of dying (*mi' pin*), and in one common funeral practice, adult mourners "die" by lying on top of one another in stacks as high as four or five people, with the corpse on top of the pile. When someone faints from the suffocating press of bodies, others pull him or her out, and someone else piles on. When an eleven-year-old girl died at Ribeirão in 1986, her affines built a home-made coffin, and relatives lay in it on top of one another, embracing her corpse on top.

Burying the Corpse

Up to this point, the funeral practices and rituals that I have described seem to have changed little since before the contact. The main differences in contemporary funerals relate to the timing and method for disposing of the body. FUNAI personnel and other outsiders pressure Wari' to dispose of corpses (by burial) much more quickly than they did in the past (when bodies were roasted). When I asked FUNAI staff about this, they all cited the terrible stench and the risk of disease from a decaying corpse as reasons to insist on a quick burial. Responding to this pressure, Wari' now hold shorter funerals than they did in the old days, when corpses often lay intact for three days. These days, corpses are usually buried within a day or so after death. Male affines dig the grave and prepare the body for burial, usually either wrapping it in a commercial cotton hammock or blanket or placing it in a coffin made of wooden planks. When someone dies in town, the hospital or clinic may return the corpse in a cheap manufactured coffin.

Each major community has a cemetery located a short distance outside the village. Some of these sites were chosen by Wari', and some were chosen by Indian agency staff. Wari' seem to attach little significance to where their cemeteries are located; their main concern is that they should be away from the zones of human activity.

Burial is attended by far less formality than the rituals that surrounded endocannibalism. When the time comes to take the corpse to the cemetery, the male affines carry it, and the other mourners walk with them to the grave. Amidst more crying, the body is placed in the grave and covered with dirt. No markers were erected in the cemeteries I have seen, and Wari' do not visit their relatives' graves. In general, they treat burial sites as places to be avoided.

The remainder of this chapter focuses on precontact funerals.

Preparations for Cannibalism or Cremation

Before the contact, if dying individuals or their relatives had felt uneasy about the idea of the corpse being eaten, they could have asked that the body be cremated instead. The affines who assisted at funerals placed themselves entirely at the service of the dead person's family, and it is inconceivable that they would not have respected the wishes of a dying individual or bereaved family. Yet I have never heard Wari' mention any resistance to having a corpse eaten rather than burned.

In all funerals except those for infants, a special decorated firewood bundle was made. This was done by the male affines, who assembled the firewood and built the funeral roasting rack in the men's house (*kaxa'*). Both the firewood bundle and the roasting rack were made of wooden house beams. A beam was pulled from the roof of each house in the village, leaving the thatched roofs sagging in tangible evidence of death's violation of the community's integrity.

The house beams were cut to the same length, bundled together, and tied with a liana called "fire vine" (*makuri xe'*). (Warriors also used this vine to tie the ritual bundle of firebrands they used to roast enemy body parts.) For funerals, the firewood bundle was made beautiful, decorated with red annatto paint and the feathers of vultures (which are associated with death) and of scarlet macaws (which are associated with the water spirits that rule the underworld where the ancestral spirits dwell). The male affines completed the preparations by cutting more firewood, ideally from trees of the same type used to build houses. It takes a lot of wood to roast a corpse and still more to burn one to ashes. Men say that cutting funeral firewood was hard work, especially in the old days, when they had only stone axes.

While the male affines made these preparations, the female affines (ideally the dead person's daughters-in-law and sisters-in-law) were hard at work grinding corn to make the dense, roasted corn "bread" called *kapam* in the Wari' language and *pamonha* in Portuguese. Wari' consider this the best food to eat with any kind of meat. In symbolic terms, the pairing of meat (which is associated with men and hunting) and corn (which is associated with women and farming) is a pattern in many Wari' rituals. In precontact funerals, corn bread was always eaten in tandem with the flesh.

6. *Wem Xu, holding leaf-wrapped packets of pamonha (*kapam*), the dense corn bread that is the proper accompaniment to meat.*

When all the preparations were finished, the helpers informed the dead person's family. The senior man in charge then sang to the helpers, calling them by consanguineal kin terms and asking them to bring the roasting rack and firewood (see Vilaça 1992:212–213). He inspected these, and when he had approved of the quantity of firewood and the beauty of the decorations, he made a public statement expressing his sorrow.'As examples of the proper sort of thing one should say on such an occasion, Jimon Maram suggested that a man experiencing the first death of a sibling or parent might say, "I never saw this firewood before." Someone who already had lost many loved ones might say, "I never want to see this firewood again."

The senior spokesman then sang again, asking the male affines to begin cutting the corpse. Moving slowly and respectfully, the helpers carried the roasting rack, the decorated firewood bundle, and additional firewood to the house where the corpse lay. They lit the fire, spread clean mats on the ground, and got a new bamboo arrow tip to cut the body.

7. *In Wem Quirió's drawing of scenes from a precontact funeral, mourners are wearing scarlet macaw feathers to honor the dead man, who was a killer of enemies. In the upper left, two relatives support the corpse between them as they dance and sing the dead man's tamara songs. The roasting rack stands ready and the fire has been kindled with the decorated bundle of firewood (shown again in detail on the right). In the foreground, three male affines are preparing to cut the bloated, rigid corpse, which has been painted with stripes of red annatto. (The swelling of the corpse and evacuation of the bowels shown here are salient images in Wari' descriptions of processes of bodily decomposition.) On the left, one man holds a mat, ready to waft away the foul odor as the corpse is cut. In the center, another holds a new reed arrow tip, ready to begin cutting, while the man on the right holds the corpse's legs steady.*

Wari' consider corpse fluids very polluting, and they emphasize how repulsive the stench of a rotting corpse is. To protect themselves from corpse fluids, the men who did the cutting painted their hands and forearms up to the elbows with black genipap and smeared their bodies heavily with strong-smelling red annatto. Later, all the people who were going to eat the flesh also covered their faces, heads, and hands with annatto to keep the pollution from entering their bodies.

Dismemberment and Roasting

By all accounts, at the moment when the corpse was taken from its relatives' arms to be cut, the outpouring of grief intensified into a loud, fevered chorus of crying and keening. Today, a similar swell of grief occurs when

8. Wem Quirió's drawing shows female affines (on the left) seated around a mat, preparing the cornbread (pamonha) and carrying palm leaves in which the corn-bread and internal organs will be wrapped and roasted. (On the far right is an enlarged detail of a palm leaf.) The body parts are on the roasting rack, and a male affine stands in front of the fire holding a stick, to prevent one of the dead man's distraught relatives from throwing himself into the fire.

the male affines take the corpse to prepare it for burial. For close kin, this is partly an emotional response to having to surrender the corpse, but as discussed in the following chapter, loud crying also is believed to help keep the dead person's ghost away.

One theme running through Wari' funeral practices is the attempt to prevent corpse substances from being lost to the earth. When corpses were cut, relatives often tried to keep the body fluids from spilling onto the ground or into the fire. As an expression of love and respect, a close kinsman sometimes lay facedown on a mat, crying and supporting the corpse on his back as it was butchered, so that its fluids would flow onto his own body rather than onto the ground.

As the cutting began, the internal organs were removed, and the heart and liver were wrapped in leaves to be roasted. Other internal organs, including the genitals and intestines, were burned in the fire.[5] The helpers cut off the head, then severed the limbs at the joints. In many respects, the manner in which Wari' dismembered human corpses was similar to the way they butcher game. The main difference, according to people at Santo André, is that whereas one makes a lateral cut across an animal's belly, one disembowels a human with a vertical abdominal incision.

After being washed, the body pieces usually were placed directly on the decorated roasting rack over the fire kindled from the special, decorated bundle of firewood. Young children's body parts were wrapped in leaves

9. Wem Quirió's drawing shows body parts roasting, along with two leaf-wrapped packets containing the internal organs. On the far right is a strand of makuri xe', *the liana used to tie the bundle of firewood.*

before roasting, the way Wari' cook soft foods like small fish and animal organs. Elders at Santo André say they usually began roasting the corpse in the afternoon, though the timing seems to have varied somewhat over time and in different regions. In the Dois Irmãos area, eating usually began at dusk and continued until dawn, so the cooking and consumption of the corpse took place during the same dusk-to-dawn period when the most important rituals at parties like hüroroin and tamara occur.

Crying continued while the body parts roasted. In this phase of the funeral, consanguines continued to express their identification with the deceased and their desires to join him or her in death. Distraught kin often tried to throw themselves into the fire where the corpse was roasting. This happened so commonly that the affines routinely assigned a young man to stand next to the fire, armed with a long pole, to stop the dead person's relatives from burning themselves. Wari' speak of such acts as attempts to kill oneself, but they were also a conventional way to express grief.

Another formal expression of love and identification with the deceased happened at funerals for people of all ages, but especially at funerals for infants and young children. Wari' say that the bodies of babies and toddlers are full of tender fat that dripped from the body parts as they roasted. To prevent this body grease from falling into the fire, the child's grieving parents or grandparents would catch it in a clay pot and, as an expression of love, smear the child's fat over their own heads, hair, and bodies as they cried. Wari' think of mortuary cannibalism as similarly expressing respect and compassion for the dead by saving their body substances from being abandoned to the earth.

Consuming the Corpse

When the body parts were well roasted, the male affines removed them from the roasting rack and placed them on clean mats in front of the close consanguineal relatives ('*iri nari*). The heart and liver cooked fastest, and these usually were cut up and eaten first. One or more of the senior consanguines (usually including the kinsman serving as family spokesman) performed the task of separating the flesh from the bones and dividing it into small pieces.

What did it feel like to watch the body of a loved one—one's own child, mother, father, sister, brother, spouse—be decapitated, eviscerated, cut into pieces? What did it feel like to sit nearby for hours, watching this loved one's body parts roast? What did it feel like to be handed the cooked flesh, the body parts that still looked human, and then have to separate the flesh from the bones, dividing it into bits that gradually, finally, lost their semblance of humanness and became no longer recognizable as the dead individual?

These are central questions, but they are questions I cannot fully answer, for there is a point beyond which Wari' become circumspect in talking about the intimate experience of cannibalism. When one asks, they fall back on conventional truisms: we were sad; we cried a lot; we felt that the body had to be eaten; the dead themselves wanted to be eaten. *Je' kwerexi'* [Thus are our bodies; thus was our custom]. Perhaps someday I or others will learn more of the details. For now, I can offer only the information that Wari' have considered it fitting to share.

Instead of talking directly about how they felt about watching a family member be dismembered, cooked, and eaten, Wari' emphasize how hard it was to let go of the corpse, how the collective keening intensified as the family cried and clung to the body before surrendering it to be cut. This clearly was an emotionally difficult experience. But once the corpse had been dismembered, eating it was considered the most respectful and honorable treatment, and the close kin ('*iri nari*) asked and pleaded with the affines to do so. More painful than having the corpse eaten would have been to have it *not* be eaten.

After the flesh was divided into small pieces, female affines brought the corn bread (*pamonha*) they had made, and this, too, was divided into small portions and placed on clean mats. One of the 'iri nari (again, commonly the man who organized the funeral) then sang to the affines, asking them to come and eat the bits of flesh and pieces of pamonha. He typically addressed the affines by consanguineal kin terms and referred to the dead person as "our" relative, using first-person plural–inclusive linguistic markers (Vilaça 1992).

The affines (*nari paxi*) did not descend greedily upon the flesh. Instead, they hung back, crying and expressing their reluctance to eat. The dead person's consanguines insisted that they should eat it. The affines cried and refused, saying over and over that they could not bring themselves to eat the person. The consanguines insisted they should. Some consanguines then might approach each of the principal eaters in turn. Embracing each other, the pair would cry together, and the dead person's consanguine would beg the affine, pleading, "You will eat, won't you?" Only after the consanguines had insisted repeatedly would the affines finally consent to eat the flesh.

Wari' reject the idea that anyone *wanted* to eat the corpse; to treat the corpse like animal meat and eat voraciously would be the ultimate insult (Vilaça 2000:93). Instead, they emphasize that affines ate because the dead person's close consanguines asked them to do so. In the scripted performances of Wari' funeral rituals, consanguines and affines alternately resisted and facilitated the act of cannibalism. Consanguines set the process in motion by designating individual affines to prepare the firewood, the roasting rack, and pamonha. But when the affines came to dismember the corpse, the consanguines clung to it, resisting the moment of letting go. Then when the body was cooked and ready to eat, the consanguines asked the affines to eat, and the affines resisted doing so.

The affines' expressions of reluctance to eat were not necessarily just a polite gesture, for most adult and adolescent corpses were so rotten as to be thoroughly revolting. Elders say that sometimes it was only with the greatest effort that they managed to force themselves to swallow the flesh. Sometimes they would leave the gathering to vomit, only to return and eat more. The decayed state of the corpse and the ritualized expressions of resistance to eating were prime markers of the recognition that the act of eating a fellow Wari' was very different from the act of eating an animal or an enemy.

Funeral "Table Manners"

Wari' eat animal meat by holding it in their hands, but at funerals, the eaters avoided touching the human flesh with their hands. Instead, they held it delicately on thin splinters like cocktail toothpicks. While the nari paxi consumed the internal organs, the 'iri nari, sitting in a separate group, cried as they removed the flesh from the bones. They placed the bones in a conical clay cooking pot and the bits of flesh on a clean mat, along with small pieces of pamonha. In a variation on this pattern, the bits of flesh were placed in a separate conical clay pot that one of the close kin held cradled in his or her lap, in the loving position in which Wari' support relatives' heads in illness or when grooming or comforting someone. With the flesh in the pot, the consanguines handed pieces directly to the eaters.

Wari' attributed no special significance to eating specific body parts, and there appears to have been no concern about who ate which parts of the corpse. Corpses of both sexes and all ages were treated basically alike.

The eaters ate very slowly and respectfully, and the eating went on for hours. The eaters alternately cried a little and ate a little, while the noneaters cried constantly. Although the eaters tried not to touch the flesh directly, their hands still became greasy with body fat, and they would wipe their hands on the heads, hair, and bodies of the dead person's close kin.

How Much Was Eaten?

When the eating was done between dusk and dawn, all the flesh would ideally be consumed by morning. Whatever remained uneaten was burned. Wari' emphasize that the ideal was to consume all of the flesh, as well as the heart, liver, and brain. In practice, the amount actually eaten varied greatly, depending on how much the corpse had decomposed before it was roasted. The longest delays between the time of biological death and the time when the corpse was roasted occurred in funerals for respected elders, whereas babies and young children were roasted sooner.

Wari' feel strongly that the family should not dispose of a corpse until all the dead person's close kin have arrived and had a chance to see the body and take part in the keening and eulogizing. I heard stories of incidents in which family fights almost broke out because a body had been buried before a certain relative was able to get to the funeral. In the past, when Wari' traveled only on foot and lived in smaller settlements dispersed over a wide territory, it could take several days to assemble all the relatives. Even after everyone had arrived, Wari' considered it appropriate (in the deaths of adults and adolescents) to wait until the third day after death before roasting the corpse. (A day is reckoned from sundown to sundown.) As mourners cried and reminisced and honored the deceased, the decaying corpse swelled up enormously. The older and more respected the deceased, the longer the interval before roasting, and the more rotten the flesh became. In funerals for adults and adolescents, therefore, a good deal of flesh seems to have been burned rather than eaten.

Children's corpses were roasted sooner and tended to be consumed in their entirety. Miscarried fetuses and stillbirths were not eaten, allegedly because they were usually already decomposed. (I heard one story, however, of a well-developed fetus that was eaten after being extracted from its dead mother's womb.) Young children have few social bonds of their own; only immediate consanguines and affines are expected to attend their funerals, and the crying does not last as long as it does in funerals for older children. Babies and toddlers often were roasted and eaten on the day they died or the day after. Because it was still relatively fresh, babies' flesh, according to the few elders who were willing to discuss this, was the most tender and palatable kind of human flesh.

Treatment of Bones and Funeral Remains

After they were done eating the flesh, Wari' disposed of the bones either by grinding and eating them or by burning and pulverizing them. In the Negro-Ocaia region, consumption of the bones appears to have been done routinely. In the Dois Irmãos area, where my study focuses, it seems to have been less common, being reserved as a special honor, primarily for men who had killed enemies. When Wari' ate the bones, they prepared them by roasting them and then grinding them into meal, which they mixed with wild honey, which is thinner (and much more delicious) than commercial honeys. The bone-and-honey mixture was drunk by the same affines who had eaten the flesh.

When the bones were not consumed, they were burned along with any remaining flesh. The clay pots, mats, roasting rack, and other items used in the funeral also were burned, along with any leftover firewood. When everything had been cremated, the male helpers dug a hole where the fire had been and swept all the charred remains into it. Using a log, they pounded everything into dust, covered the hole with dirt, and swept the ground to eradicate all traces of the funeral. Finally, they replaced the household sleeping platform over the spot where the ashes were buried.

Destroying Material Reminders

After the funeral, relatives burn the dead person's house. The residents of neighboring homes alter the appearance of their own houses by covering up their old doors and making new ones on a different side of the house. Existing paths are abandoned and new ones made. All the dead individual's personal possessions are burned or removed from the household. In the past, virtually everything that had belonged to the deceased was burned: baskets, bows and arrows, mats, clay pots, feathers, fighting sticks, festival attire. Today, clothing and photographs are also thrown into the fire, and when a schoolchild dies, relatives ask the teacher to hand over all of the student's books, papers, and drawings to be burned.

These days, less easily destroyed or expensive store-bought possessions, such as kettles, machetes, and shotguns, usually are given to nonconsanguines. Chickens, ducks, and other fowl may be killed, but they are more often given away. To say that possessions are "given" away is a bit of a euphemism, for while everyone recognizes that the family must part with the dead person's possessions, they are also very aware that some people take advantage of this, exhibiting an avarice that borders on disrespect. People at Santo André say this attitude is getting worse, and a number of bereaved individuals have complained bitterly to me about the greed of nonrelatives who descended upon their household right after the funeral to carry off whatever they could get their hands on.

A measure of how much significance Wari' attach to erasing material traces is the fact that they also destroy any food associated with the deceased. Crops that the dead person planted and stores of corn or other crops that he or she harvested are burned or uprooted and thrown into the forest. This has a serious impact on the bereaved family, for with their house and food supplies destroyed, they must rely on the charity of relatives to take them into their homes and feed them. Bereaved adults with children to support still work to produce food, but family diets inevitably suffer. Supporting one's kin in their time of mourning is one of the strongest obligations of Wari' family relations, though some complain that these days "people don't help their relatives like they used to."

The imperative that Wari' feel to erase tangible traces of a dead person's identity and former presence extends to the way they talk about the dead. In addition to not speaking their names or calling them by kinship terms, Wari' depersonalize the dead, referring to a deceased individual only in the plural as *oro jima*, "the ghosts," or *jami mijak*, "white-lipped peccary spirits." If Wari' use kinship terms in reference to a dead relative, the relationship is collectivized. For example, instead of saying "my father," one always says "our father."[6]

Behavior During Mourning

Close relatives of the deceased cut their hair and use no body paint during the period of active mourning, which tends to last for about a year after a death. Close relatives, especially women, also continue to keen for several months after someone dies. Wari' may cry and keen spontaneously any time they feel moved by sorrow, but recently bereaved individuals keen periodically during the day, especially in the early morning and at dusk. As time passes, the frequency of keening gradually diminishes.

While in mourning, Wari' observe behavioral restrictions similar to those associated with illness. Mourners withdraw from social interaction and do not run, dance, attend parties, shout, or sing. Reserved comportment expresses one's grief and shows respect for the dead. At Santo André, people criticized a family in which the teenagers and their older married sister flaunted these norms by playing their radio loudly and dancing in front of their house only two months after their sister had died.

With their home, crops, and food reserves destroyed, the dead person's immediate family has little reason to stay in their home village, especially since it is full of painful reminders. Before the contact, Wari' often abandoned an entire village after an adult died, or at least stayed away for a number of months. After the contact, the change to larger, permanent settlements made it impractical to relocate an entire village. These days, usually only the immediate relatives of the deceased go away to stay with relatives elsewhere. In Wari' life histories, family members' deaths are one of the most common reasons for moving to a new community.

Especially in the first weeks and months after a death, mourners do little or no work and produce little food. From the time when a close kinsperson falls seriously ill until long after the death, individuals curtail or drastically reduce their normal activities of hunting, fishing, and farming. This pattern of diminished food production continues to some degree until the period of formal mourning ends. Wari' mourners observe no specific food restrictions, but they eat less than normal because, they say, they simply are not hungry, and besides, there is not much food in a bereaved family's home. Although there is no rule against eating meat, mourners hunt and fish less than usual and consequently eat less meat and fish than usual. As we will see in Chapter 11, a return to hunting and a celebratory meat feast mark the end of mourning.

CHAPTER FIVE

EXPLANATIONS
OF EATING

Before examining in more depth how Wari' beliefs and values related to their former practice of eating the dead, it is useful to consider some of the theories that westerners have proposed to explain cannibalism in other societies. Scholars have approached cannibalism from several distinct perspectives, each of which raises a particular constellation of issues to consider. A materialist perspective would focus on questions about cannibalism's dietary role: Did Wari' eat human flesh because they needed the protein or other nutrients from human corpses? A psychoanalytic perspective would focus on questions about emotional drives: Did Wari' endocannibalism express aggression, ambivalence, identification, or desires to hold on to others by taking them into one's own body? Although my conclusion is that none of the models commonly used to describe cannibalism explains much about Wari' mortuary practices, these models have been so prominent in western thought about cannibalism that it is worth taking time to consider to what extent they do or do not apply to the Wari'.

The Dietary Question

There are a number of well-known cases of people who resorted to eating human flesh when facing starvation. The popular film *Alive!* portrayed the excruciating dilemmas faced by members of a Uruguayan college rugby team after a plane crash high in the Andes mountains stranded them for months without food. California's Donner Lake is named after the famous Donner Party, a band of pioneers trapped by Sierra Nevada snowstorms in the winter of 1846, among whom some survived by eating the others. Until recently, students at the University of Colorado at Boulder could order a "Packerburger" at the student union's Packer Grill, named after Alfred E. Packer, who survived in a similar manner when he and his companions were snowbound in the San Juan Mountains of western Colorado in 1874.

These incidents of "hunger cannibalism," in which human flesh was used as food, were aberrant acts that violated the moral norms of the societies to which the people who ate human flesh belonged. In contrast, mortuary cannibalism is an institutionalized form of cannibalism, a practice considered morally acceptable in the societies where it is practiced. Anthropologists have argued about whether dietary needs were the motive for institutionalized cannibalism in certain societies. One of the most rancorous debates focused on the practice of human sacrifice among the Aztecs of central Mexico in the fifteenth century. Aztec priests ritually slaughtered thousands of war captives and offered their hearts to the Aztec gods. Portions of the sacrifice victims' flesh were eaten by priests and nobles, as well as by the warrior who had taken the captive and the warrior's relatives and friends. Anthropologist Michael Harner (1977) suggested that this use of human flesh might have helped the Aztecs cope with famines and food shortages, particularly a shortage of animal protein that, he argued, resulted from a combination of factors, including population growth, environmental circumscription, the depletion of wild game, and the lack of domesticated herbivores. Marvin Harris (1977, 1985:199–234), the well-known cultural materialist, took this argument further and attempted to show how the use of human flesh provided incentives for warriors and helped sustain the power of the elites.

This materialist interpretation of Aztec cannibalism provoked a heated controversy. Many scholars disagreed with Harner's and Harris's assumptions and data about population levels and ecological conditions in the Valley of Mexico and pointed to contradictions in the argument (cf. Berdan 1982, Ortiz de Montellano 1978). In a famous rebuttal, Marshall Sahlins (1978:52) criticized the "Western business mentality" behind materialist interpretations that, he claimed, treat the concern to achieve a bottom-line profit as the dominant motive in human behavior. Sahlins argued that Aztec human sacrifice should be understood in terms of its complex cultural logic and religious meanings, not reduced to a strategy for getting some meat.

Regardless of the problems with protein shortage as an explanation of Aztec exocannibalism, the question of whether dietary needs motivated Wari' practices deserves consideration.[1] For the Wari', both exo- and endocannibalism sometimes involved consuming substantial amounts of flesh, and it is reasonable to ask whether eating human flesh was a response to nutritional needs or an adaptation to the ecological circumstances of Wari' life.

Wari' Views of the Gastronomic Qualities of Human Flesh

Wari' children sometimes ask their grandparents what it was like to eat human flesh. The answers I heard to this question were always the same: "*Ak karawa*," the elderly person said [It's like (animal) meat]. When Wari' describe human flesh as being similar to animal meat, they are referring to its taste and texture. In gastronomic terms, Wari' do not seem to emphasize any fundamental difference between human and animal flesh. They use the same word, *kwere-* ("body" or "flesh"), for animal flesh (*kwerein karawa* or *kwerekun karawa*) and human flesh (*kwerekekem wari'*), and they talk about the qualities of human and animal flesh in similar terms. When I asked directly about how human flesh tastes, elders described certain corpses they had eaten as having been tough, tender, fatty, or bitter-tasting. Old people, everyone agreed, tend to be lean, tough, and dry, while babies are tender and fatty.

Meat is the food Wari' value most highly. In addition to its delicious taste and unparalleled ability to satisfy hunger, Wari' especially appreciate the fat in meat, which they consider essential to good health and vitality. Yet although they recognize that human flesh resembles animal flesh, they consider it barbaric to treat a person as food. In fact, a defining characteristic of certain monsters in Wari' mythology is that they stalk and kill people just in order to eat human flesh. With one exception, I have found no evidence that Wari' ever treated the flesh of their fellow Wari' simply as food.[2] There are a few stories about famous incidents in which someone did kill and eat another Wari' (always from a different subgroup). In these cases, the killer intentionally treated his victim like food as a way to make a public statement of hostility and disdain for the victim's subgroup. These incidents loom large in Wari' discourses about cannibalism, for they are counterimages that embody what the eating of corpses at funerals was *not* supposed to be.

Yet even if they say they never ate the flesh of fellow Wari' to satisfy their hunger, Wari' know it could be possible to do so. In precontact funerals, they went to great lengths to differentiate their eating of the dead from gastronomic cannibalism. The elaborate rules and conventionalized gestures for handling, preparing, and consuming corpses highlighted the difference between eating a Wari' corpse and eating animals or enemies. Vilaça (1992) has suggested that the practice of delaying the roasting of corpses until the flesh was decayed beyond palatability also had the purpose of marking mortuary cannibalism as a *non*gastronomic activity. Yet whether or not Wari' wanted to think of it as food, those who ate human flesh clearly would have received some protein, iron, and other nutrients.

The Nutritional Value of Human Corpses

Anthropologists have tried to calculate the nutritional value of human flesh. One estimate suggests that a corpse provides slightly more than one hundred grams of protein per kilogram of body weight, assuming that 40 percent of body weight is wasted in the butchering process (Dornstreich and Morren 1974:7).[3] By this estimate, a fifty-kilogram (110-pound) adult corpse might yield five thousand grams of protein. In Wari' funerals, the practice of eating bits of corn bread along with the flesh might have enhanced protein intake, since corn and meat contain complementary amino acids. The liver and heart are rich in iron, and bone meal is a good source of calcium. The wild honey with which the bone meal was mixed tends to be rich in vitamins, which would have enhanced calcium absorption.

It is difficult to estimate how much flesh an individual would have ingested at a Wari' funeral, for the amount that was eaten varied greatly, depending on how rotten the flesh was and how many people took part in eating it. Babies and young children who were roasted soon after their deaths were consumed in their near entirety by a small number of individuals, whereas adult corpses usually were rotten, and the little that was actually eaten was divided among many people. Occasionally, however, an adult might be roasted while fairly fresh. (This seems to have happened sometimes when a person died after a long illness during which all the relatives already had spent many days crying around the sickbed.) It seems reasonable to assume that, in general, an individual would have consumed more flesh at funerals for young children than at funerals for adults, and this concords with the recollections of a few men who described going home from children's funerals with a full stomach, in contrast to the hunger for real food they felt after other funerals. However, satiation clearly was the exception, not the rule.

If funerary cannibalism contributed to Wari' diets, this benefited only part of the population. Children did not eat human flesh, and women seem to have eaten less than men overall. Women from the Negro-Ocaia region have said they did not eat corpses because they disliked the stench. Women from the Dois Irmãos region say that they had no such reservations and that women did eat at funerals. However, it was considered acceptable for a female affine (but not a male affine) to decline to eat if she felt she simply could not do so, and some women say that if the flesh was too repulsively rotten, they did not eat but just cried with the dead person's close relatives. Enemies, according to my Dois Irmãos informants, were eaten exclusively or primarily by older men. Thus the overall pattern was that the nutritional inputs from cannibalism went only to adults, and to men more than to women.

Mortuary cannibalism also may have had *negative* effects on Wari' nutrition. Even when decay was far advanced and the stench was overpowering, male affines still forced themselves to swallow bits of the flesh, and this sometimes made them so nauseated that they had to leave a funeral several times to vomit. Vomiting and diarrhea provoked by eating rotten flesh would have depleted the body of nutrients and electrolytes and interfered with nutrient absorption. Nutrition also may have been impaired by the way a death disrupts normal food-producing activities. The dead person's close relatives eat and drink little and cry intensely for days. Other members of the community and mourners who come from elsewhere also eat less than usual for a while, since no one hunts or fishes much until after the funeral. The protein and other nutrients from human flesh and bones may have compensated somewhat for the dietary disruption that a death causes, but it is not clear whether there was any net gain in nutritional inputs.

Although those who took part in eating the dead at funerals clearly might sometimes have received some nutritional benefits (especially at funerals for young children), it makes little sense to claim that Wari' practiced endocannibalism *because* they needed or wanted to use human flesh as food. Two major factors militate against such an interpretation. First, there is little reason to assume that the precontact population suffered significant protein shortages. Wari' controlled a large territory with low population density and abundant game, fish, and Brazil nut resources. In the decades before the contact, all their subgroups' territories bordered on unpopulated forest areas where game was plentiful. Elders say that outright hunger was rare before the contact, although certainly there were lean times. The greatest seasonal dietary stress came at the end of the dry season, in October and November, before the new corn had ripened. This was the time of year when communities dispersed into small family groups that moved to areas where palm hearts, Brazil nuts, game, and fish were abundant. Kwashiorkor (protein deficiency disease) is unknown among the Wari', and New Tribes missionaries who were present at the first contacts have said they observed no signs of malnutrition. This is consistent with medical studies of other groups of newly contacted native Amazonians in similar situations. From the late

1960s through the early 1980s, scholars argued vigorously over the idea that protein is scarce in the Amazonian rainforest and that certain cultural patterns, such as warfare or cannibalism, might be adaptations to protein scarcity. However, neither medical examinations nor dietary studies have ever documented protein deficiency in a relatively undisturbed native Amazonian population living in circumstances similar to those of the precontact Wari'. On the contrary, researchers have found adequate or more than adequate protein intake.[4] While it is impossible to evaluate the quality of precontact Wari' diets with any precision, there is little reason to think they suffered from either clinical protein deficiency or sustained food shortages.

A second argument against the idea that dietary needs motivated Wari' cannibalism lies in the fact that they burned or discarded large amounts of potentially edible flesh. In funerary cannibalism, the two- or three-day delay before roasting many corpses often left them so rotten that little flesh was eaten. Wari' never tried to preserve their fellow tribesmembers' flesh to eat later. When faced with "too much to eat" at a funeral, which sometimes happened when several people died at once in a massacre or epidemic, the eaters consumed as much as they could and then burned the rest.

Even in eating their enemies, Wari' wasted a good deal of flesh. Warriors usually took only the head and limbs of the enemies they killed. Men say they left the body trunk behind because it was too heavy to carry and would have slowed them down in getting away from the scene of the slaying. While this may have been true when the killer was alone, it does not explain the failure to take the whole corpse when the enemy was slain by a group of warriors and the body parts could have been divided among them to carry home, as hunters do with large game such as tapirs. If Wari' had seen enemy flesh primarily as food, it seems unlikely that they would have thrown away so much of it. The fact that they did suggests that getting meat was not the major motive for killing and eating enemies.

This is not to say that Wari' would pass up an opportunity to eat lots of enemy flesh when it was convenient to do so. The biggest feast on human flesh I have heard about seems to have occurred in the late nineteenth or early twentieth century, when warriors from a foreign tribe tried to attack an Oro Nao' village in the Negro-Ocaia region. Their speech is said to have been partially intelligible to Wari', so they probably spoke a Chapakuran language.

Wari' dubbed these enemy warriors Oro Nene (*nene* connotes gullibility) in memory of how easy they were to trick. As the story goes, some Oro Nao'

(Wari') men intercepted the Oro Nene warriors before they attacked. "Why not be friends instead of enemies?" the Oro Nao' suggested. They proposed a chicha-fest to mark this friendship, and the Oro Nao' women set to work grinding corn to make beer. While waiting for the beer to ferment, the Oro Nao' put their new friends to work using stone axes to fell trees to clear fields. Then when the beer was ready, the Oro Nao' men killed all the Oro Nene. They invited Wari' from neighboring villages to come see the bodies, and after a raucous celebration in which men and boys took turns shooting arrows at the corpses, there was a feast from which people went home sated. In 1986, Wari' were reminded of this story when a windstorm toppled the last big, old tree that had been left standing, chopped halfway through by the stone axes of the gullible Oro Nene.

This story suggests that Wari' were not averse to consuming substantial amounts of enemy flesh. Although incidents like this feast on the unfortunate Oro Nene seem to have been rare, enemy body parts were always roasted while fresh, and with none of the ill effects caused by rotten flesh, there could have been a net gain in protein for those who ate enemy body parts. However, it is difficult to see protein acquisition as the major motive even for Wari' exocannibalism, in view of how routinely they wasted so much enemy flesh. This pattern of wastage in all forms of cannibalism among the Wari' is diametrically opposite to the way they treat animal meat, which is always roasted as soon as possible and consumed entirely. With human flesh, however, wastage was the rule, not the exception. Combined with the lack of evidence for a shortage of protein before the contact, this fact makes the argument for a materialist interpretation of Wari' cannibalism weak. Clearly, social and cultural considerations played a bigger role than nutritional functionalism in shaping Wari' practices.

Psychoanalytic Perspectives

Many of the most compelling questions about cannibalism relate to subjective experience. How does it feel to eat another human being? Is there a natural revulsion against eating one's own kind? What motivates someone to do so? The only ones who can really answer such questions are individuals with personal experiences of people eating. Yet most of the scholars whose ideas have shaped western academic theories of cannibalism have had little or no access to informants from societies where cannibalism was a normative practice, and many have not paid much attention to the ethnographic data on cannibalism either. Instead, psychoanalytic models have tended to rely mostly on analyses of the fantasies and aberrant behavior of people in western societies, where cannibalism is stigmatized and anyone who practices it is seriously deviant.

Wari' testimonies about their personal experiences with cannibalism provide a rare opportunity to examine some of its subjective dimensions. To look at endocannibalism from Wari' points of view, however, requires a shift away from some of the assumptions in which most academic interpretations of cannibalism have been grounded. First, most theorists treat cannibalism as a dyadic relationship between the person who eats and the person who is eaten. For Wari', however, mortuary cannibalism was a fundamentally collective activity, one of the practices that organized relations among families, not between individuals. Second, scholars have tended to assume that the motives for cannibalism are located in the eater, in that individual's personal desire to consume the other person. Although they have suggested diverse kinds of motivating desires, ranging from hunger to aggression to desires to hold on to the deceased, most theories of cannibalism share the assumption that it is primarily an act of self-gratification based in some deep-rooted impulse in the individual who does the eating.

Wari' disagree. They categorically reject the idea of mortuary cannibalism as a form of self-gratification motivated by individual desire. On the contrary, they point out that eating the dead was often quite unpleasant. They say that the ones who benefited from the eating of the corpse were not those who ate it, but those who did *not* eat it: the dead person and his or her close kin. As they see it, what individual eaters gained from eating the corpse was the satisfaction of having acted properly to fulfill a major social duty. Wari' endocannibalism was not a one-way transaction in which an eater acted upon the one who was eaten; rather, it was part of a broader set of social transactions and mutual commitments between the dead person's family and the families with whom they had intermarried.

With its two distinct forms of cannibalism, the Wari' case also highlights the importance of not lumping all forms of cannibalism together into one model. When psychologically oriented theorists have looked at ethnographic data on cannibalism, they often have paid more attention to enemy eating than to mortuary cannibalism. There has been a tendency to treat exocannibalism as the prototype form of cannibalism and to assume that the motives for eating enemies must also, at some level, operate in the eating of relatives. Given this bias toward thinking about cannibalism in terms of eating enemies, it is not surprising that themes of hostility, anger, and aggression pervade western theories of cannibalism. From Freud's 1913 essay,

"Totem and Taboo" (1981b) to Eli Sagan's *Cannibalism: Human Aggression and Cultural Form* (1974), psychological models that seek a single, universal motive for cannibalism have tended to interpret all forms of people eating as an expression of the eater's hostility or ambivalence toward the individual who is eaten. When theorists have paid any attention to native people's statements about cannibalism as an act of compassion or respect for the dead, they have tended to dismiss such ideas as forms of self-deception that hide the fundamentally ambivalent, egocentric, antisocial nature of all cannibalism. Even among anthropologists, enemy eating has received more theoretical attention than mortuary cannibalism, especially from scholars looking for a universal pattern of psychological motivations. British social anthropologist I. M. Lewis (1986), for example, argued that both endo- and exocannibalism could be subsumed under a single model, as acts of oral and genital aggression in which the eater expresses desires for dominance over the one who is eaten.

Western psychoanalytic models are difficult to test among nonwestern peoples, for culture shapes how individuals experience family relations, emotions, and the symbolic elements that are the foci of psychoanalysis. The difficulty of applying western models cross-culturally is compounded enormously when, as in the Wari' case, cannibalism is no longer practiced and researchers cannot observe the behaviors and emotions surrounding it. Recognizing these limitations, my objective in the discussion that follows is not to prove or disprove a particular psychoanalytic interpretation, but to identify some of the evidence and lines of argument that should be taken into consideration in thinking about how certain models might apply to Wari' endocannibalism.

Eating as an Act of Aggression

When I returned to Berkeley after my first stint of fieldwork with the Wari', I went to talk to a well-known folklore professor with a resolutely Freudian outlook. Half a minute into my description of Wari' endocannibalism, he bluntly informed me: "Aggression; it's about aggression. Every time you put something in your mouth, it's aggression." This is one of the most familiar ideas about cannibalism: that it expresses hostility toward the human being who is eaten. Wari' agree that eating human flesh can express hostility, and elderly men explain their own participation in exocannibalism in exactly these terms: "We ate the enemies [*wijam*] because we were angry [*mana'*] at them." They say they acted out their hatred by treating enemy corpses like game. Actually, enemies were treated less respectfully than animals, for whereas Wari' are careful not to waste or mistreat animal meat or offend animal spirits, they left major portions of enemy corpses to rot and ridiculed and abused enemy body parts. Little ritual surrounded the eating of enemy flesh, and the "table manners" for eating enemies were explicitly intended to express hostility and disrespect. Enemy body parts were divided among various individuals, who carried them home and ate them unceremoniously. Wari' say that when they ate enemy flesh, they held big chunks in their hands, tearing the flesh off the bone with their teeth, while they grunted and made rude comments expressing their disdain for the enemy.

The consumption of affines at funerals was a different matter, and Wari' adamantly deny that hostility or aggression were factors in it. When I put this question to Jimon Maram, for example, he responded by saying that hostility does not belong at a funeral and people who are on bad terms with the deceased are barred from attending. This happened, he said, at a funeral a few years earlier, when a senior kinsman of the deceased ordered a man to leave on the grounds that "you did not love him; it is not good that you come here."

Wari' are aware that hostile or uncaring sentiments toward the deceased nonetheless could be present at a funeral. In their insistence on a rigid protocol for eating the corpses of fellow Wari'—allowing the flesh to rot, handling the corpse ceremoniously, initially refusing the invitation to eat, not touching it with the hands, eating slowly and crying while eating—they went out of their way to mark the consumption of flesh at funerals as different from other acts of eating that did express hostility toward the one who was eaten.[5]

Eating as an Act of Respect

Wari' insist that eating can have more than one meaning: it can express aggression, but it also can be an act of respect and compassion for the individual or thing that is eaten. When they talk about eating as an act of respect, they commonly illustrate this by contrasting it with the dishonor connoted by burying or abandoning a body. This idea comes through in a story about the Corn Spirit (*jaminain mapak*), which explains why one should not leave corn lying on the ground:

Long ago, a man was walking to his field carrying a basket of corn seeds to plant. A corn kernel fell to the ground on the path. The man did not see it and went on. The corn seed began to cry like a child. Another man came along and found it crying on the ground. He picked it up and ate it. In doing so, he saved it, showing that he felt sympathy [*xiram pa'*] for it. The man who ate the seed planted his field, and it yielded great quantities of corn. The man who had left the seed on the ground planted his field, but nothing grew.

This tale expresses the idea that leaving a spirit-being on the ground in the forest connotes disrespect, whereas eating it expresses respect. In this context, eating is an act of salvation that pleases the thing consumed, so that it bestows abundance on the person who ate it. Wari' handle corn and meat (foods with humanlike spirits) carefully, and keeping them away from direct contact with the soil is part of this respectful treatment.

Similar ideas about eating as an act of respect for the object that is eaten are evident in food taboos associated with the category of animals called *jami karawa,* whose spirits are really human beings. These animal spirits can cause illness, and Wari' try to avoid offending them. When a hunter kills a jami karawa animal, he and his family must take care to prepare and consume the carcass properly. Jami karawa are angered by offenses such as: delay in butchering and cooking the animal's carcass; disrespectful treatment of the carcass, such as (for certain animals) being cooked in water instead of roasted; cooking meat together with incompatible foods (specifically, foods that also have spirits, such as corn or honey); failure to have a shaman remove the magical annatto and other fruits the animal carries in its body; and failure to distribute shares of its meat to all the relatives who should receive it. When a hunter kills an animal, his young children are supposed to eat the head, especially the eyes. Game are said to run toward hunters whose children eat the head and away from hunters whose children refuse to do so (cf. Everett and Kern 1997:498–500). What is notable about the rules surrounding the treatment of meat is that what offends jami karawa is the improper treatment of their carcasses, not the consumption of their flesh. To *not* eat its meat—to let its body parts rot—would be a sure way to provoke the spirit's wrath and vengeance. Eating properly demonstrates respect for the one whose flesh is consumed and pleases spirits so they will allow hunters to kill them again in the future.

* * *

The fact that Wari' insist on representing the funerary consumption of their dead as an act of respect, affection, and compassion means little from the perspective of western psychoanalysis. Cultural practices can express meanings of which their practitioners are unaware, and anger, ambivalence, and sadistic urges can hide behind a veneer of affection. Did Wari' mortuary cannibalism express covert hostility? This question can be considered from two directions, from the perspectives of the two distinct groups of actors in Wari' funerals: the affines (*nari paxi*) and the consanguines (*'iri nari*).

Affines and Aggression

The obvious place to look for aggression and hostility in Wari' endocannibalism is in relations among affines, since it was affines who ate one another. Did cannibalism express or mediate affinal tensions or conflicts?

Wari' generally treat relations among affines as a matter of complementarity and mutually beneficial reciprocity. Affinal relations ideally are supposed to be cordial and cooperative, and to a large extent, this holds true in practice. Almost all marriages are arranged or approved by the families involved, and Wari' parents are careful to approve marriages for their children only to members of families with whom they enjoy good relations. As in most societies, relations with one's affines are rarely as intimate as with one's own siblings. Men and women generally prefer to work with their close consanguines, but they often work with affines, too. Many affinal relationships appear to be based in genuine friendship and affection. Affective bonds between brothers-in-law generally are relaxed and positive, provided that the sister/wife involved is content with the way her husband treats her.

Wari' express solidarity in idioms of consanguineal kinship and shared body substance. Consanguinity is a metaphor for trust and intimacy, and in daily life, Wari' tend to call their affines by consanguineal kin terms.[6] In doing so, they acknowledge that they are closely related to one another and express friendly feelings for one another. But this is also an implicit recognition that trust and intimacy tend to be stronger in relations among consanguines and that relations to affines are more likely to involve some distance or ambivalence. This recognition is also reflected in the way Wari' call male strangers or unrelated men with whom they want to establish amity or fictive kinship by the term *nem*, "sister's husband" (Vilaça 1992).

While Wari' emphasize treating affines like consanguines and maintaining cordial relations with them, they also are aware that many of the most common social conflicts grow out of problems between husbands and wives. As in most societies, tensions among families related to one another by marriage often stem from discord between marital partners, especially accusations that one spouse has committed adultery or that a husband has neglected or threatened his wife. Actual physical violence against women is rare, perhaps partly because Wari' men respond so quickly to any threat against a sister, daughter, or other close kinswoman.

Conflicts among affines are a theme in a number of Wari' stories and myths, but other stories emphasize conflicts and betrayals among close consanguines. Among the families of Santo André, relations to consanguines outside the nuclear family (such as aunts, uncles, cousins, or grandparents' siblings) have been at least as problematic as relations among affines. Tensions in relations to consanguines seem to generate far more anxiety and emotional distress than tensions among affines, for to feel neglected or disliked by one's blood kin is the worst thing imaginable for Wari'.

Though Wari' may experience conflicts with both their consanguines and their affines, they deal with these two sets of problems differently. Conflicts among consanguines tend to be sublimated; instead of leading to direct confrontations, problems in relations among close family members often show up in the form of illnesses or seizures. The inevitable response is an outpouring of physical and emotional support and expressions of affection and caring from all close kin, regardless of prior tensions in any of the relationships. Serious conflicts among affines, in contrast, tend to be confronted directly and resolved either by talking through the problem or by the mixita fighting described in Chapter 2.

There is nothing unique or especially unusual in the structure or dynamics of Wari' affinity. Wari' recognize the potential for conflict in relations to their affines, and they have ways to deal with it. Since similar affinal tensions exist in most other societies, the mere existence of affinal oppositions and tensions does not go very far toward explaining Wari' mortuary cannibalism. I see little evidence to support an argument that hostility or aggression motivated Wari' to eat their in-laws.

Wari' see the task of eating the corpse at a funeral as a service that affines owed one another. This reflects a larger pattern in precontact affinal relations, the tendency to ask affines (especially close male affines) to perform death-related tasks that family members could not or did not wish to do themselves. One example is the precontact practice described in Chapter 3, in which, when a woman had suffered repeated late-term miscarriages or stillbirths, a male affine was asked to bury her most recent stillborn infant's corpse in the forest. Another example is euthanasia (mercy-killing). Before the contact, an elderly person who was terminally ill with no hope of recovery, someone who was suffering greatly and wanted to die, would announce the decision to die and choose a male affine to do the killing. This usually was done using a tree bark called *ka karama*, which Wari' say has potent medicinal properties. After stuffing grated bark into the sick person's nostrils, the male affine covered the mouth and pinched together the nostrils with one hand while squeezing the throat with the other. Death was said to be rapid and relatively painless.

Wari' see the precontact obligation to eat affines' corpses in similar terms, as a responsibility to act at one's affines' request to take care of emotionally difficult, death-related tasks. As they see it, one ate the corpse out of a sense of duty, not desire.

Consanguines and Ambivalence

An alternative approach to the question of aggression is to ask whether the desire for the corpse to be eaten came not from the affines but from the dead person's close consanguineal relatives, the people who did not eat it themselves but urged the affines to do so. This might make more sense, since psychoanalytic models tend to see cannibalism as the product of the emotional impulses or fantasies of individuals who are deeply affected by a loss. Although in the Wari' case the family members most affected by a specific death did not eat the corpse, Sagan (1974) has suggested that cannibalistic impulses may be sublimated and expressed in other forms, and urging others to eat might easily be one form of sublimation. In searching for the psychological motive for Wari' endocannibalism, should we look to the close consanguines' emotions?

This may be a more fruitful approach, since it is closer to what Wari' say about the dynamics surrounding endocannibalism. They emphasize that affines ate the corpse because the dead person's close consanguines insisted that they do so. They locate the emotional force behind cannibalism not in the relationship between the eater and the person who was eaten, but in the relationship between the eaters and the family of the one who was eaten.

In considering why Wari' would want their close relatives' corpses to be eaten, orthodox psychoanalytic theories suggest two major impulses: ambivalence and incorporative desires. Ambivalence is the simultaneous existence of love and hate towards the same object. Sagan proposed one of the most explicit models of how ambivalence relates to what he called "affectionate cannibalism," that is, cases like Wari' endocannibalism in which people say they consume the dead as an act of love or compassion. Sagan suggested that "affectionate cannibalism" involves emotions "very similar to our own feelings toward dead relatives: affection, sorrow, and the desire to preserve and remember the virtues of the deceased." Such emotions are very different from the aggressive eating of enemies, but nonetheless, he commented, "[o]ne cannot help feeling that there is some connection" between the supposedly affectionate eating of kin and the aggressive eating of enemies. The link between endo- and exocannibalism, Sagan suggested, is emotional ambivalence toward the deceased. Mourning always involves a mixture of affection and anger. "When someone dies and leaves us behind, we cannot help but feel that we have been abandoned; we cannot react to this situation without intense feelings of anger at the person who has thus left us deprived of his or her support" (Sagan 1974:26, 22–23, 28).

How do people deal with this mixture of anger and affection for the dead? Sagan suggested that such ambivalence is analogous to the stage in early childhood when the "undeveloped ego of the small child reacts to all undesired separation from the sources of love and physical sustenance as if it were abandonment" (1974:27). The child responds with anger to the withdrawal of the mother's breast, and this anger coexists with desire for reunion with the lost object. One way to satisfy the twin impulses of aggression and affection is to incorporate the object orally, by biting or swallowing the breast or fantasizing about eating the mother. Sagan suggested that "affectionate cannibalism" is based in a similar impulse:

> The undeveloped imagination of the cannibal does not deal very adequately with metaphorical usage. He is compelled to take the urge for oral incorporation literally. He eats the person who, by dying, has abandoned him. This act of literal oral incorporation has an affectionate and an aggressive dimension. As with all of us, the aggressive aspects of the situation are not conscious with the cannibal; he gives voice only to the affectionate feelings involved in this action (1974:28).

According to Sagan, societies, like children, grow out of this phase as they mature and move up the ladder of cultural development: "As the imagination develops, the need for literal implementation of psychic urges decreases" (1974:28). In more "advanced" societies, rituals sublimate such impulses into substitute forms that satisfy the desire for oral incorporation in other ways. Instead of eating or mutilating the corpse, mourners may feast on an animal, cut or mutilate their own bodies or clothing, or drink alcohol while standing around the corpse at a wake.

Hopefully it goes without saying that Sagan's characterization of "primitive" mentality as incapable of metaphorical thought is roundly contradicted by the rich symbolic lives of people like the Wari'. Still, his model of ambivalence merits consideration, for ambivalence was and is part of the emotional mix experienced by Wari' mourners, just as it is for mourners in North America, Europe, and elsewhere. Wari' commonly express feelings of loneliness and abandonment after a kinsperson's death, although instead of verbalizing anger toward the deceased, they more often direct their expressions of anger outward, against the sorcerer (usually from a different community), enemy foreigner, or animal spirit they blame for causing the death.

The best evidence I have found for the existence of ambivalence or covert anger toward the dead themselves appears in images of what happens to the spirits of the newly dead during their own funerals. Wari' believe that when a human spirit first awakens in the unfamiliar surroundings of the underworld, it is disoriented (*jimao*) and homesick. The spirit leaves the underworld and walks back to the surface of the earth in search of its home and family. However, the spirit's vision and hearing are confused and distorted. Approaching its own funeral, the spirit hears the crying and keening wails of grief but misperceives these (*kerek xirak*, "to see incorrectly"; *taraju xirak*, "to hear incorrectly"). Some older people say that, in the days of endocannibalism, the smoke billowing around the roasting corpse clouded the spirit's vision. Looking at the mourners, the spirit mistakenly sees its own relatives shaking fighting sticks (*temem*), threatening to beat the returning spirit. Instead of the verbal outpouring of love and sorrow in the crying and keening, the spirit hears its kin shouting, "Get away from here! . . . We're angry! . . . We don't like you!" Feeling rejected by its own kin, the spirit sadly leaves to go back to the underworld.

Wari' recognize this driving away of the spirit as one of the necessary, though secondary, effects of crying. They say that, while crying primarily expresses sorrow, love, and honor for the deceased, the sound of crying also drives away the ghost so that it will not carry away any of its living loved ones for company in the underworld.

In this cultural scenario, it is the dead individual who confuses affection and anger. Psychologists, however, might interpret this as a projection of anger that the living feel toward the relative who has deserted them by dying. This imagery is the clearest indication I have found of ambivalence toward the dead. Aside from this, I see little else in Wari' discourses or funeral customs to connect the eating of the dead to overt, covert, or displaced anger.

Desires to Hold on to the Dead

Another major theme in psychoanalytic interpretations of cannibalism is the impulse for oral incorporation: the desire to unite with the object that is eaten, to act out a fantasy of holding on to the dead by absorbing them into one's own body (Abraham and Torok 1994:111). A lurid example of oral incorporative fantasies made headlines in 1991, when Jeffrey Dahmer was arrested for multiple acts of murder and cannibalism in Milwaukee,

Wisconsin. Dahmer was convicted of having killed seventeen men and boys after having sex with them or before having sex with their corpses. He ate some of his victims' body parts, kept some in his freezer, and collected the skulls of his favorites. Dahmer "told the police that he ate only those young men he liked: he wanted them to become part of him" (Askenasy 1994:205). Psychologists who testified on behalf of Dahmer's defense portrayed him as an intensely lonely individual who tried to overcome his feelings of isolation and powerlessness by merging himself with another person. "Killing was not the objective," Dahmer told interviewers on the television program *Dateline*. "I just wanted to have the person under my complete control to do with as I wanted" (Askenasy 1994:207).

The desire to hold on to the dead need not take the extreme form it did in Dahmer's pathology. Freud and some of his successors have seen desires for incorporation as a normal part of the mourning process. In "Mourning and Melancholia," Freud (1981a) argued that the trauma of losing the object of one's affection leads to the desire to incorporate the object within oneself in order to hold on to the loved one. By swallowing the deceased, one takes possession and makes him or her part of one's own body or psyche, identifying oneself with the deceased, preserving the tie with the deceased by "setting up the abandoned object within the self" (Kracke 1993:80). Incorporating the lost love object is a way to "buy time"; by making the dead physically part of themselves, bereaved individuals can take time to work out their emotions. "Given that it is not possible to liquidate the dead and decree definitively: 'they are no more,' the bereaved become the dead for themselves and take their time to work through, gradually and step by step, the effects of the separation" (Torok 1994:111).

Many psychologists have found cannibalistic fantasies to be common elements among bereaved Europeans and North Americans, and the idea of cannibalism as a way to hold on to the dead by making their bodies part of one's own body has been used to explain cannibalism in some nonwestern societies also. Sanday (1986:45–46) interprets cannibalism as "part of the drama of becoming a self," in which desires for oral incorporation are linked to "the suppression of the object in the predication of the self." She identifies this theme in the myths and cannibalism practices of a number of societies, especially where cannibalism is associated with images of union with a maternal body.[7]

In looking at oral incorporation as a possible motive for Wari' endocannibalism, we run up against the problem that the close kin—the people who best fit the Freudian model of emotional trauma and incorporative desire—

were the ones who did *not* take part in the eating, who did not try to make the corpse part of their own bodies. Of course, one might suggest that the consanguines sublimated and projected their own desires onto the affines, who acted out the consanguines' oral-incorporative fantasies. But this dilutes the strength of the argument and calls for a powerful explanation of why Wari' consanguines did not simply eat the dead themselves. After all, in many other societies, the corpse was eaten by close consanguines. Among the Wari', if close family members' oral-incorporative impulses were the motive for wanting the corpse to be eaten, why didn't they eat it themselves?

One might imagine various answers to this question. But a basic problem with applying such a model arises from the fact that there is so little evidence to indicate that, either consciously or unconsciously, Wari' experienced cannibalism as a way to hold on to the person who was eaten. The oral incorporation model is based on the idea that what is eaten is *retained* in the bodies of the living, but this is not an idea that Wari' express in any form. The notion of holding on to the dead by making them part of living people's bodies has never come up in my conversations with Wari', nor have I seen it reported by other ethnographers. I have never heard any Wari' comment on the fact that living people carry elements of dead people inside themselves. Wari' talk about cannibalism as an act of destruction and erasure, not retention. They represent cannibalism as a way to eradicate the corpse and sever ties between the living and the dead, not to preserve the corpse in the body of the eater. Consistent with this emphasis on eradication, Wari' considered cremation—an act of destruction without incorporation—an acceptable substitute for cannibalism.

An orthodox psychoanalytic interpretation of how oral-incorporative impulses are expressed cannibalistically does not shed much light on Wari' motives. But if we take a broader view of the act of eating, we find psychoanalytic insights that do resonate with Wari' cultural themes and point to connections among several domains of Wari' thought and social action.

Disassemblage and Regeneration

One of the legacies of Freudian psychoanalysis has been a tendency to treat eating in narrow terms that focus attention on the act of swallowing/ingestion as the critical activity. But "our relationship to our food is much broader and richer than mere biting, chewing, and swallowing" (Gottlieb 1993). In clinical work with clients in New York City, psychoanalyst Richard Gottlieb noticed that his patients' cannibalistic fantasies often focused on events that led up to eating—being stalked, captured as prey, dismembered, eviscerated, drained of blood, prepared as food. Such fantasies also dwelt on concerns with what happens to the remains of the person who is eaten, both the swallowed and the discarded portions. Similar concerns crop up in cannibalistic imagery from diverse sources, such as the biblical story of Jonah and the whale, European vampire tales (Gottlieb 1991), children's stories such as "Little Red Riding Hood," the tale of Frankenstein, and religious imagery, especially medieval Christian debates over the Resurrection and the fate of the human corpse. A theme running through these various sources is the image of a human body being created or re-created intact and alive after it has been destroyed or fragmented (swallowed, dismembered, buried, decayed, drained of blood, or reduced to pieces). The body's destruction is part of a scenario that leads to its eventual regeneration and restoration to wholeness, in recurring clusters of meanings that revolve around "experiences of object loss, separation, and grief, on the one hand, and cannibalistic imagery that included ideas of fragmentation and re-assembly of the body on the other hand" (Gottlieb 1993:17).

Michele Stephen (1998) has pointed out that reassembling, restoring, or regenerating the dead is a cross-cultural theme in many societies' mortuary rites that involve literal or symbolic cannibalism or other methods of destroying or fragmenting the corpse. Interpreting this theme from the perspective of psychoanalyst Melanie Klein's models of an infant's attachment to its mother as the primary human relationship, Stephen argues that the death of a close loved one plunges bereaved individuals into chaotic emotional states that mirror, or reactivate, infantile reactions to the loss of the mother's breast. Rage, hatred, and aggression are expressed in destructive fantasies of biting, tearing up, and destroying the mother, and these alternate with or are balanced by guilt-driven reparative fantasies of restoring or reassembling the object that has been destroyed. In mortuary rites from various cultures,[8] Stephen sees a similar pairing of cultural imagery of cutting up and eating or otherwise destroying the corpse, and images of subsequently restoring the dead individual to wholeness.

Was Wari' endocannibalism based in the combination of aggressive and guilt-driven psychological processes mirroring infantile attachment dynamics that Stephen and Klein describe? In the absence of more direct evidence of rage, aggression, guilt, oral-incorporative fantasies, or a focus on mothers or maternal bodies in Wari' mortuary practices and mourning, I hesitate to accept this as the answer. But focusing on links between the body's destruction and its subsequent reconstitution is a fruitful avenue for exploring Wari' endocannibalism from western psychoanalytic perspectives, for this is a theme that resonates through several domains of Wari' thought.

One example in which images of consumption and regeneration abound is the myth of Hujin (see Appendix B), which tells how Wari' learned about their destiny to be re-embodied as peccaries after they died. A man named Hujin was captured by a carnivorous spirit in the underworld who ate him and tossed his bones in the air. As the bones fell, the flesh rematerialized on them. The carnivore ate Hujin again, tossed his bones up in the air, made the flesh reappear, and ate him once more. This went on and on, until a shaman caught Hujin's bones and restored him to wholeness. The experience of having been eaten by the spirit and then restored to wholeness gave Hujin the power of a shaman, the ability to move back and forth between his society and the realm of underworld spirits.

When Wari' men become shamans, they also have an experience of being killed and then restored to a physically and spiritually transformed, newly empowered state. A man gains shamanic powers when an animal spirit attacks and "kills" his spirit, an event that usually takes the form of a serious illness or accident involving loss of consciousness. Some shamans say the animal spirit ate them; others say only that it killed them. The animal spirit then revives the man and implants substances in his body that endow him with shamanic powers.

Another image of bodily destruction and regeneration is the belief that someone who is killed by being cut into pieces can restore himself to wholeness. Wari' say this happens only when a man is attacked by an enemy outsider (*wijam*) outside Wari' territory. If the enemy hacks the Wari' man's body into many small pieces (when they describe this action, people invariably pantomime a vicious flailing-about with a machete), the spirit of the victim's blood (*jami kikon*) jumps out of his body and sits on a log nearby, watching his body be cut to pieces. The killer flings the pieces of his corpse about, scattering them all over. After the killer leaves, the blood-spirit collects the pieces and puts them back together.

When the reassembled man manages to make his way back home, he is extremely fragile. He could literally fall apart at any moment. To make his body strong and solid again, he must rest a great deal and drink large quantities of sweet corn chicha, a beverage symbolically associated with blood and nurturant domestic relations. After about a year of such care, his body will have returned to normal. During this period of transition, no one can say a word to him about his experience of having been hacked to bits; if anyone mentions it, he will fall apart again, crumbling into pieces on the spot.

Wari' tell of how this happened to certain men who went away to live among Brazilians or Bolivians. In 1987, a middle-aged widower who had been gone for years, working as a laborer in the boomtowns of eastern Rondônia, returned to Rio Negro-Ocaia. Rumors flew about how he had been killed in a fight with a Brazilian who had hacked him to pieces with a machete. After his blood-spirit put his body back together, so the story went, the administrator in charge of FUNAI's regional office discovered him and escorted him back to Guajará-Mirim on the bus.

When people at Santo André who had told me this story heard that I was about to go upriver to do some interviewing at Rio Negro-Ocaia, they panicked. "Do *not* say *anything* to him about being killed and chopped up!" one after another warned. A small stream of visitors stopped by my house to make sure I understood that "if you say even one word, he'll fall apart and die." As I was carrying my backpack down the path toward the boat, Tokorom Mip intercepted me and threatened to stop me from leaving unless I swore not to speak to the man at all.

At Rio Negro-Ocaia, I kept my promise and observed the man in question only from a distance. From what I could tell, he seemed to be something of a misfit. Far more acculturated to Brazilian ways and more fluent in Portuguese than most Wari', he seldom spoke to anyone. Although he was living with a daughter who cared for and fed him, he appeared withdrawn and uncomfortable. People treated him with deference, and no one seemed to expect him to do anything other than rest and recuperate from his traumatic experiences in the outside world.

Wari' tend to use body metaphors to describe psychosocial states, and these ideas about the physical fragility of people who return after spending years in the alien outside society are poignant metaphors of psychosocial alienation. The scenario of the body's reassemblage evokes a vision of a transition from alienation to social reintegration, and the practical effect of this belief is to create a supportive environment for the returnee during his transition back into community life. The need for such men to rest and drink sweet chicha reduces physical and social demands on them and requires that they be integrated into a household with female kin to feed and care for them.[9] The imperative for others not to mention what happened to them reduces pressures to remember or talk about traumatic experiences in the outside world.

The theme of dismemberment and destruction as a prelude to reconstitution and regeneration runs through a number of domains of Wari' culture. In the imagery associated with death and the rituals of mourning, it is a core idea in concepts of the dead being regenerated as perfected immortal beings who can take on the bodies of white-lipped peccaries. To understand how this theme fits into Wari' experiences of bereavement, we first need to explore how Wari' think about the human body and why images of the body are such a powerful focus for emotional attachment, remembering, and grieving.

PART III

BODILY
CONNECTIONS

CHAPTER SIX

SOCIAL ANATOMY

One bright October afternoon, I wandered through the nearly deserted village of Santo André to see if anyone was home at the house of Manim Oro Eo and his wife, Tocohwet Pijo' Oro Jowin. Their household was always a busy place, with chickens scratching in the yard and babies underfoot. This afternoon, the only person there was their daughter Diva, a middle-aged widow. Kneeling on a mat beside a large slab of wood on the clean-swept earth in front of their house, she was grinding corn to make chicha. After chatting for a few minutes, I offered to help; she grinned in amusement and turned the grinding stone over to me. I was still new at this, and it took all my concentration to steady the heavy stone as it rocked from side to side. When I stopped to scoop another handful of kernels into the center of the slab, I glanced up at Diva and was startled to see her eyes filling with tears as she sat staring at the ground. After a while, she brushed away a tear and said, "That's good, Beth; that's enough." We scooped the cornmeal into a kettle, poured in some water, added a couple of sticks to the fire, and set the chicha to cook.

"Come here." Diva motioned to follow her into the house. She reached under one of the bark-covered platform beds, pulled out an old cardboard suitcase, and sat down with it on her lap. Inside was a jumble of clothing: torn, faded T-shirts, a short blue cotton skirt.

"My daughter's things," she explained.

"These belong to *Elsa?*" I exclaimed. Elsa, Diva's twenty-year-old daughter, was a strikingly beautiful young woman with a penchant for store-bought clothing. Through friendships with outsiders, she had accumulated a multitude of new skirts, blouses, and dresses—a wardrobe that was the

10. Rosa, Diva's sister, grinding corn.

envy of all the girls in the village. It was hard to imagine Elsa saving the ragged garments in the suitcase.

"No," Diva said softly. "My other daughter, the one who went away and didn't come back. Look." She reached into the suitcase pocket and pulled out a manila envelope. It contained a set of large, glossy black-and-white photographs. In the first picture, a stocky, bright-eyed teenage girl solemnly met the camera's gaze head-on. Two more photographs of the same girl followed, and then a different image: a grainy, out-of-focus gravestone. Then a close-up, clear enough to read the inscription: "Inácia Oro Nao."

Diva's hands were shaking. Her voice shook, too, with an edge of anger knifing through sorrow. "The doctors took her away; FUNAI took her." Then the story emerged: Inácia was born with a minor physical deformity. One of the Brazilian physicians who visited Santo André with FUNAI's traveling medical team persuaded her family to let them send the girl to Rio de Janeiro for cosmetic surgery. Weeks later, word came that she had died of bronchitis. Somewhere in Rio de Janeiro, she had been buried. Someone in that faraway city sent these glossy photographs to her mother.

"She was strong and healthy when she left here," Diva lamented. "Look at her! My daughter was strong; she had lots of fat on her body. She ate and ate. I gave her lots of food, all kinds of food—meat, fish, chicha. My daughter ate a lot! And she helped me; she worked hard." Diva gestured toward an old broom in the corner. "My daughter wasn't lazy; she swept the floor with that broom. She killed fish for us to eat. She helped me grind corn to make chicha. Like you did." I winced and wondered, is that what reminded her just now?

"My daughter knew how to work; she was really strong. And FUNAI says she got sick and wasted away!" Diva snorted. "*Bronchitis!* How could my strong daughter die fast like that?

"That's why I don't like him," she went on, naming the government official whom she held responsible. "When he comes here, I ask why he didn't bring back my daughter's body to me. The doctors took her away and cut her. They cut her, and she died."

Tears streaming, Diva angrily held up a handful of crumpled garments. "This is all I have. My daughter's clothes! And look here . . ." She pulled out a paper booklet, a penmanship book filled with lines of *os*, *ms*, *ps* — the repetitive traces of hours spent in a grade-school classroom. Carefully, she put the workbook and pictures back in the suitcase.

"I keep my daughter's things, all her things. They didn't bring back her body; her body stayed far away. I think about her every day; I remember her every day."

The door opened, and Elsa came in giggling, her long black hair wet from bathing, balancing her baby on one hip and a wide metal pan of wet laundry on her head. When she saw her sister's suitcase in her mother's lap, Elsa instantly grew solemn. She set the washbowl on the floor and moved to Diva's side, placed her hand on her mother's shoulder, and bowed her head. For a long moment, they cried softly together.

It was a gesture I would see again, too many times, this posture of grief and empathy for the bereaved. At that time, early in my fieldwork, it was still unfamiliar, and I didn't know that I, too, should have leaned on Diva's shoulder and cried with her. Instead, I sat there awkwardly, not knowing what to do or say. Then the emotion flooding through the dimly lit room washed away my fear of committing a cultural faux pas; I did the only thing I knew and put my arms around both women and hugged them.

*   *   *

The sorrow and anger that Diva expressed are commonplace Wari' responses to the loss of a loved one, but her way of dealing with her daughter's death was not. Inácia's family were the only Wari' I knew who kept a dead relative's possessions intact.[1] They also were the only ones who continued to speak directly about a dead person, using Inácia's name and calling her "daughter" and "sister." It was not that they doubted that she was really dead. Rather, what seemed to gnaw at them was the unfinished business of her death, or rather, the unfinished business of their relationship to it. In the absence of the girl's corpse, it had been impossible to hold a funeral, impossible to mourn properly. Later, after I learned how thoroughly other Wari' families destroyed their dead loved ones' possessions, the suitcase under Diva's bed came to seem like a horrendous anomaly, the black hole of a mother's love turned back on itself.

* * *

It may seem odd to begin this account of Wari' attitudes toward corpses and mourning with such an atypical case. I do so because Diva's anger over what was wrong about her daughter's death and her unresolved feelings about it call attention to some of the basic concerns in this study: the importance that Wari' ascribe to seeing and holding the dead person's body and knowing what happens to it; the desire to control the disposition of the corpse; and the subjective connections between body and memory, between tangible reminders and the grieving of close relatives. Diva's recollections of her daughter ("I gave her lots of food . . . she swept the floor . . . she killed fish for us to eat . . .") also convey something of the significance that exchanges of nurturance—giving and receiving food, doing work to support others—have in Wari' family relations.

To understand why Wari' used to consider it essential to destroy the corpse and why they saw cannibalism as the best way to accomplish this, we must first understand how they construe and experience the bodies of those they care about. How do bodies fit into people's relations to one another? What meanings does the body carry in composing the person? This chapter explores Wari' ideas about how body substances and bodily experiences connect the members of a family to one another. These ideas help to answer several questions about their endocannibalism practices: Why did Wari' avoid eating the corpses of their own consanguines? Why are a husband and wife defined as consanguines to each other, so that one did not eat the corpse of one's spouse? What happened when Wari' made exceptions to the rule against cannibalizing consanguines? The concepts examined in this chapter also lay the groundwork for exploring the broader question of the emotional attachments that mourners feel to the bodies of their dead and the role that bodies play in memory and the transformation of memories.

Permeable Bodies

Wari' think of human bodies as permeable and interactive. They do not see the skin as a limiting layer that separates people from one another into discrete, autonomous units; rather, they see human skins and bodies in general as porous and open.[2] Substances from outside the body pass easily into the bloodstream, and other elements pass out of the body, especially through perspiration and sexual fluids.

For Wari', blood is the most important body element, for its composition and circulation are primary determinants of health and growth. Blood also conveys qualities of social identity, such as kinship, ethnicity, and, in the case of animals, species identity. Blood's dual role as a major component of health and a major component of identity makes it central in Wari' conceptions of persons and social relations. Blood is, as anthropologists have noted in many other native Brazilian societies, a substance that mediates between "physio-logic" and "socio-logic" (Seeger, da Matta, and Viveiros de Castro 1979).

Breast milk, semen, vaginal secretions, and sweat are thought to be blood analogs, produced from and interactive with the blood. These fluids can pass from one person to another through the skin and body orifices. When a baby nurses, when lovers have sex, or when skins touch intimately, exchanges of fluids take place. Over time, as elements associated with the bodies of others accumulate in one's own body, the composition of one's blood changes. Some fluids, such as the blood of childbirth or liquid from a close consanguine's corpse, are very potent, and their effects on vulnerable individuals can be quick and dramatic. Other fluids take a long time to accumulate and have milder effects.

Wari' believe that the composition of the blood affects the flesh and body as a whole. People who exchange body fluids with each other gradually develop common blood and flesh, which contributes to the creation of common identity. I use the term "shared substance" to capture this broad sense of common essences developed through exchanges between individual bodies.

In the United States, people talk about consanguineal kin as "blood relations," but we mean this more metaphorically than literally. When someone receives a blood transfusion from a stranger, does that make the blood donor and the recipient kin to each other? Most North Americans probably would say no, for we think of genes, not blood, as the substance that defines kinship. Since genetic relatedness is established at the moment of conception, when one sperm meets one egg, biological kinship is fixed; there is nothing one can do to redefine who one's biological relatives are. For Wari', kinship is literally more fluid. Biological relatedness is based on sharing blood and analogous body substances. Since the composition of one's blood can change in certain ways, kinship and other blood-based identities also can change to some extent. Blood and body substances thus serve as an idiom for thinking and talking about changes in identity and social relations.

Substance Shared Between Parents and Children

Wari' consider the first and most enduring bodily connections to be those that develop between parents and their offspring, not only before birth, but also afterwards. The substances shared within a nuclear family derive first from elements that form the fetus. Wari' ideas about conception tend to be rather vague, but the point on which Santo André residents agree is that conception occurs when a quantity of male semen unites with a woman's reproductive blood. Since semen (*warakixi'*) is a transformation of male blood, conception is essentially the union of female and male blood. Maternal blood and paternal semen have distinct roles in composing the fetus: the mother's blood forms and nourishes her fetus's blood, while semen forms and nourishes its flesh and bones.[3] In daily speech and in keening for the dead, Wari' women often refer to their husbands as *kwerekekem homajü,* "my children's body (or flesh)," and they speak of their children as *arain taxi',* "bone of my husband."

In western models of conception, one sperm fertilizes one egg, and a fetus develops through more or less automatic biological processes that involve only the bodies of mother and fetus. Wari', in contrast, see the creation of a fetal body as a prolonged process requiring inputs from others beyond the mother-child dyad. Like many other Amazonian Indians, Wari' believe that one act of sexual intercourse is not enough to cause pregnancy; rather, the embryo forms when a quantity of semen accumulates in the womb after multiple acts of sexual intercourse within a relatively short time period. Women ridiculed me for suggesting that a woman might get pregnant after having sex just once. "Don't people know how to make babies in America?" they laughed incredulously. Tokorom Mip was sure they didn't, so he taped instructions to send to my husband: "You must *work* to make a child, Roberto. Have sex; have sex a lot, and Beth will get pregnant." If that didn't work, he recommended smashing an egg on my back when I wasn't looking.

Constant inputs of nourishing semen are considered essential throughout gestation, and elders advise young couples to have sex often during pregnancy to make a healthy baby. Santo André women illustrated this point by comparing the cases of two women whose husbands died while they were pregnant. One widow took a lover and gave birth to a fat baby girl, whereas the other widow remained celibate and gave birth to twins so scrawny and weak that she had to give one to the missionaries to nurse back to health. If more than one man has sex with a pregnant woman, all these men are considered to be the baby's biological fathers, since their semen contributed to forming the fetal body.

Semen's role as fetal nourishment means that creating a human being is a collective project that involves multiple contributions of nurturance from at least two individuals (mother and father) linked to two different kin networks. Echoing Marilyn Strathern's (1992:61) observation about how New Guinea natives use images of human bodies to represent social relationships, each individual Wari' body-person is "an icon of a relationship" between its mother and father(s) and their relatives. The physical body that comes into being is not an asocial, "natural" entity; from the earliest moments of life, the body itself is a social product (Conklin and Morgan 1996).

The process of creating shared substance does not end at birth, but continues throughout the life cycle as an individual absorbs substances from other people. The corporeal substances that link children and their parents at birth are amplified by exchanges that take place in the course of family life. Wari' emphasize how a baby grows from the food (especially game) that its father provides for its mother to eat, which builds her breast milk and nourishes their baby. They also emphasize that blood elements pass through the skin from father to child, especially during sleep. Wari' parents and their prepubescent children always sleep together, with the children nestled in the middle and the parents on either side, their bodies curving protectively around the children. In the intimacy of this circle of sleeping bodies, and in the touching, holding, and grooming that are constants in daily life, elements pass from body to body.

Physical interconnectedness between parents and children is the conceptual basis for prohibitions against killing certain animals and eating certain foods that Wari' parents are supposed to follow until their children are around seven years old. Wari' believe that certain game, fowl, and fish cause illness and deformity in small children. Not only should children avoid eating these animals, but their parents should, too, and fathers should not kill them, because contamination passes easily among nuclear family members in breast milk, sweat, semen, and menstrual blood. For example, if a man kills one of these harmful animals, the animal's spirit-body, or parts of it, may enter the hunter and pass to his children during sleep. When a hunter has sex with a nursing mother, harmful spirit elements contained in his semen may enter her blood, pass into her breast milk, and contaminate her baby's blood.

Such restrictions on hunting highlight men's status as fathers, keeping them ever aware of their paternal responsibilities and reinforcing public recognition of the child's relation to the father and his kin (Kensinger 1981: 166). Not just the mother's husband, but all her male lovers (if she is involved in extramarital relations), are supposed to follow the same rules to protect her fetus or nursing infant. Shamans sometimes use this idea as an indirect way to censure adultery, for when an adulterous woman's child gets sick, a shaman often will blame her child's illness on an animal killed by her lover.

Sharing biosocial substance within the family is a normal and essential part of health, growth, and sociality, but it puts children at risk of illness agents that pass to them from their parents' bodies. All consanguineal kin share some body substance, but the most direct bodily connections are those reinforced on a daily basis among parents and children who sleep and eat together. Wari' see the bodies of family members not as autonomous, disconnected entities, but as parts of an organic, interactive whole.

Body Fluids and Social Fluidity

As an individual matures and engages in new kinds of interactions with others, the composition of his or her body changes also. Exchanges of blood-based body fluids (through breast-feeding, sexual intercourse, and the killing of enemies) establish relationships that Wari' recognize as being similar to, though weaker than, the consanguineal links that exist at birth. At Santo André, one young man called a certain Brazilian woman his "other mother" (*xikem na*) because she had nursed him when his own mother was incapacitated during the early postcontact epidemics. "When my mother was sick, the Brazilian gave me her breast to suck. So she's my mother also," he explained. "That's why I have some wijam [outsider] blood." In recognition of their relationship, this young man occasionally sent small gifts to his "other mother."

Wari' also consider it possible to have multiple biological fathers, since any man who has sex with a pregnant woman contributes semen to building the baby's body in her womb. An example of this situation was a middle-aged man from Santo André named Wem Xao. The first time I interviewed him to record his family genealogy, he gave the name of his long-deceased father and then added, "My other father [*xikun te'*] is Maxun Kwarain; that's why he lives with me." Wem Xao explained that Maxun Kwarain had told him that he had had sex with Wem Xao's mother while she was pregnant with Wem Xao. Thus, he was a biological father to Wem Xao.

Wari' men almost always acknowledge their paternity for all the children their wives conceive. But a woman's other lovers also are recognized as "other" biological fathers. I have never heard a Wari' man broadcast his paternal relation to a child while the child's mother's husband is living with her. But if her husband dies, these other biological ties may be invoked by the widow to claim support from her child's "other" father. They also may be invoked by an "other" father to legitimize his claim on the child. Wem Xao's "other" father, Maxun Kwarain, was a widower who had never sired a child with any of his three wives. After his last wife died, he needed support, for because he was crippled, he could not hunt, fish, or farm. His only close living relative was a brother in his seventies who barely managed to feed his own wife and three young daughters. By asserting his tie to Wem Xao, Maxun Kwarain aligned himself with a household headed by a younger man whose family was able to feed and care for him. This is one example of how the variety of processes Wari' recognize for creating biological relatedness can broaden the social safety net, offering alternative idioms of relatedness on which individuals can draw to legitimize alternative arrangements for giving and receiving support.

In Marriage, "There Is One Body"

Changes in body substance are associated with moves between social categories at a number of points in the Wari' life cycle. One example is the idea that marriage turns two unrelated spouses into consanguines (*'iri nari*) to each other. Consanguinity develops gradually as wife and husband absorb each other's sexual fluids. A woman's vaginal secretions accumulate in her husband's body, and his semen accumulates in hers. Over time, this transforms both partners' blood, so that spouses come to share common blood and, by extension, the "same" flesh. In the marriage ceremony that has developed at Santo André since the contact, senior relatives (especially parents of the bride and groom) lecture the bride and groom on the changes and responsibilities that marriage brings. In the two weddings I have attended, the young couples' parents and other relatives invoked this idea of mutual bodily transformation to emphasize the interdependence and totality of the marital bond. Whereas a North American church wedding culminates with the preacher's proclamation "I now pronounce you husband and wife," Wari' speakers say, "*Xika pe' na kwere*" [There is one body (between you)].

This idea that marital bonds are forged in exchanges of blood-based body fluids is reflected in an informal ritual that used to be performed frequently at the birth of a girl whose parents had promised her in marriage to an older boy or man. In this ritual, immediately after she is born, before the baby has been washed, the newborn's family summons her husband-to-be and places the still-bloody baby girl in his arms. Her birth blood (which Wari' consider very potent) passes through her fiancé's skin, imprinting their union in his body. A doctor who has worked for many years in the Sagarana community told me that after he has helped deliver female babies, Wari' women have often pointed to his bloody hands and giggled, "*Narima pin nem*" [She (the baby) has become your wife]. For a bridegroom-to-be, this betrothal by blood is a first step in the process by which he and his future wife eventually will become "one body." For a girl, a parallel imprinting occurs when she first has sexual intercourse and a man's semen merges with her blood. The single blood/flesh that a husband and wife develop redefines them as consanguines, blood relatives to each other. At funerals, the widow or widower of the deceased is classified as 'iri nari and sits with the other close consanguines of the dead person and cries with them. And when endocannibalism was practiced, the dead person's spouse, like other close consanguines, did not eat the corpse.

Sharing Substance with Animals and Enemies

The idea that shared body substance establishes a kinship relation also appears in ideas about shamanism and warfare. A Wari' man becomes a shaman when an animal spirit (*jami karawa*) takes elements out of its own body and implants these in the man's body. A key element is annatto (*Bixa orellana*), the fruit from which red body paint is made. Annatto is symbolically linked to blood and is a marker of human (Wari') identity.[4] Each jami karawa animal spirit carries in its body its own special annatto fruit and seeds, as well as other fruits, plants, and favorite foods, such as beetle grubs. Animal spirits carry these substances in specific places in their bodies, especially in the hands (or hooves or paws), the chest, and the joints of the limbs. Many of these spots are points where Wari' believe that blood pools or many blood vessels converge. The magical fruits and other substances contain essences of the animal spirit's power, and a Wari' shaman acquires these powers when an animal spirit implants them in his body. A human shaman, acting in his animal spirit capacity, also can take substances out of his own body and implant them in another man to make him a shaman.

Like the practice of imprinting a prospective husband with his future wife's blood, transfers of substance in shamanic initiation may represent a betrothal, for some shamans say that their animal spirit companion promises one of his daughters to be the shaman's wife after the shaman dies. Shamans' spirits have a different postmortem destiny than ordinary people's spirits do. Instead of becoming a white-lipped peccary after he dies, a shaman's spirit becomes an animal of the species with which the shaman identified.

Incorporating an animal spirit's substance establishes a kind of kinship and close identification between a shaman and his companion animal spirit species.[5] Wari' shamans are not supposed to kill or eat the flesh of their companion species.[6] A deer-shaman, for example, cannot eat venison; a fish-shaman cannot eat fish; a peccary-shaman cannot eat peccary meat, and so on. Shamans say that if they violated this rule and ate their companion species, they would get sick and might die. (This notion is echoed in the myth of Hujin, in which a fish-shaman commits suicide by roasting and eating his own son, who was born as a fish.) The shamanic practice of not eating one's companion species is consistent with the rule against eating one's close blood relatives.

Another expression of the link between blood and the creation of kinship is the belief that when a warrior kills an enemy, the enemy spirit's (invisible) blood enters the killer's body. Maxun Kwarain emphasized that enemy spirit-blood entered through the killer's genitals, where layers of enemy blood alternated with layers of the killer's semen (a blood-plus-semen combination reminiscent of the Wari' model of conception). After absorbing the enemy spirit-blood, the killer went into a period of ritual seclusion during which he drank huge quantities of sweet corn chicha in order to tame the enemy spirit so that it would stay in his body the rest of his life. Wari' men say this merging of their bloods made the warrior and the spirit of the enemy he killed *ak 'iri ka nari*, "like real kin." This was explicitly a father-child relationship, for the enemy spirit was said to become the child of the warrior, whom the enemy spirit called "my father."[7] Just as a father did not eat his child's corpse, a warrior did not eat an enemy he killed. If he had, the killer would have gotten sick. This is how Wari' explained to me why enemy body parts were eaten only by individuals who did not take part in the killing.

In marriage, shamanism, and warfare, Wari' believe that individuals incorporate each other's body fluids or analogous body substances and become kin to each other. In all these relationships, those who share body substance do not eat each other: a married person did not eat the flesh of the spouse whose sexual fluids he or she had absorbed; a warrior did not eat the enemy whose spirit-blood he had incorporated; and a shaman is not supposed to eat the companion species whose magical fruits he has incorporated. A similar logic applied to not eating close relatives.

Why Avoid Eating Consanguines?

When Wari' explain why 'iri nari, the dead person's close consanguines, did not eat the corpse, they emphasize two related ideas: that it would be fatal to eat a close consanguine, and that intense grief is incompatible with the idea of eating a family member. The belief that one will get sick and even die if one eats a relative's flesh makes sense in relation to ideas about shared substance, for eating someone whose body is similar to and linked to one's own would be tantamount to auto-cannibalism, eating oneself. The genealogies I collected turned up an actual suicide based on this principle. A family described a relative of theirs, a bachelor who lived in the Lage area before the contact. When his na (mother or mother's sister) died, the young man was so grief-stricken that he wanted to die himself. He cut a piece of flesh from her bloated belly, swallowed it raw, was struck with intense vomiting and diarrhea, and died. Wari' cited this incident as proof that close consanguines could not eat a corpse.

From a western medical perspective, the likeliest explanation for this man's death is dehydration. Dehydration is always a risk for Wari' mourners, since they eat and drink little while crying and keening for days. Fluid loss from the vomiting and diarrhea provoked by the putrid flesh would have depleted his body of liquid and disrupted his electrolyte balance. The psychological trauma of violating one of his society's strongest cultural prohibitions undoubtedly exacerbated the physical stresses.

Wari' give a different medical explanation: consuming his mother's flesh caused an intense contraction in the man's heart, which set off a process (described by the verb xao) in which the heart and blood circulation slow down. Diarrhea and dehydration (which Wari' see as the results of blood imbalances) are common side effects of the xao process. Ingesting a corpse's raw flesh or fluids can make anyone sick, but Wari' say it kills only close relatives. The closer the kinship tie, the more lethal the effect.

The idea that the effects of consuming human body substance depend on the degree of relatedness between the one who eats and the one who is eaten is consistent with other Wari' beliefs about blood and illness. Blood has ambiguous and ambivalent meanings. On one hand, it is the stuff of which shared consanguineal substance is made and the basis of health and physical and emotional well-being. At certain times in the life cycle (especially infancy and puberty), incorporating body fluids from other individuals stimulates growth and promotes vitality. At other times, in other situations and relationships, other people's blood is dangerous.

Various forms of blood have different effects, ranging from innocuous to mildly polluting to potentially lethal. Contact with normal venous blood (such as bleeding wounds) carries little risk. Sexual fluids (semen and vaginal secretions) are mildly polluting (*homirixi'*) to the opposite sex, and newlyweds of both sexes are at risk of illness (*xao*, respiratory congestion and emaciation) until they build up their tolerance to their partner's fluids. Men are more vulnerable to sexual contamination than women, for Wari' say that women's blood is "strong" (*hwara opa'*) in contrast to the weaker blood of men and children. Whereas menstrual blood is not considered very dangerous, the blood of childbirth, postpartum hemorrhaging, and newborn infants is dangerous to adult men in general. One of the biggest risks of menstrual and birth blood is that its scent attracts jaguars. To prevent young children from accidentally being contaminated by nursing or sucking on their fingers, mothers who are menstruating or experiencing postpartum bleeding are advised to wash their thighs and breasts frequently.

Like corpse substances, menstrual blood and sexual fluids are most harmful to close relatives. A woman's menses do not affect anyone outside her immediate family, and Wari' take no special precautions to avoid menstrual contamination outside the home. Within the nuclear family, a woman's menses can cause mild illness for her own husband and prepubescent children. In the past, when Wari' used body paints daily, when a woman's period began, she, her husband, and their young children all applied fresh body oil and annatto (red paint), whose odor is believed to repel jaguars attracted to the blood scent. Adolescents are unaffected by their mothers' menses, for young men do not sleep with their parents, and after menarche, girls develop more of their own blood. Disconnected from intimate links to their parents' bodies, adolescents are no longer vulnerable to illness agents transmitted through them.

The idea that certain body fluids are dangerous only to close consanguines reappears in beliefs about incest. Mating between closely related individuals produces offspring with weak blood, and it also weakens the blood of the two sexual partners, making them grow thin and emaciated.

This danger was one of several arguments that a father used to justify his refusal to let his son marry the girl he loved. The two were deeply in love, had a baby daughter, and had been faithful to each other for years. Nonetheless, the young man's father adamantly opposed their marriage, for the two young people were cousins, which Wari' consider too closely related for marriage. In late 1986, the lovers finally got their wish when the man's father moved away from Santo André and, as he left, gave his consent to the marriage. The young man then moved in with his wife and her parents.

Santo André's teenagers were thrilled at this triumph of romantic love over parental opposition, but many older folks took a dim view of this turn of events. Village gossip was laced with gloomy predictions for the newlyweds' future. Once, when the couple in question walked past with their little daughter perched on her proud father's shoulders, an older woman whispered, "Look—they're getting thin; their fat is all finished! They're going to get sick!" Personally, I thought the young couple looked the very picture of health and glowing happiness, and I said so. She glared at me. "No," she insisted, "they're going to get thin and sick. Just watch; you'll see."

The common thread running through these ideas about incest, menstruation, birth, and the dangers of eating consanguines is the idea that the dangers of human body substances are *relational,* based on the corporeal co-identity of close kin. This perceived danger is part of the answer Wari' give to explain why they did not eat their own close blood kin in precontact funerals, and it reinforced the emotional reasons not to do so.

Affines and the Dangers of Corpse Substances

Eating corpses was less dangerous for affines, for whom the risks related mostly to pollution. Wari' consider corpses the most polluting form of human substance, for they embody decay and dissolution, the antithesis of growth and health. When older people describe how corpses changed as they lay unroasted during the funeral, they emphasize qualities of "otherness" diametrically opposite to the normal, proper condition of living human beings: the strong, putrid odor, the pallid skin color, the release of the bowels, the bloating of the abdomen.

Corpses were most polluting in their raw, unroasted form, before the fire "dried up" the body fluids. Wari' say that as a corpse lies on its mat, all the blood drains into the central body cavity, where the red part settles out, becoming a dark, glutinous substance called *tarakixi'.* They call the clear serum that remains *kuji kom,* "rotten water," and they say that accidentally swallowing it can make anyone sick. The scent of human corpse blood is also highly attractive to jaguars. To protect themselves, the men who cut and dismembered the corpse painted their hands and forearms up to the elbows with black genipap and red annatto and smeared annatto on their faces as well.[8] Wari' believe that genipap has protective qualities that neutralize contaminants and that the smell of annatto prevents jaguar attacks. To prevent babies from ingesting contaminants as they sucked on their fingers, they used to paint babies' hands and forearms with genipap, just as corpse cutters painted themselves.

Wari' consider blood and other body substances to be physiologically potent only in their raw (uncooked, untransformed) state. Roasting dries and neutralizes raw body fluids, rendering them less harmful. For this reason, roasting is the best way to cook any flesh that contains dangerous blood. Game and fish that are exceptionally bloody or whose blood causes illness or deformity must be roasted, while animals with more innocuous blood can be boiled. Wari' also think of roasting as a more respectful treatment and say that certain animal spirits may be offended if humans consume their body fluids.

In precontact funerals, after the flesh had been roasted, Wari' considered it polluting but not illness inducing for the affines who ate it. Although those who ate tried to avoid touching the flesh directly, no one escaped the stench, which permeated everyone's skin. When the funeral was over, the eaters went to a nearby stream, where they bathed thoroughly, rubbing their skin to remove the odor of death and then applying fresh body oil.

Ideas about body substance can be only part of the explanation for why Wari' avoided eating consanguines' corpses, for as discussed later in this chapter, there were times when some Wari' did eat consanguines. Another part of the answer involves emotional relations to the deceased.

Emotional Reasons Not to Eat Consanguines

Over and over, Wari' told me that when they are crying in grief over a relative's death, they are not hungry and simply do not feel like eating. From an anthropological perspective, this principle of not eating during a kinsperson's funeral seems to reflect the broader cultural pattern in which oral activities are symbolically associated with social integration, while states of sadness and sickness are associated with diminished oral activity. Eating in general, and meat eating in particular, express happiness and involvement in communal life. When Wari' are sick or in mourning, they typically speak, eat, and drink little and lie silent and lethargic, unresponsive to those around them. The sick person's siblings, parents, grandparents, and grown children empathetically subdue their own behavior: they eat and drink little, speak quietly, and do not sing, shout, run, dance, or attend parties. When a close relative is ill, Wari' often lose weight and become thin and pale. The practice of not eating at a close relative's funeral makes sense in terms of these cultural attitudes and the symbolic equation of happiness with eating. As an anthropologist, I felt more comfortable with this explanation than with the statement "We just don't feel like eating."

I recall with some embarrassment how little credence I gave to what Wari' said about their lack of desire to eat when grieving intensely. When people told me this, I tended to brush the explanation aside and question them again, pressing for some deeper motive that I could fit into a nice symbolic analysis. On more than one occasion, Wari' became annoyed at my refusal to accept their statements about the bodily sensations of grief. "Don't you know anything, Beth?" Tocohwet Pijo' exclaimed incredulously. "When we are crying, we just don't feel hungry; we don't want to eat anything!"

Two years later, when my own brother died, I realized how naïve I had been. In the depths of my own raging grief, eating was the last thing I felt like doing. The flood of tears left a sick feeling in my stomach, as if it were simultaneously heavy and hollow. In the first days after he died, food looked strangely foreign, and the thought of eating was nauseating. Undoubtedly some people have different reactions; perhaps for some, grief intensifies hunger or food cravings. My own body, however, testified to the subjective reality that Wari' had described: with grief came a physical disinclination to eat.

While Wari' accepted—indeed expected—this reaction as a normal part of the experience of grief, my own culture did not. In the small town in southwestern Iowa where my parents grew up and where we went to bury my brother, people offer food as an antidote to sorrow and as an expression of social support. Before the funeral, friends and relatives inundate the bereaved family with casseroles, salads, and desserts. After the burial, everyone drives straight from the cemetery to a "lunch" held at a town meeting hall or a relative's home. At the lunch after my brother's funeral, the hearty eating and determinedly cheerful conversation about crops, cars, jobs, boyfriends, 4-H projects, and college plans—about everything, that is, except my brother and his death—were worlds away from Wari' ways.

In Iowa, when a recently bereaved individual manages to eat, people see this as a good sign, an indication that the person is coping well. Among the Wari', eating much of anything soon after a close relative's death would be seen as gross disrespect, a sign of a lack of feeling and an absence of sorrow. Strong emotional attachments preclude eating soon after a death. Wari' consider the idea of eating at a close relative's funeral to be irrational. They think it even more irrational to suggest eating the dead relative himself, to whom close kin feel intimately linked. Though they insisted that affines should eat the corpse, it would have been emotionally impossible for close family members to bring themselves to treat the loved one as if he or she were food. The task thus fell to affines, who were the only clearly defined group of people at the funeral who had commitments to supporting the dead person's family but were not intimately connected to the deceased by the intense bonds of emotion and body substance that made cannibalism impossible for close family members. Wari' consider it pointless to ask why it was the affines and other nonrelatives who ate the corpse. No one else could do it.

Exceptions to the Rule

There were at least two exceptions to the rule against eating the corpses of consanguineal kin. Grandchildren sometimes ate bits of their grandparents' corpses, and babies killed at birth were consumed by their mothers' own kin.

I first heard about the practice of eating one's own grandparent or classificatory grandparent in a conversation with an elderly man at Santo André who mentioned that when his father's mother (*jeo*) was dying, she summoned him and asked him, as a favor, to join in eating her corpse. "She *wanted* me to eat her," was the only explanation he gave. Subsequently, I heard of another case of a grandmother asking her grandson to eat her, and Vilaça uncovered similar accounts in the Negro-Ocaia region. The physical danger of consuming consanguineal substance that Wari' emphasize in other contexts does not seem to have been a concern. When grandchildren ate grandparents, my Santo André informants emphasized, they did not eat much, only token bits of flesh. Vilaça (2000:93) reports that it was specifically tiny bits of the brain that grandchildren (and, according to some informants, sometimes young children of the deceased as well) were given to eat at the same time as the affines ate the rest of the brain. Her informants explained this as an attempt to preserve the memory of the grandparent in the children, who did not remember well and would soon forget the grandparent.

Though the eventual goal of the year-long series of mourning rituals is to contain and attenuate memories, the months immediately after a death are a time to remember deeply and honor the dead, and this practice suggests a concern for drawing young children into that process. A similar concern is evident in changing attitudes toward photographs of the dead. I have always tried to remove pictures of dead people from the sets of photographs I give to Wari', assuming that such pictures would evoke painful memories and would have to be burned. But the last time I saw my friend Maria, she asked for pictures of her great-uncle, Maxun Kwarain, who had recently passed away. She said her children were too young to have known him and it was important for them to remember. Other young parents joined in this conversation and insisted that they, too, wanted pictures of their dead grandparents. The Wari' emphasis on controlling and attenuating memories has always been in tension with desires to remember the dead, and attitudes may be shifting in the younger generation.

* * *

A very different exception to the rule against cannibalizing consanguines occurred in cases of infanticide (the killing of unwanted babies soon after birth). Infanticide was not common among the Wari' before the contact. They did not use infanticide to control their population, limit family size, or space births. They did not kill twins, and they did allow some infants with visible congenital deformities to live. The only situation in which Wari' used to consider infanticide justified, as far as they have admitted to me, was out-of-wedlock births to very young girls.

Before the contact, there were not many unmarried mothers because most girls married young, often before they began to menstruate, and there were strong social pressures on men to marry the mothers of their children. When a man refused to do so, or when marriage was out of the question (for example, because of incest rules), pregnant unmarried girls and their mothers sometimes induced abortions with a hard massage or pummeling of the abdomen. Wari' also believed that the mother's family had the right to decide whether or not to allow the baby to live. The young mother herself seems to have had little say in this decision. Some families decided to let the baby live, especially when the unwed mother was older and better able to care for herself and the child. But sometimes the family decided that the infant should be killed. A male relative (often an older brother or uncle of the girl who gave birth) performed the killing, which was supposed to be done immediately after birth. Breastfeeding marked the baby's acceptance into the group; once this had begun, infanticide normally was out of the question.

The mass epidemics and social chaos of the contact era also provoked several aberrant episodes in which young orphans (mostly infants or tod-

dlers) were killed. Killing children has never been a socially accepted practice among the Wari', and all the incidents of which I have heard occurred
under the exceptional stresses of the early postcontact period, when hundreds of people were dead or dying. Especially in the Negro-Ocaia and
Lage/Ribeirão areas, epidemics wiped out whole families overnight, leaving
dozens of orphans. Food was short in supply, and everyone was disoriented
and demoralized.[9] Even during these most desperate times, the vast majority of orphans were cared for—often at considerable personal sacrifice—
by relatives, usually relatives of the child's mother. Some children, however,
had no surviving close adult kin, or at least none able or willing to care
for them. Some babies died because there was no lactating woman to nurse
them, and several young orphans were killed by their own kin. Wari' who
have talked to me about these killings have expressed a range of attitudes.
Some see the families' actions as regrettable but justified; others consider
them despicable. In particular, some of the murdered orphans had older siblings who were too young to prevent the killings. Now grown to adulthood
without the company of a younger brother or sister, these individuals harbor
deep bitterness about their relatives' coldheartedness.

The rejected orphans seem to have been killed mostly by strangulation
and smothering, which Wari' consider the most humane method for killing a human being. However, one Oro Waram man angrily described what
happened after his parents died in the epidemics of the early 1960s, when
he was about five years old. His mother's relatives took him in, but they did
not want to care for his little sister, who was about two years old. An uncle
killed the little girl by shooting her with an arrow. To her brother, this was
like rubbing salt into a wound, for Wari' say bows and arrows are for killing
only animals and enemies.[10]

Wari' treated the corpses of rejected orphans and infanticide victims in
ways that defined them as nonpersons, and they consumed them according to the rules of *exo-*, not *endo-*, cannibalism. The victims received no
funerals, nor did anyone cry publicly for them. The young mothers of babies
killed at birth often seem to have felt sad and resentful, but though they
might cry privately, they were expected to acquiesce impassively to their
family's decision. Like animals and enemy outsiders, infanticide victims and
murdered orphans were cut up and roasted immediately. In marked contrast to the treatment of Wari' corpses at funerals, rejected children were
eaten by their own blood relatives, even including the man who did the killing. A baby killed at birth typically was consumed by its mother's closest
kin: the mother's older siblings, parents, and other close relatives who lived

nearby, such as grandparents, uncles, or aunts. Of the adults in the immediate family, only the infant's mother always refrained from eating its flesh. Treating the corpse this way made a dramatic statement about the family's rejection of the child as a person and as their kin.

The baby's corpse embodied a contradiction, for its blood linked it to the maternal relatives who were to going to eat it. The family dealt with this problem by negating their physical ties to the child. They drained the blood from the corpse, cut up the body parts, scrubbed them with sand, and washed them in a stream until the flesh was "white," cleansed of every trace of blood. Devoid of maternal substance, the bloodless flesh (composed only of its genitor's semen) could then be eaten by its mother's relatives.

These incidents show another, more brutal facet of the Wari' use of the body and body substances as an idiom through which to communicate messages about individuals' social positions and relations to others. Just as relatedness and belonging are defined partly by affirmations of shared body substance, such ties can be negated by destroying shared substances.

The manner of eating also communicated a message of rejection, for such babies' corpses were treated like enemy outsiders. The eaters handled the tiny body parts casually, holding them in their hands and eating the flesh off the bone. Elders say that as people ate infanticide victims, they made rude comments about the irresponsible man who had fathered the baby without marrying its mother.

A story of precontact killing and hostile cannibalism between Wari' subgroups shows a similar point about the social messages communicated by the "table manners" used for consuming human flesh. This incident allegedly took place at a time when the Oro Mon and Oro Waram subgroups were on such bad terms that they were approaching open warfare. An Oro Waram man found an Oro Mon man and his Oro Waram Xijein wife gathering Brazil nuts a long way away from their village. The Oro Waram man shot and killed the man, then took a knife and cut a big piece of fatty flesh from the stomach. He carried this chunk of flesh home and roasted and ate it, telling others in his village that it was Oro Mon meat (*karawa nukun Oro Mon*). By treating the flesh so casually and equating it with animal prey, the killer made a powerful statement about his disdain for the other subgroup. The Oro Mon who first told me this story cited it as evidence of what he claimed was the innate barbarism of the Oro Waram.

The principles and practices involved in handling, preparing, and eating the flesh of enemies and animals contrasted markedly with the principles and practices associated with eating fellow tribesmembers' corpses at funerals. These distinctions in how to prepare and eat animals, enemies, and fellow Wari' provided a symbolic vocabulary that people used to make statements about their attitudes toward the individual who was eaten. The respectful gestures of endocannibalism marked the individual being eaten as *wari'*, "one of us," a person with whom the eater recognized a relationship based on kinship or exchange obligations. The table manners for eating enemies expressed just the opposite: the eater regarded the individual he or she was eating as a nonperson, someone with whom the eater recognized no exchange relationship or social obligation. This idea of acting on the physical body to express, affirm, or alter relationships is a central theme in Wari' responses to death.

CHAPTER SEVEN

EMBODIED IDENTITIES

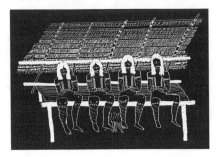

One of the striking aspects of Wari' funeral practices is the amount of attention and emotion focused on the corpse. From the moment of death until
the body is disposed of, relatives hold the corpse, clinging to it and throwing
themselves upon it. The keening, crying, and eulogies all take place around
the corpse and are directed toward it. With such intense affirmations of
caring focused on the physical body in the first stages of a funeral, it may
seem paradoxical that, in the past, Wari' then proceeded to assault the integrity of the corpse in a most radical way, cutting it into pieces that were
eaten or burned and pounding the charred remains into dust.

What complex meanings does the human body hold for Wari', that they
should have treated their loved ones' corpses this way? This chapter explores some of the ideas and sentiments associated with the body. The main
point is that, in the body, Wari' do not see just the outer form of the person or a symbol or metaphor for identity; rather, they see the body as a site
where personal identity and social relationships develop. Relations to others
do not exist in some abstract space located between two bodies; they develop in and through the physical body itself. Conversely, the body develops
out of the give-and-take of fluids, foods, and other forms of nurturance that
are the tangible stuff of which Wari' social life is comprised.

Wari' ideas about the human body's social qualities reflect the relational
notions of personhood that are characteristic of many other native Amazonian societies.[1] Especially among native peoples of Brazil, concepts of the
person tend to have a strong relational emphasis: an individual's social ties
define his or her status as a person or nonperson, and many aspects of identity and individual capacities are thought to depend on developing certain

kinds of interactions with others. Cross-culturally, notions of relational personhood tend to be associated with body imageries that emphasize how changes in someone's physical body reflect changes in his or her social position and identity (Conklin and Morgan 1996).

This chapter begins by examining the meanings associated with two major aspects of the Wari' person, the spirit (*jami-*) and the body (*kwere-*). This lays the groundwork for understanding the problems that death poses concerning the fate of the corpse and the spirit, and how Wari' think about the harmful effects of prolonged mourning. Since Wari' bodies are created through social relationships, when relationships and identities must be disassembled and transformed, one way to help accomplish this is to disassemble and transform the physical body itself.

Wari' ideas about the composition of the person reflect tensions at the heart of social life between the need for interdependence and the desire for autonomy. In a pattern similar to Ernestine McHugh's (1989) description of another sociocentric society, the Gurungs of Nepal, the conflicts that Wari' experience between social demands and individual desires are reflected in the contrast between the idea of a body composed of substances acquired from other people, and the idea of the individual spirit as an autonomous, socially unconstrained consciousness.

Wari' ideas about the body tend to emphasize the notion that physical vitality is created through interdependence and interactivity. In Wari' society, reciprocity based on involvement in numerous relationships of giving and receiving is the key to personal and collective security. The highest-status individuals are those who have an extensive social network, with many grown children who bring in-laws and grandchildren into the family. Those who have strong ties to many others are able to mobilize help for the work of clearing a field, building a house, or making a beer barrel for a party. Status also is based on less material forms of giving: having knowledge and skills to pass on to others, i.e., knowing songs and stories and the proper way to do things, especially the proper way to conduct festivals, funerals, and (in the past) warfare. For Wari', participation in social exchanges is the essence of life.

As McHugh observed among the Gurungs, the downside of a cultural emphasis on social integration, solidarity, generosity, and the imperative to fulfill obligations is that many people experience these social demands as oppressive. Wari' are constantly asked to share the few possessions they have; anyone who enters someone else's house can ask to be given almost anything in sight, except essential tools and staple foods like corn. Refusing a request is likely to provoke resentment and criticism, so people try to hide food and possessions and deceive others about how much they have. This maintains a veneer of social harmony, but since everyone knows that everyone does it, there is always an undercurrent of mistrust and insecurity in relations among Wari' households. Though people usually feel that they can count on support from their closest relatives, relationships are less secure beyond the nuclear family, and antipathies and resentments may simmer. In this atmosphere, concrete manifestations of caring, commitment, and support are important for what they show about the degree to which one can count on a particular relationship.

Wari' tend to use ideas about the human spirit to express insecurities in their relations to others, especially close relatives. Whereas ideas about the making of the body tend to emphasize social connectedness and interactivity, concepts revolving around the spirit address more problematic issues related to interpersonal tensions and the fragility of social bonds. Ideas about human spirits highlight the ways in which alienation and egocentric desires separate individuals from one another.

Spirit (*Jami-*)

All human beings (both Wari' and non-Wari') have a spirit, and so do certain animals and natural phenomena. The spirit is the vehicle of consciousness and self-awareness, and it is closely related to visual perception. Spirits normally reside in the body, invisible and imperceptible.[2] When a spirit leaves its body (which happens during dreams, serious illnesses, or deep emotional malaise), the body loses consciousness in part or in full. If a spirit manifests itself apart from its body, this phenomenon is described by the verb *jamu* and by the words *takom'* or *takom' hot,* meaning "to untie" or "free" something. Beliefs about the human spirit express a sense of persons as fragile beings, for individuals cannot control their own spirits, and spirits can willfully desert their bodies. Ideally, an individual's spirit will remain invisible and never manifest itself; Wari' say that someone whose spirit never leaves his or her body will live to be old. Spirit separation exposes individuals to great danger and is always cause for alarm. "*Takom' na jima, mi' pin ta na,*" Wari' say [The spirit is loosed; (she or he) is going to die].

A number of Wari' tell of uncanny encounters with a spirit double that looked like a living person they knew.[3] After seeing that person working in a field or walking on a path in the forest, they returned to the village and, unnervingly, found the real person there. No one sees his or her own spirit, but some people tell of having heard it chopping a tree in the forest. Following the sound to its source but finding no one there, they knew that it had been their own spirit. Such incidents are terrifying, because any event in which a spirit manifests itself apart from its body is a premonition of death. Several people are said to have developed cancer or debilitating illnesses after encountering their own spirit double.

Spirits tend to linger in spots where their bodies habitually sit or sleep. Young children are especially susceptible to spirit loss, since their spirits are not yet firmly fixed in their bodies and are apt to wander away. Quimoin was mindful of this one afternoon when her family and I were about to start walking back to Santo André after we had been living near their corn fields at Hon Xitot for a couple of weeks. When we had packed up our belongings and were about to leave, she called her two youngest children to stand by the sleeping platform. With a palm frond fan, Quimoin swept the length of the bed, sweeping toward the children and calling out, "Hurry up! Come follow us!" reminding her children's spirits to accompany their bodies on the journey home.

The spirits of Wari' adults normally leave their bodies only in dreams. Wari' consider events in dreams to be as real as events in waking life. When someone dreams of another person, the other person's spirit is said to be present also, so that he or she is dreaming the same scene. Dreaming about someone can indicate that the person is in danger of dying, and this makes Wari' reluctant to talk about their dreams or even admit to having any.

When dissociated from their bodies, people's spirits are apt to wander off to the forest, where they may be captured by a sorcerer. Wari' say that any man with malicious inclinations can become a sorcerer. Everyone knows how sorcery is done, though no one admits to actually doing it. Sorcerers can capture someone's spirit only when it leaves its body in a dream, and they attract their victims by manipulating individuals' selfish desires. To lure a spirit into the forest, the sorcerer builds a miniature traditional bed (*tapit*) and a small palm screen upon which he hangs attractive gifts of meat, fish, honey, and other tempting foods and miniature objects. If he wants to capture a man's spirit, the sorcerer also offers bows and arrows and, these days, cigarettes and shotgun shells. If he wants to capture a female spirit, he might add baskets, cooking pots, cloth, perfume, or needles and thread. Wari' images of sorcery project a vision of being able to acquire desirable material items without being bound by obligations of reciprocity. Sorcery beliefs encapsulate the danger of selfish desires that are not constrained by the patterns of mutualism that structure most exchanges in Wari' society.

Spirits leave their bodies when they are unhappy, usually because they feel unloved, criticized, mistreated, or neglected by their kin or (especially among the elderly) when the longing to reunite with dead loved ones becomes stronger than the will to live. The belief that unhappy spirits will abandon their bodies reinforces norms about the proper treatment of vulnerable family members. Fretful children are placated quickly for fear that the child's unhappy spirit will depart. People say that you must give food to children and old people and that you should not beat children, wives, or the elderly, because if you do, their spirits will depart. When a young woman died at Lage in 1986, some of her neighbors speculated that this had happened. "Her husband was having sex with another woman," they told me. "He beat his wife, and her spirit said, 'My husband doesn't love me, and I don't have a father, brother, or any real kin here.' Her spirit left her body, and she died."

The idea that spirits are easily lost when people feel alienated or become disconnected from others reflects a concept of health and well-being as synonymous with social integration. Wari' ideas about the human spirit acknowledge the fact that disruptive, alienated, egocentric feelings exist. But at the same time, ideas about the spirit reinforce the moral order of their world, emphasizing that nurturance (especially food giving) and expressions of respect and caring are the bonds that keep loved ones' spirits tied to their bodies.

These models of the person present a set of ideas and images in which different aspects of the way Wari' experience themselves as social beings can be expressed. As is probably true in all societies, an individual's sense of the world and sense of the self are never constant. Sometimes we see ourselves connected to others, integrated with our family and community. Wari' express such feelings in their discourses about bodies, food, and the sharing and exchange of substances. Connections to others also are expressed and experienced in directly physical ways, for bodily contact is a primary affirmation of social attachments and affection. Among close kin and friends of the same sex, people of all ages, both male and female, unselfconsciously hug, touch, and lean against one another. It is common to see twenty-year-old male cousins sprawled across one another in sleep, or an elderly woman cradling her tired middle-aged son's head in her lap. Grooming others to remove lice is a constant activity. For Wari', close relationships are tactile relationships. This physicality extends into illness and death, in which sick people are touched and held and corpses are embraced.

Connectedness is just one dimension of the experience of oneself as a social being. At other times, Wari' feel detached or alienated from those around them, and they express this sense of separateness in their discourses about spirits, illness, and sorcery. Whereas the body is associated with communal ties and the sensations of touch and smell, the spirit is associated with individuation and the senses of vision and hearing.

Bodily Bases of Identity and Personality

One of the striking things about spirits as conceived in Wari' cosmology is how little they contribute to the formation of personal identity. Although the jami spirit is the animating element of individuation and the source of consciousness, it is not the source of the main qualities that distinguish individuals from one another. Spirits are rather generic entities that possess only the most basic features of identity, such as gender, age, and kinship ties. All Wari' spirits act more or less alike, as do all spirits of a particular animal species. An aggressive man's spirit acts no differently from a shy man's spirit; the behavior of a greedy woman's spirit is indistinguishable from that of a generous woman's spirit. When someone dies, his or her spirit retains only minimal features of the identity the person had when he or she was alive.

When Wari' try to explain someone's behavior or eccentricities, they usually do not say much about mind or spirit. Instead, they talk about the body, for while the body is the site of connections to others, it also is a source of individuality and the distinctions that set people apart from one another. The body/flesh imbues individuals with character and personality, with qualities that are not innate (present at birth) but are acquired during one's lifetime, the socially created and self-developed aspects of the individual. Why, for example, is that man so quick to anger? "*Je' kwerekun*" [His body is like that]. Why is another stingy about sharing meat? "*Tara; je' kwerekun*" [Who knows? It's the way his body is]. Why is that girl promiscuous? "*Je' kwerekem*" [Thus is her body]. Adults shrug off children's mischief with the observation "*Je' kwerekekem hwijima'*" [Children's bodies are like that].

The human body also is a locus of what we call culture, the patterns of behavior that are learned and shared within social groups. To say "It is our custom," Wari' say, "*Je kwerexi' ka wari' 'iri ka*" [Thus are our bodies (or flesh) that we truly are]. This phrase is not just metaphorical; it expresses a sense of the body as a locus of those aspects of identity and behavior that are culturally shaped. When Wari' talk about what makes them different from Brazilians and other outsiders, they point to bodily differences. These are not necessarily obvious differences in appearance; Wari' are lighter skinned than many non-Indian Brazilians, and many Brazilians have "Indian" features. The bodily differences that Wari' emphasize involve the composition of body substances, of which body odors are a prime sign. Wari' are highly sensitive to odors; they consider one's scent as distinctive a marker of personal identity as one's visual appearance or voice. A number of people have told me that they can identify someone by smell alone. Individual scents reflect what has been taken into the body, including food, drink, skin oils, and body paint. Wari' say that non-Indians stink because of the beans, rice, cane liquor, soaps, and medicines they consume.

Part of the definition of being Wari' is having Wari' blood, a Wari' body. I discovered how literally Wari' can mean this one afternoon in 1986, when a Brazilian anthropologist was visiting Santo André. As we chatted with a group of young women, this visitor remarked that one of her great-grandmothers had been an Indian. "You have Indian blood!" the Wari' girls exclaimed approvingly. "That's good!" Then they asked whether I also had Indian blood. Feeling rather left out, I flirted momentarily with the idea of inventing a Native American ancestor, but honesty won out. "No, I don't have Indian blood," I replied and added, "I'm sad that I don't."

Some wistfulness behind my words must have been obvious, for Teresa placed a comforting hand on my arm. "Don't be sad, Beth," she said. "You can get Wari' blood. If you want to, you can become Wari' [wari' pin], just like us."

"Yes," chimed in the others. "It's easy to get Wari' blood."

How in the world, I wondered, could that happen?

"Just take a Wari' husband and have a baby here," the young women said. They explained that a non-Wari' woman "becomes Wari' " when she gives birth to a child fathered by a Wari' man. As they understood it, if the baby is born in Wari' territory, both the baby and its mother are considered to have Wari' blood and to be Wari'. For women, ethnic identity (a blood-based quality) can change, because when a woman is pregnant, her blood merges with the blood of the fetus in her womb. The mother's blood takes on qualities of her baby's blood, including her child's ethnicity. According to Santo André villagers, if a child has only one Wari' parent, its ethnicity is determined by its place of birth. This process works both ways: when a child of mixed parentage is born outside of Wari' territory, the child and its mother are considered to have the blood and identity of outsiders (wijam).[4]

It may have been no coincidence that it was Teresa who drew attention to this idea, for people at Santo André had been using it to criticize Teresa herself. In 1985, Teresa and her widowed mother had scandalized the community and shamed their family by getting pregnant from trysts with two Brazilian men. Both women gave birth at a maternity ward in town, and although they returned home to raise their babies in exemplary Wari' fashion, members of the community (especially their own relatives) commented frequently and pointedly that the two women were no longer really Wari'. They had lost their Wari' blood and had become wijam, non-Wari' outsiders. Teresa's own grandmother was vehement about this. Watching the two babies toddling after their mothers one afternoon, she exclaimed, "Look at them—they're completely wijam!" When I countered by saying that I didn't think they looked very different from other Wari' children, she glowered and hissed, "Their blood is not Wari'; their bodies are completely wijam! And so are their mothers!"

These statements about blood and identity seemed to make little practical difference in how people treated Teresa and her mother. Teresa's grandmother delighted in playing with her "wijam" grandchild and great-grandchild as much as any other doting Wari' matriarch. It was, rather, that talking about the foreignness of the bodies of the mothers and babies offered a way to express criticisms indirectly, in a pointed but nonconfrontational manner. More direct public statements about the women's wanton behavior would have put them on the spot to defend themselves and might have led to harsh words that could have escalated into the kind of overt conflict that Wari' try to avoid. Statements about blood and bodies, however, were inarguable; they called for no response, and none was given.

These ideas about blood-based changes of ethnicity reflect the primacy of physical body substances in defining social positions among the Wari'. So firmly is identity rooted in blood that even an American anthropologist might conceivably "become Wari'," regardless of how poorly she spoke the native language or conformed to local cultural norms. Of course, Wari' also recognize behavioral components of ethnicity. When a missionary, a FUNAI worker, or an anthropologist speaks their language well or acts in a culturally appropriate manner, people comment approvingly that the outsider is 'ak wari', "like Wari', like one of us." But language and cultural competence alone will never make an outsider 'iri (truly) Wari'; that requires a bodily transformation. The body is essential in defining connections or the lack of connections to the social group.

Flesh (Kwere-) and Blood (Kixi'-)

The word kwere- means both "body" and "flesh," and this dual significance reflects a tendency to conflate these aspects of the physical person. Wari' think of the body as integrated and interactive, a systemic whole rather than a composite of separate organs and limbs. A substance that enters any part of the body (especially the blood) may affect the body as a whole.

Blood (*kixi'-*) is the key to health and growth. It is produced in the heart (*ximixi'*), which transforms food into blood. The most important blood-building food is sweet corn chicha, which is closely identified with blood and female production and reproduction. Other foods, especially meat and the livers of certain birds, also build blood, and nurses and teachers have taught Wari' about the healthful benefits of drinking powdered milk. Corn chicha, however, continues to be seen as essential for building the blood and maintaining good health. Since 1981, when FUNAI ordered the village of Santo André to be built at its present site, which is a long way from soil that can grow corn, villagers have been forced to rely more and more on manioc. They see the fact that they eat much less corn these days as a major reason for poor health and weakness in their community.

Blood-building foods produce *homain ximixi'*, "fat of our hearts." When someone does not drink much liquid, especially chicha, the heart shrinks and produces less blood and fat. When blood flows freely, the heart expands and makes more fat. Growth, strength, and resistance to illness are thought to depend on body fat. Individuals with lots of blood have big hearts that produce lots of fat and keep them healthy; thin people have small hearts and little blood or fat, so they get sick easily. Strong, plentiful, free-flowing blood confers qualities that Wari' value: fatness, strength, resilience, resistance to disease, and the ability to work hard.

Mind, Thought, and Emotion

The Wari' body is not just material substance; it is also a source of thought, emotion, knowledge, morality, and personality. Wari' do not think of mind or mental processes as separate from the physical body. Many of the functions that westerners locate in the mind, such as learning, personality, and the development of habits, are seen by Wari' as physical events that take place in the body, especially in the eyes, brain, and heart.

This view of the interdependence of the physical and mental, or psychological, aspects of the person is evident in the idea that each of the territorial subgroups that made up precontact Wari' society—the Oro Nao', Oro Eo, Oro Jowin, Oro Waram, and so on—had a distinct flesh, blood, and physique that are still apparent in their descendants (Meireles 1986:345). Wari' tend to be vague about exactly what these physical differences are, and they conflate physical and behavioral traits. For example, when I asked one man how the blood and flesh of the Oro Nao' differ from the blood and flesh of the Oro Jowin, he explained that the Oro Jowin are more aggressive and quicker to start a fight. When I asked a woman how the physical bodies of the Oro Waram differ from the bodies of the Oro Nao', she responded by imitating differences in their speech. When I asked an Oro Mon man to explain his claim that Oro Jowin behaved differently from his own people, he demonstratively thumped his upper arms and chest. "Can't you *see?*" he asked incredulously. "Oro Jowin *bodies* are different from ours; their *blood* is different!" The distinctions that I was accustomed to making—between body and behavior, between substance and personality—were meaningless to Wari', for whom the social, biological, and cognitive-emotional aspects of the person are inseparable.

Wari' see the brain and eyes as closely connected. To the brain they attribute cognitive processes linked to visual recognition. The existence of a phenomenon is defined primarily in terms of sensory, especially visual, perception. The verb *kerek* means both "to see" and "to know" in the sense of being acquainted with something or someone. As a postverbal modifier, *kerek* means "to experience, to try (something new)." To know someone is to have *seen* him or her. The importance ascribed to vision contributes to the emphasis on eradicating visual reminders of the dead so that these sights will not bring the dead to mind.

Wari' consider the heart to be the primary physiological locus of psycho-mental processes, including rational thought and emotion. They think of the heart and lungs as interconnected; with each breath, the heart expands and contracts. Respiration is a pathway to the heart, and the verb *wereme* means both "to breathe" and "to think." Being rational or having good sense is expressed by the phrase "to have a heart." Of a woman making a sensible choice, people say, "*Ma' nam ximikam*"—literally, "She has a heart." As a tenderfoot ignorant of the tropical forest, I exhibited an apparent lack of common sense that often evoked the laughing observation "*Om nem ximüm, Beth!*" [You have no heart!]. Many emotions are expressed as cardiac processes. In excitement, "*Hwap na ximixi*'" [Our hearts move fast]. When worried, "*Toron na ximixi*'" [Our hearts are groaning]. When someone is confused or disoriented, people say, "*Xat xat na ximikon*" [His heart is wandering around]. These phrases are more than metaphors; they express the idea that emotions are inseparable from cardiovascular processes, so that psychological states are closely related to physiology. An individual with lots of strong blood is courageous and energetic and has a positive outlook on life, while weak blood and slow circulation make people thin, weak, sickly, incapable of working hard, and prone to lethargy, depression, and anomie.[5]

When the heart constricts, circulation slows. The blood, Wari' say, flows out of the limbs and head and collects in the chest cavity and joints, where it thickens (*xao*) and coagulates into dark, gelatinous clumps (*tarakixi'*). Wari' understand these changes in blood and heart functioning to have serious side effects: emaciation, fatigue and lethargy, dehydration, rapid, labored breathing, respiratory congestion, and sometimes muscular seizures. Fever and diarrhea are interpreted as blood disorders, and high fever is thought to exacerbate the xao process, turning the blood thick and dark. Less common circulatory disorders include a condition called *kup* that is almost always fatal, involving hematemesis (vomiting blood), uncontrolled nasal bleeding, abdominal swelling, and rigid muscular contractions.

When all the blood has thickened into tarakixi', the heart ceases to pump, and the person dies. Wari' consider the cessation of circulation the definitive sign of death and the immediate cause of all deaths. One way they describe the moment of biological death is "'*Om pin na karapitaxi*'" [Our blood vessels are finished]. A corpse's blood pools in the abdomen, where it changes into "rotten water" (*kuji kom*), and the corpse swells up huge (*mom*) with this decaying blood.

Emotions (especially negative emotions) are believed to have direct effects on the heart and thus on the blood and overall bodily vitality. Sadness and unhappiness cause the heart to constrict (*xi'*). Until the coming of western nurses and doctors, who will intervene to save lives whenever possible, it was not uncommon for elderly Wari', especially shamans, to announce the intention to die and then to do so forthwith. Wari' explain such deaths by saying that sadness and the desire to die constrict the heart. Mourners who grieve intensely are said to experience similar cardiac constriction. As the heart shrinks, it produces less blood and fat, so grieving individuals grow thin and waste away. Intensifying this effect, mourners often eat and drink less than normal, and old people who want to die may stop eating or drinking at all. This leads to dehydration, which Wari' see as reinforcing the negative cardiac process: as the circulation slows, blood moves out of the extremities and pools in the chest and joints, the skin and eyes become dry, and breathing grows shallow and finally ceases altogether.

So certain are Wari' of this medical model of how grief affects the body that the failure to waste away in a loved one's absence is taken as a sign of lack of affection. In 1987, I was criticized for this reason. My husband had returned to the United States the previous July. I missed him a great deal, but

11. Manim, resting during a honey-gathering expedition.

I was determined to present a cheerful face and carry on in the stiff-upper-lip mode that I imagined to be the ethnographer's proper modus operandi. As months passed and I remained alone, one after another of my Wari' friends began to make oblique inquiries about the solidity of my marriage.

Late one afternoon, I had just finished swimming and was climbing up the river bank when Manim marched over and planted himself in my path. "Do you miss your husband?" he demanded. Taken aback, I stammered my by-then-standard reply: "Yes, I miss him very much; I cry every night."

"You're lying!" Manim snorted. "Look at you: you're fat and strong! When we Wari' miss someone, we get thin. We have no blood; our fat is finished. When a Wari' husband goes away, his wife gets sick and dies. If you *really* miss someone, you *die!*"

Pointedly glancing up and down my body, he shook his head in disgust, turned on his heel, and stomped away, muttering, "No, Beth, you don't really love your husband!" Dumfounded, I stared after him as water dripped off my wet hair and clothes and pooled in the dust around my feet. I wasn't sure whether to laugh or scream in frustration. The fact that I was down to about 105 pounds at the time made his criticism feel especially unfair.

Wari' consider illness to be a normal, even expected, response to the absence or loss of a loved one. Their models of human physiology offer ready explanations of how emotional stresses lead to illness, bodily wasting, and death. By locating thought and emotion in the physical body (specifically, in the heart), they avoid the Cartesian split between mind and body that has been so prominent in western concepts of the individual and also in some native societies, such as among Gê speakers in central Brazil (da Matta 1976, Melatti 1976). For Wari', it is impossible to treat mind and body as independent components of the person; cognitive and physiological processes are facets of the same organic phenomena. One's bodily state depends on one's emotional state, which in turn depends on the state of one's relations with others.

Growth, Health, and Vitality

The Wari' term that comes closest to the Anglo American concept of "health" is *hwara' opa'*, a verb meaning "to be big, to be strong." Hwara' opa' connotes a capacity for hard work and productivity; productive vitality, not the absence of disease, is the core of the Wari' notion of health. A person who is hwara' opa' is active and works to produce food and support his or her family. A man who is hwara' opa' has strength for the hard work of clearing fields and the courage and vitality to protect his people. A woman who is hwara' opa' has strength for producing and processing food, for bearing and caring for children. Vitality is strongly associated with blood. Children are not hwara' opa', because their blood is weak, so they have little fat or strength. Likewise, elderly people are not hwara' opa', because their bodies have become weak and flaccid (*maram*), with soft, brittle bones. Although both children and the elderly do some work, they lack the vitality of adults in the prime of life.

Wari' pay a great deal of attention to weight loss and gain as an index of individuals' health and productive abilities. Substantial, fleshy physiques are highly valued, and fatness is considered pleasing and attractive to the opposite sex. Once, when some girls were looking at photographs of my family, they came across an old picture of me when I had been twenty pounds heavier and, by North American standards, unattractively plump. "So that's why Roberto married you!" one girl exclaimed. "We couldn't understand why he wanted a skinny wife like you," confessed another. "Now we see— you used to be fat and pretty!"

The value placed on fatness reflects the connection Wari' see between blood and work capacity: strong blood creates strength for work, and hard work enhances blood circulation. When people work hard, they breathe hard, their heart pumps faster, and their blood circulates more quickly. This produces more body fat, which in turn increases resistance to illness. Conversely, laziness and inactivity slow the circulation, so fat and flesh waste away. Sick people are caught in a vicious circle: their weak blood makes them unable to work, and the resulting inactivity slows their circulation, making them more vulnerable to disease.

A case in point is Marissa, a young wife who was notorious for her disinterest in cooking, gardening, or any form of domestic work. To me, the girl seemed to be depressed. Her parents had died two years earlier, and left without close relatives, she had married at the age of twelve, much younger than most Wari' girls marry these days. Her husband and his family treated her affectionately and made few demands on her limited energies, but as years went by and Marissa continued to spend most of her time lying around the house, people outside the family began to comment. Instead of criticizing her laziness, they excused her lethargy by attributing it to her weak blood. Yet some also pointed out that if Marissa did more work, her blood would grow stronger, and she would be healthier and better able to do a woman's work.

These beliefs about blood reinforce the notion that hard work is in an individual's own best interests. The idea of being healthy but indolent—that is, unproductive and not making tangible contributions to social exchange—is unthinkable. Wari' see food production and collective well-being as dependent on the physical vitality of a community's members, and they are concerned with molding and channeling individual bodily capacities (especially the quality of blood) into socially productive forms. As Viveiros de Castro (1979:47) observed with regard to the Yawalapiti of Brazil's Upper Xingú region, what happens "inside" the body is of interest to the society as a whole.

The Social Creation of Bodies and Persons

"It takes a whole village to raise a child," says the African proverb that Hillary Clinton made famous. For Wari', one might paraphrase this to say: "It takes a whole social network to create a healthy, mature body." Physical growth and development depend on incorporating vitalizing substances that come from other people, animals, or enemies. Before the contact, every major change in social status, each of the various moves between social categories that structured an individual's passage through life—puberty, motherhood, enemy killing, shamanic initiation, and old age—involved changes in body substance. Body transformations are not just metaphors for changes in status and identity; they are part of what makes these social transitions happen.

Wari' see the trajectory from birth to death as a process in which an individual moves from dependency on the nuclear family to an increasing biological and social autonomy, with more capacity to take part in social exchanges, do productive work, gestate and raise children, act in a moral manner, and acquire cultural knowledge. An individual's status as a person grows fuller and more complete as his or her social relations grow more complex over the course of a lifetime.

In the passage from birth to death and beyond (when the human spirit joins the world of the ancestors), physical growth, maturation, development of strength, and acquisition of moral and cognitive capacities come about through the control of exchanges between the interior body and the outside world, especially the manipulation of substances that should or should not enter or exit the body: blood and its analogs (such as breast milk, vaginal secretions, and semen), food (especially corn chicha), and the blood and flesh of certain game and fish. The social process of constructing the body is most apparent at major transition points—including pregnancy, when the fetal body comes into being; early infancy, when a newborn becomes a social person; female puberty and childbirth, which make women full adults; the killing of an enemy, which used to be essential for attaining full manhood; and shamanic initiation, which gives men the powers of animal spirits. As Wari' see it, each of these biosocial transitions involves the incorporation of body fluids or other substances from another individual who is in a category different from oneself—be it a parent, lover, child, enemy outsider, or animal spirit. Incorporating the other's substance transforms one's own body, social position, and capacities for action.

Over the course of the life cycle, the Wari' body-person is made and remade through processes in which intensified interactions with other individuals (mediated by transfers of body fluids, foods, or chicha) alternate with periods of seclusion (in which the individual withdraws from social interactions and strengthens or stabilizes his or her body by monitoring the substances that enter it). Periods of transition, during which individual bodies are made or remade, are closely associated with the social space and symbolism of the *xirim*. In its narrowest sense, the word *xirim* refers to the palm-thatch roof of a house; but Wari' extend the term to signify the whole interior domestic space in a family home and, by extension, the social space of the village. Individuals withdraw into the interior of their houses during periods of making and remaking their bodies and relationships. The act of staying inside the house is described by the verb *to' hwet*, "to remain," which contrasts with the act of "going out" (*hwet mao'*), an act that marks the conclusion of the formal period of mourning. Seclusion in the *xirim* also occurs during transitions involving the unmaking or disassembling of the Wari' body-person and relationships, such as in illness, death, and mourning. Tracing these ideas about the social fabrication and transformation of the body-person in periods of transition and seclusion lays the groundwork for understanding the social significance attached to the bodies of the dead and the complex of ideas and symbols associated with funerals, endocannibalism, and mourning rituals.

Child Development

Wari' babies enter the world metaphorically sheltered by the *xirim* (house), for Wari' call the placenta *xirikam/kon pije'*, "the house of the child." At birth, the newborn trades the womb's all-encompassing protection for the shelter of its mother's body and home. Newborns and their mothers remain secluded in their home for about six weeks after birth. During this time, the infant constantly is close to its mother's body, held in her lap or lying on a mat beside her. In social terms, this is a liminal period during which both mother and newborn have minimal contact with people outside the immediate family. Closely related women and children may visit briefly, and neighbors may take a peek at the new baby, but adult men (other than the baby's father) usually do not see newborns or their mothers until they emerge from seclusion weeks later. The imperative to respect this postpartum seclusion is reinforced by men's fears of the birth blood that fills the bodies of newborns and their mothers, for if a man other than the child's father were to touch mother or newborn, their blood could imbalance his own and make him sick.

Wari' emphasize that the most important objective of the postpartum seclusion is to build and strengthen the baby's blood as it nurses at its mother's breast. They stress the father's role in providing foods (especially certain kinds of blood-building game) that are considered especially important for making strong breast milk. On the day of a birth, older people watch to see if the father kills the right kind of game to feed his wife. Mothers get nourishing food, rest, and care from female relatives who help around the house. Seclusion probably improves the infant's survival chances by protecting the newborn inside the home, warmed constantly by contact with its mother's body.

Newborns are not considered complete social persons, and they have little individual identity in this liminal period just after birth. The sense of them as still "in process" is conveyed by the practice of referring to newborns by generic terms, not personal names, until they are about six weeks old. In the Lage/Ribeirão area, newborns are called *arawet,* which means "still being made." In the Dois Irmãos area, they are *waji,* a term that connotes immaturity. (Green, unripe fruit is called *oro-waji.*) A baby and its mother are seen almost as a single unit, extensions of each other's biological substance and social identity. This physical merging begins during pregnancy, when Wari' view the bloods of mother and child as a unified substance, and after birth, this blood unity is reinforced as the infant absorbs its mother's breast milk.

Physical consubstantiality has a social parallel in the treatment of mother and infant as a single unit. This is expressed in the practice of female teknonymy. When a newborn receives a personal name, its mother's name changes to her baby's name, prefixed by a referential pronoun (*kam* or *kon*) indicating possession. The mother of a baby girl named Jap, for example, becomes Kam Jap, which means "belonging to Jap" or "with Jap." This practice has diminished since the 1960s, for it has been discouraged by government administrators who found it too confusing for censuses and record keeping. But even though mothers of young children officially retain their own names these days, many Wari' still refer to them using the teknonymous form.

Postpartum seclusion relaxes gradually over a period of several weeks, as the mother's bleeding and the potency of the birth blood diminish. About six weeks or so after birth, the mother and child begin to go out of their house for short visits with other women and children. No special ritual marks this emergence into social life, but around this time, the baby usually is given a name and thus begins to acquire a public identity. Wari' explicitly link this practice of delayed naming to the uncertainty of neonatal survival. Traditional personal names usually are the names of dead relatives, and Wari' tend to wait several years after a death before reusing a dead person's name. They say that hearing the name too soon after a death makes people sad. After a few years, a dead person's name may be used again, but if the child then dies, this name usually will not be used again for several more years. Parents say that they delay naming newborns until they have survived early infancy to avoid wasting good names on babies who die soon after birth.[6]

Acquiring a personal name and being carried into the public space outside the family home is a first step toward the infant's acquisition of a social identity independent of its parents. Wari' see this process of individuation as occurring simultaneously on social and physiological levels. As children mature and eat nourishing foods (especially corn and meat), they gradually develop their own blood and body substance, distinct from the blood and bodies of their parents.

Biosocial individuation brings vulnerability. Wari' believe that baby fat, which nursing infants develop from their mothers' strong blood and breast milk, confers some resistance to disease, but when toddlers stop nursing (typically around two years of age), they lose their baby fat, and their blood becomes weak, thin, and yellowish. Children between about two and five years of age are thought to be more susceptible to illness than any other age group. By the time they are about seven years old, children have developed their "own" blood, which is stronger than the weak blood of toddlers and less vulnerable to elements that pass through their parents' bodies. With puberty, the blood of adolescents becomes more fully differentiated from the blood of their parents.

Making a Woman's Body

Prepubescent children of both sexes are called by the generic term *hwijima,* "kids." When a girl develops breasts, she begins to be called *xojam,* and when she bears a child, she becomes *narima',* a full adult woman. For boys, physical signs of puberty are less precise. Wari' generally note growth, deepening voices, and genital development as evidence that boys are becoming young men, who are referred to as *xo' tarama',* "recently man" or "recently grown," and *xo' hwara',* "recently big." Later, they become *napiri,* full adult men.

Adolescent physical maturation begins naturally, but Wari' traditionally have believed that certain social interactions are essential for creating an adult with fully developed physical capacities and moral and intellectual skills. For both girls and boys, this involves a transformation of adolescents' blood that stimulates growth and maturation and enhances their health, strength, and resistance to disease. The catalyst to this transformation is another individual's body fluid, taken into one's own body through the genitals. For young women, this happens with their first experience of sexual intercourse. For young men in the past (when Wari' still warred against their neighbors), the parallel event involved taking part in the killing of an enemy, which Wari' believe caused the enemy's spirit-blood to enter the boy's body.

Wari' have no female puberty rites or initiation ceremonies; the changes that come with female puberty are physical and social. When their breasts begin to develop, girls find themselves the object of a new kind of masculine attention, for breast development is thought to signal readiness for sexual intercourse, and in the past, most girls married soon after their breasts began to develop.

A girl's first experience of sexual intercourse is thought to transform her blood, body fat, and physical vitality. People say that prepubertal girls "have only a little blood" and consequently are thin, weak, vulnerable to childhood illnesses, and unable to work hard. When a girl first has sex, the infusion of semen (a nourishing, growth-promoting substance) stimulates her blood so that it increases in quantity and changes in quality: she grows fatter and taller and gains the strength to do women's work. Most importantly, semen stimulates her body to produce menstrual blood, the essence of female fertility.

Wari' believe that menarche (first menstruation) occurs only after a girl has lost her virginity. Throughout a woman's life, each menstrual period is seen as the product of sexual intercourse. Even in the face of evidence to the contrary, many people insist that only sexually active women menstruate; virgins and widows and divorcées who remain celibate do not have periods. When an unmarried female missionary told Wari' women that she menstruated even though she was a virgin, they said it was impossible. Privately, both women and men admit that virgins and celibate women may have some vaginal bleeding, but they say this is not "real" menstruation but "only a little blood that flows for no reason (ao ximao)." Real menstruation depends on having sexual intercourse.

While premarital sexual experimentation is a fact of life for many teenagers, most parents and elders still affirm the ideal that a girl's first sexual partner should be the man she will marry. This ideal of female virginity at marriage may have been attained more often in the past, when girls married earlier, often before they began to menstruate. A girl's first lover is said to be 'iri taxikam, "her true husband." Manim's wife, Tocohwet Pijo', proudly told me, "Manim is my 'iri taxi'; he was the first one." She complained, "Now these girls have sex randomly [wan ximao]. In the old days, we knew how to behave."

Underlying this ideal of virginity at marriage is the notion that a husband grows and nourishes his young wife's body as it develops in much the same way that a father's semen grows and nourishes the body of his child in its mother's womb. The positive value associated with this idea that sexual intercourse stimulates female development was highlighted in a scandal that erupted one night at Rio Negro-Ocaia in 1987. A man who was a notorious womanizer deflowered his wife's niece in the same bed where his wife and daughter were sleeping. The girl did not object, but his wife woke up, jumped out of bed, and cursed her husband with a loud string of epithets so choice that, for weeks afterwards, Wari' women delighted in telling and retelling this juicy tale.

The next morning, community sympathy seems to have supported the wife and her sister (the mother of the girl involved), who were seen as justifiably outraged at the husband for insulting his wife by having intercourse with someone else in the same bed where his wife lay sleeping. Incest was not an issue, since the girl (the wife's sister's daughter) was in an affinal category that Wari' consider appropriate for marriage. In the past, a first wife's niece might have become the second wife in a polygamous marriage or might have married the widower if her aunt had died.

The girl's father initially claimed to be unperturbed. As the story came down to us at Santo André, he brushed off this incident and disavowed any interest in fighting over it by saying that he welcomed his daughter's deflowering under any circumstances. Having been "opened up" to receiving growth-promoting semen, she would now grow fat, tall, strong, and healthy. The Wari' who repeated this story took it for granted that a girl's first experience with sexual intercourse would stimulate her growth. Wari' see male and female bodies as interdependent and interactive. Menarche and menstruation are not events that take place in an autonomous female body; they require a man's participation. Creating a woman's body capable of production and reproduction is a social project predicated on cross-gender cooperation.

Making a Man's Body

For Wari' boys before the contact, the transition to adolescence began when they moved out of their family homes and into the men's house (*kaxa'*) around the age of eight to ten. Wari' had no age grades, but when older men decided that several boys in the village were ready to move into the men's house, they gathered the boys together and pierced their earlobes with a thorn. Eventually, these boys would be able to wear the short wooden earplugs (*maxowat*) that all adult Wari' men wore before the contact. After moving into the men's house, boys changed their hairstyle from the short cut with bangs worn by women and children to the adult male style of long hair parted in the middle. Although youths slept in the men's house, they continued to consume food and drink prepared by their female relatives, which young sisters carried to their bachelor brothers in the men's house. After the contact, Wari' stopped building men's houses[7] and stopped piercing boys' ears. Only a few male elders still wear their hair long. Today, the transition from boyhood to manhood is much less clearly defined than it was in the past.

In the days when Wari' were still at war with their neighbors, a second major stage in adolescent male development occurred when a young man first participated in the killing of an enemy outsider.[8] Killing an enemy transforms the killer's blood, for Wari' believe that the victim's blood and spirit enter the bodies of everyone who witnesses the killing, regardless of whether or not they actually shoot the enemy. Enemy spirit-blood has vitalizing effects on male blood that parallel the effects of semen on adolescent girls' blood. In boys, the infusion of invisible enemy blood stimulated a growth spurt. In seasoned warriors, each new infusion of enemy blood made them grow fatter, stronger, and more resistant to disease.

To retain the vitalizing enemy blood in their bodies, men and boys went into ritual seclusion behind a screen of woven mats erected to enclose the men's house. They spent the entire period of seclusion lying together in one or more giant hammocks (*xijat*) woven of strips of palm bark. (This was the only context in which Wari' used hammocks before the contact.) To nourish and stabilize the enemy blood in their bodies, the men and boys drank copious quantities of unfermented corn chicha. The goal was to fatten up, since strength and vitality depend on body fat. A fat belly also proved that a man really had killed an enemy, and a man who did not fatten was considered a fraud. By all accounts, the men and boys really did grow quite plump as they gorged themselves on pot after pot of the chicha that their female relatives worked long hours to make.

For Wari', bodily domains and moral domains are interdependent.[9] Fattening enhanced a man's strength and health, and also his courage and self-confidence. Ritual seclusion made boys into *napiri*, adult men. Their orientation to their new roles was reinforced in conversations with the older men in seclusion, who lectured them about their new responsibilities as napiri and told tales of warfare, raids, and famous warriors' exploits. Boys also were taught the ethical ideals associated with being napiri, the expectation that they would comport themselves proudly, with dignity, at all times. They learned that henceforth they would be expected to control their emotions, especially expressions of anger, and that they must avoid dirt and pollution and practice scrupulous hygiene. A man who failed to follow these rules would grow weak and sick and might die. The basic message was that social virtues and proper interactions with others are rewarded with physical well-being, while improper behaviors are punished by a loss of health and vitality.

When members of a war party emerged from seclusion weeks later with their plump, well-rested, beautifully oiled bodies, they were highly desirable as sexual partners. Wari' believe that the vitalizing enemy fat passed out of the warriors' bodies in their semen and into the bodies of the first women with whom they had sex. These women, in turn, would grow fat and healthy, so that the killing of an enemy benefited members of both sexes, infusing new vitality into the collective social body.

Modes of Consumption: Absorbing Blood, Eating Flesh

Wari' beliefs about the positive effects of enemy spirit-blood might be considered a sort of symbolic exocannibalism if we think of cannibalism not simply as an act of swallowing something orally, but more broadly as the incorporation of body substance from another human being. But Wari' also ate enemy flesh, and it is worth considering the coexistence of these two distinct forms of incorporating enemies. A key difference between them is that, whereas enemy spirit-blood had transformative effects on the killers who absorbed it, the enemy's roasted flesh had no corresponding effect on those who ate it. Enemy flesh was an inert substance. Wari' appreciated it for the meat and fat, but eating it did not bring any physical or metaphysical transformation.

Wari' beliefs about the nontransformative nature of roasted enemy flesh contrast with the ideas of certain other peoples in South America, Melanesia, and elsewhere, who are said to have eaten their enemies in order to acquire the enemy's courage, vitality, or life force. Exocannibalism based in such ideas exemplifies what Maurice Bloch (1992) calls the "conquest of external vitality," the practice of appropriating elements from beings outside one's own group to create in oneself a state that transcends (at least temporarily) the constraints of mundane biological degeneration. In the Wari' case, external vitality was captured not by eating enemy flesh, but by absorbing and transforming the enemy's spirit-blood. Wari' views of the revitalizing properties of enemy spirit-blood are consistent with the perspectives of other native South Americans who have seen enemy outsiders as a kind of natural resource, a source of generative relationships or transformative powers to be appropriated for the benefit of oneself and one's society (see Fausto 1999). Among the Tupian-speaking Araweté of central Brazil, for example, eating enemy flesh was believed to enhance individual vitality, so that "an eater of enemies lives a long time, is immune to disease, and is physically strong" (Viveiros de Castro 1992:256). A key trope in the construction of indigenous Amazonian identities is what Viveiros de Castro has called "ontological predation"—the formation and transformation of self-identity, individual agency, and collective empowerment based on the killing and consumption of others external to the self.

Illness, Old Age, and the Attenuation of Personhood

Healthy, productive adult Wari' bodies are maintained by active engagement in society. A woman who does not have sexual intercourse loses her fecundity; a man who fails to act as a proper napiri falls ill. When people do not work hard (implying diminished productivity and disengagement from social exchange), their blood grows weak, and they get sick. Maintaining physical health depends on active involvement in social life.

The process of creating healthy adult Wari' bodies is essentially a process of socializing the body as it absorbs health-enhancing fluids, foods, and other substances produced by others. Illness and death reverse this process: the body-person is desocialized, cut off from the flow of positive exchanges. As Terence Turner (1980:116) observed for the Kayapó of central Brazil, " 'Health' is conceived as a state of full and proper integration into the social world, while illness is conceived in terms of the encroachment of natural, and particularly animal, forces upon the domain of social relations."

The characteristic behaviors of sick Wari' express this attenuation of sociality. Seriously ill individuals lie silent and lethargic, unresponsive to the relatives clustered around them. Conversely, the return of interactivity, especially oral interactions (speaking, accepting food or drink), is taken as a sign of imminent recovery. The equation of illness with social disengagement is reflected in the idea that a sick person's spirit or body loses its qualities of personhood and humanity. Wari' attribute most serious illnesses to an aggressive attack on a person's spirit by a human sorcerer or an animal spirit. The sorcerer lures his victim's spirit out of its body and away from the village to an isolated spot in the forest, where he ties it up. The social isolation of the victim's spirit has a physical parallel in the victim's bodily behavior: sorcery victims typically withdraw into themselves, refuse nourishment, and stop talking.

Animal spirit attacks take people's spirits out of the human domain in a different way. When an animal spirit (*jami karawa*) attacks someone, its victim's human spirit begins to turn into an animal of the same species as the attacker. Shamans say that as the animal spirit aggressor consumes the person's internal organs, the person's human spirit gradually takes on features of the animal attacker. One shaman, for example, described how he looked into a sick girl's body and saw that her spirit was covered with brown hair and had a tail like that of the capuchin monkey spirit that was eating her. When Wari' are seriously ill, they sometimes make grunting and moaning sounds that others interpret as alarming evidence of animalization.

Like illness, old age brings diminished sociality and the beginning of a transition to a nonhuman or extrahuman category. The elderly are called *hwanana,* which is the same term used for ancestors. Elderly people, and especially elderly women, often seem to dwell more and more on thoughts of joining lost loved ones, which they express especially in talking about their dreams of white-lipped peccaries and longings to join the herd. In this sense, old age moves toward another kind of animalization, which is completed after death, when the human spirit joins the underworld domain of animal spirits from which it will eventually emerge as a white-lipped peccary.

* * *

Wari' strategies for coping with illness emphasize rehumanizing the sick person's body and spirit by strengthening and affirming the individual's connections to other people. Curing draws on principles related to the making of the body during life cycle transitions. Illness can be seen as a weak form of seclusion, and the ways Wari' deal with it reflect some of the same concerns and techniques observed in the seclusions of enemy killers and new mothers and the semiseclusion of new shamans. The way Wari' respond to serious illness in the family also can be seen as a kind of premourning behavior that anticipates some of the sentiments and actions characteristic of bereavement.

If sickness develops out of attenuated or alienated sociality, curing requires reintegration of the patient into the community. Shamans attempt to expel the intrusive animal spirit from the patient's body or (although this is difficult and seldom accomplished) free the patient's spirit from the sorcerer's captivity. Red body paint made of annatto is a key marker of human (Wari') identity, and a shaman takes annatto and palm oil out of his own body (where his companion spirit implanted them) and rubs these on the patient. Family members verbalize their love and kinship with the sick person, affirming his or her social connections and belonging. Through a variety of strategies, Wari' try to restore health by drawing the sick person back into the flow of social life.

As Mary Douglas (1966) and others have observed, the human body often serves as a symbol of society, a material metaphor for how social groups are organized. Wari' affirm more dynamic experiences of the body as a site where social relationships actually develop and change over time. The behaviors of family members who cluster close around a sick person suggest the degree to which notions of shared substance have subjective tactile and emotional correlates in individuals' experiences of the bodies of those for whom they care. Physical touch or the absence of touch, bodily postures, and modes of comportment are salient expressions of the state of a person and his or her relationships. Connections to others are forged in and through the body.

In the body, Wari' see not just the outer form of the person, but the physical sum of his or her experiences, character, and relationships. The physical body is a social product created out of the give-and-take of nurturance, the flow of social exchanges in daily life. At a deep experiential level, concepts of the body as the site where personality and relationships develop seem to merge with the emotional significance of bodily contact, physical touch, and the giving of food as affirmations of caring and acceptance. The body is where Wari' express and experience the tensions between individual desires and interdependence, between longing and belonging.

CHAPTER EIGHT

BURNING SORROW

The deep attachments Wari' feel to the bodies of those they love and with whom they live come to the fore when death poses the problem of what to do with the corpse. This chapter explores why Wari' consider the persistence of the corpse to be problematic and why they used to consider it imperative to destroy the bodies of their loved ones.

The intensity of meanings that Wari' associate with the corpse may be difficult for westerners to understand, accustomed as we are to thinking that the essence of an individual resides in immaterial qualities like mind, consciousness, personality, or spirit. In this view, the loss of consciousness or spirit at the moment of death takes away most of an individual's important qualities, leaving behind a corpse perceived as an empty, almost meaningless body shell. We treat the corpse respectfully, but in it we see little more than the remnant of a life that has been extinguished.

Wari', in contrast, perceive the body as a tangible product of the dead person's relationships and a repository of much of his or her identity. They express their sense of attachment to the bodies of their close kin in a variety of ways at funerals in which the corpse is the physical and emotional center of activity. Mourners embrace and caress the corpse, press themselves against it, and at times treat it almost as if it were alive. 'Iri nari (the close consanguines and spouse)—those who are of "one flesh" with the deceased—express their physical identification with dead individual in the gestures toward suicide and in the ritual action in which mourners form piles of living bodies with the corpse on top. While Wari' consider expressions of attachment to the corpse and to images of the deceased appropriate during a funeral, they consider such attachments counterproductive if they persist long afterwards. They say that the rituals of mourning and the normative behaviors expected of mourners explicitly aim to attenuate and transform mourners' sense of attachment to the deceased. One way they do so is by acting to alter both the dead person's physical remains and mourners' visual images of the deceased. As a site where social relatedness and identities are forged and signified, the body is also a site where these can be negated and recomposed.

Death and the Problem of Attachments in Lowland South America

In a classic essay published in 1907, Robert Hertz (1960) observed that every death creates three primary "actors": the corpse, the soul, and the mourners. Relations among these three entities can be envisioned as a sort of triangle composed of three sets of interactions: between the corpse and the soul of the deceased, between the soul and the mourners, and between the mourners and the corpse. What happens to one of these relationships may affect the other two. Throughout the world, many people believe that the fate of the spirit is connected to the fate of its corpse, and images of what is happening to the corpse often parallel images of what is happening to the dead person's spirit.

Hertz's model offers a useful framework for understanding why some lowland South American peoples have thought it essential to transform corpses by eating or burning them. The mourners' act of destroying the corpse is thought to sever or attenuate the other two relationships in the triangle: the connection between the body and spirit (soul) of the dead person, and the connection between the spirit and the living mourners. Many native South Americans feel that both of these connections are potentially threatening to the well-being of living people. The perceived dangers revolve around two related phenomena: the problem of ghosts and the problem of excessive grief.

Death brings a rupture in relations between the dead and those who knew them, but it is seldom a clean break. The lives and emotions of the living are bound up with the individual who suddenly is gone from the world, and adjusting to this change takes time, especially for those who loved the dead person or were involved in long-term relationships with him or her. On the other side of this relationship, many South American Indians believe that the spirits of the recently dead also have trouble adjusting to their new situation as long as they remain emotionally attached to the people, places, and bodies of their former lives.

The problem of attachments looms large in native South American thinking about death. Living people can encounter the dead in two ways: as ghosts, or as mental images in memories or dreams. Both kinds of encounters are potentially harmful. Ghosts are dangerous because they may try to carry away their own relatives for companionship in death, and some native people also believe that ghosts cause illness. Memories and emotional ties are problematic if they prevent living people from being able to return to their normal, productive routines and social activities, or if they make the spirits of the dead want to remain among the living. Some native Amazonians place more emphasis on fears of ghosts, while others (including the Wari') see the greater danger in mourners' tendencies to dwell on memories of the dead.

Ghosts and Grief

In a number of lowland South American cultures, the problem of ghosts is closely intertwined with the problem of grief. This is apparent in the twin explanations that many Amazonian Indians commonly give for the practice of destroying dead people's property and ceasing to use their names: to drive away ghosts, and to help mourners forget the deceased (Kracke 1988:213–214). Waud Kracke observed that among the Kagwahiv, a Tupian group that lives near the lower Madeira River in north-central Brazil, these two different rationales are given "so interchangeably that it almost seems as if they are different ways of phrasing the same thing" (1988:213–214; and see Kracke 1981:262).

"According to the Wari'," Vilaça (1992:228) has noted, "the destruction by fire of all reminders of the deceased is, in the first place, a protection against the sadness that is felt upon seeing something that belonged to the deceased or that was touched, used or made by him; but it is also a way to avoid the coming of the ghost." I once asked Maxun Kwarain, who was widely regarded as the most knowledgeable shaman, why Wari' always gave these two reasons for burning dead people's houses and possessions. To me, sadness and ghosts seemed like two entirely different ideas, but people seemed to treat them as if they were interchangeable. He replied that ghosts (*jima*) do not appear at random, but only to individuals who dwell on memories of the dead. "If a father thinks a lot about his son who died, the ghost of the dead one comes," Maxun said. "If he does not think about him, it [the ghost] does not come."

Not all Wari' share Maxun Kwarain's explicit recognition of the notion that memory itself attracts ghosts. But everyone knows that it is the ghosts of close relatives from whom one has most to fear. The few Wari' who claim to have actually encountered a jima almost always say it was probably the spirit of a kinsperson or neighbor. Wari' do not seem to worry much about the ghosts of people whom they never knew, as if they implicitly recognize the mind's power to create the realities it experiences.

Anthropologists who work with other Amazonian Indians have made similar observations. Glenn Shepard (n.d.:13) notes that among the Matsigenka in the Madre de Dios region of southeastern Peru, ghosts "are not anonymous spirits from bygone generations. They are always close relatives of their victims, typically a spouse, parent, sibling, or child." In Peru's Bajo Urubamba region, Peter Gow (1991:186) found that native people believe that a ghost can be seen only by someone who knew the individual in life: "The souls of the dead thus depend on the contacts they built up during life in order to act after death." The dead soul is disembodied memory, drawn back to earth by its own memories of life there and manifested to those who remember the person it used to be. Thus, mourners who are haunted by their memories of the dead may find themselves haunted more literally as well, visited by the ghosts of those on whom their thoughts dwell.

The link between grief and ghosts is the act of remembering, which perpetuates psycho-emotional attachments between the living and the dead. Some native Amazonians see memory not merely as the subjective experience of a lone individual, but as a force with tangible effects on the material world. This is consistent with the emphasis that native Amazonians place on the power of thought and mental states (see M. Brown 1986, Sullivan 1988:375–383). Dreams, visions, desires, and emotions are widely believed to have the capacity to shape reality. Native ideas about the power of mental states intersect with ideas about the bodily bases of thought, emotion, and knowledge, to make mind-altering and body-altering processes inseparable (McCallum 1996a, Pollock 1996). This is one reason Amazonian peoples devote so much attention to developing and controlling knowledge, emotions, and visionary experiences, and why consciousness-altering hallucinogens, tobacco, and fermented beverages have been used more intensively in lowland South America than anywhere else in the world.

Recognizing how aware lowland South America's Indians are of the power of what we call mind, emotions, and visions, it is not surprising to find widespread concerns about the effects of memories of the dead. In particular, a number of peoples believe that thinking too much about the dead can attract their ghosts or create an opening through which ghosts can become manifest in the world of the living.

For Wari', the connection between memory and ghosts is one factor contributing to their feeling that it is important for mourners to attenuate their remembrances of the dead, but it is not the factor they emphasize most. In contrast to many other Amazonian Indians, Wari' are not terribly worried about ghosts. They do not believe that jima cause illness, and although the recently dead are thought to long for their loved ones on earth and desire their companionship in the underworld, very few actual deaths are blamed on ancestral spirits or ghosts. Instead of the danger of ghosts, Wari' place far more emphasis on the dangers of dysfunctional grief perpetuated by obsessive remembering and mourning. Nonetheless, though ideas about driving away ghosts and dissociating spirits from their former lives do not explain much about Wari' endocannibalism, fear of ghosts is part of the mix of emotions that comes into play in response to a death in the community. These fears reinforce the felt need to destroy physical traces of the dead, including the corpse, in order to distance the dead from the living.

Ghost Fears and Dissociation

Wari' believe that one form in which dead people's spirits appear on earth is a frightening specter called *jima*.[1] Jima can be invisible, or they can appear as insubstantial apparitions composed of eerie, flickering light. Jima ghosts are devoid of individuality: they all look more or less alike, with an appearance that resembles certain aspects of a decomposing corpse. Jima have full-sized, human-shaped bodies, but their heads are huge, grotesquely swollen, with bulging eyes. Their skin is cold, smooth, slippery, and hairless, because the hair falls out as the corpse rots. When a jima appears, people speculate about which dead relative or neighbor's ghost it was, but they usually say it is impossible to know for sure, because jima all look alike. A few Wari' have had close encounters with jima, and their stories are terrifying. The jima is said to grab its victim and hold on with awesome strength, trying to pull the person's spirit away. A jima's hands are very cold and covered with a slippery poison that makes the victim's head swell up enormously, like the head of the jima. A man from Tanajura described how a jima had clutched him on the riverbank and held him as he struggled for what seemed an interminable length of time. Finally, he escaped and ran home, exhausted and covered with sweat. His head was swollen, and he felt miserable the following day.

Jima lurk in dark places, waiting for someone to pass by alone. For fear of them, Wari' seldom go out alone at night. Jima also may attack and impregnate women who sleep alone; children often expressed worry over my habit of sleeping alone in the dark. Jima avoid the light and appear only on moonless nights; like animal spirits, they dislike the smell of *naran*, the resin that Wari' burn to light their houses. For this reason, many families sleep with a light burning all night. On dark evenings, the sense that jima might be lurking nearby becomes almost tangible, and families huddle together around small fires. At times, the darkness seems to press close, and strange sounds and eerie screeches echo from the forest. On one such night, an elderly woman sensed an evil presence around her nephew's house. Grabbing a burning leaf packet filled with resin, she thrust it angrily toward the edges of the house platform, crying out, "Why have you come, ghost? Go away!"

Although Wari' fears of jima are real, little actual misfortune or mischief is blamed on them. Of the 399 precontact deaths on which I collected data, only one (the sudden death of a young boy) was a case in which an informant identified the cause of death as an attack by jima—in this case, the ghost of a dead grandfather who carried away his grandson's spirit.[2] So insignificant are jima as a perceived cause of sickness and death that many Wari' insist that jima do not really kill anyone, but just frighten people.

Wari' fears of jima are strongest in the first days and weeks after a death, for this is a liminal period during which neither the dead person's spirit nor the bereaved family has adjusted to the new state of affairs. The dead person and the loss of the dead person are constantly on the minds of the living, while in the underwater realm of the ancestors, the newly dead person's spirit is said to be homesick for the people and places it knows. Even after the spirit accepts the fact that it no longer belongs to the world of the living, nostalgia for its former life may continue and motivate it to return as a jima.

Distancing Spirits by Destroying Remains: An Explanation for Cannibalism?

Wari' say outright that one reason they burn the house and personal possessions of the deceased and change the appearance of neighboring houses and the layout of paths is to confuse the newly dead person's jima so that, unable to find its former home, it will not linger in the village but will return to the otherworld. If the burning and destruction of physical remains drives away or discourages ghosts, was this also a motive for destroying the corpse by eating it?

For some other South American Indians, the answer seems to be yes.[3] The Guayakí and Cashinahua (who used to practice flesh cannibalism) and the Yanomami (who consume only the bones) explain their practice of endocannibalism partly as an attempt to sever the spirit's connection to its corpse, liberating or banishing the spirit so it will not harm living mourners (Albert 1985:524–525, P. Clastres 1974, McCallum 1996b:70). But in each case, endocannibalism is also directed toward shaping mourners' psychology, their emotions or memories of the deceased. Pierre Clastres (1974) reported that Guayakí spoke of the danger posed by the spirit in terms of its effect on mourners' psychological state, asserting that the lingering presence of the dead person's soul causes the living survivors to feel great anxiety and anguish, which Clastres identified as the fear of being harmed by the ghost. In order to return the community to a state of psychological tranquility (which Guayakí value highly), everyone except the closest blood relatives took part in eating the corpse.

Meireles (1986:427) concluded that Wari' mortuary cannibalism also was "based in the idea that the dead person's soul must be banished, to avoid the risk that it might afflict the living." However, none of the Wari' I have met agree with this interpretation. I have never heard any Wari' say that cannibalism drove away the dead person's spirit, nor did any of my informants spontaneously suggest that eating the dead prevented ghosts or spirits from returning to earth. Rather, when asked whether eating the corpse had that effect, a few agreed that it might be possible. Others insisted that cannibalism had nothing to do with banishing ghosts. As evidence, they cited the fact that the ghosts (jima) of people who are buried today do not return to wander the earth any more frequently than those of people who were cannibalized or cremated in the past.

Vilaça suggested a more subtle interpretation: that roasting was a dissociative mechanism that liberated the dead person's spirit from his or her body so that the spirit could make a full transition to the afterlife (1992:70–71, 233, 243, 262). The best support for this argument comes from the way Wari' treat animal carcasses. They believe that one must roast and eat certain game animals quickly so that the animal's spirit will not linger in the vicinity.

An incident I observed at Santo André in 1987 also suggested that roasting liberates an animal spirit from its body. Two white-lipped peccaries were shot by hunters whose families were temporarily residing at Hon Xitot, a farming area about ten kilometers from the main village. White-lipped peccaries are said to contain the spirits of Wari' ancestors, and their meat is supposed to be shared widely. On this occasion, the hunters and their families ate it all themselves. Back at Santo André, there had been little meat that week, and there was grumbling about the hunters' selfishness.

The issue took on a new dimension when the shaman, Maxun Kwarain, reported that he had dream-journeyed to Hon Xitot and talked with the peccary spirits, who turned out to be the spirits of an aunt and uncle of the hunters who shot them. As the female peccary head lay on the roasting rack talking to the shaman, she griped about the poor way she was being treated. One of her complaints was that the hunters had delayed roasting her and that the cooking fire was too small, just smoke with little heat. Only a good, hot fire can free the spirit from its carcass, the shaman explained. The peccary-ancestress found herself stuck in a lukewarm lump of dead flesh, and she was not at all pleased about it. She also criticized the hunters' selfishness, saying that she wanted all her relatives at Santo André to share in her meat, not just the hunters' families. After Maxun Kwarain awoke from his dream-journey, he relayed the peccary's sentiments to others. Early in the morning, I found him sitting on my porch. "Get your tape recorder," he ordered. He wanted to record the new song that the peccaries had taught him, a song condemning the hunters' improper actions.

Maxun Kwarain's account of the female peccary's complaint about being stuck in her carcass, waiting to be freed by fire, suggests that roasting liberates a spirit from its body. This may have been an idiosyncratic interpretation, for most Wari' say that an animal's spirit jumps out of its body at the moment it is killed. After a spirit has left its carcass, it may linger in the vicinity. As long as some of its flesh (particularly its eyes) remains, the animal spirit may hang around, waiting to take revenge on the hunter or his family if they mistreat its carcass. Deer (especially *kotowa,* a species of brocket deer) are said to be most vengeful; when a hunter kills a deer, his children are supposed to eat the eyes first. Among other things, this makes it harder for the deer spirit to find those who killed it. If a roasted deer head remains uneaten and intact at nightfall, Wari' place a basket or mat over the head so that the deer spirit cannot see them through the eyes.

Resonances of this idea that animal spirits remain attached to their carcasses also emerged in an incident that Vilaça described, in which fifty white-lipped peccaries were killed in one day at Rio Negro-Ocaia and several people got sick with diarrhea after eating lots of meat. One shaman blamed the sickness on the slowness with which people consumed the meat. As long as even one peccary head remained uneaten, he told Vilaça, the peccary spirits would linger in the village, afflicting people with illness. Other shamans disagreed and said that the peccaries' spirits already had departed from their bodies and from the community at the moment when their carcasses began to be butchered. The rumbling of thunder that had been heard at that moment was said to have signaled their departure, for thunder is the sound of the drum that Naxo, a fish spirit, plays whenever the white-lipped peccary spirits emerge from the river or go home to their underwater abode (Vilaça 1992:68–69).

Just as there is no consensus about exactly when an animal spirit leaves its body behind, there is also no consensus about exactly when a dead person's spirit finally dissociates itself from its corpse. Wari' suggest various scenarios: the spirit separates when its body dies, when the corpse or carcass is dismembered, when roasting begins, or when the flesh has been eaten entirely. Vilaça (1992:69) suggests that "[t]his lack of definition about the exact moment of the liberation [of spirit from body] appears to reflect, not an incoherence among informants, but [the idea of] an analogy between cooking and devouring, as processes related to the destruction of the body." The relation between a human spirit and its human body cannot be a simple matter of the spirit being imprisoned in the corpse, since all Wari' agree that death occurs because the spirit has already left its body and gone to the underworld. What, then, is the relation between what happens to the corpse and what happens to the spirit?

* * *

In precontact Wari' funerals, the cutting and roasting of the corpse were thought to parallel the revival of the spirit in the underworld, where it had fallen into a deep sleep (*itam*) after drinking corn beer at the hüroroin festival in the underworld. At dawn on the final day of a hüroroin party, male hosts revive their unconscious male guests from their "death" in itam by bathing them with warm water (an act called *pixat* or *jök xain*). This bath begins at the feet and proceeds upward, bringing each body part back to life. When the water reaches the head, the men open their eyes and return to consciousness. In the same way, Towira Towira, the leader of the underworld party, revives the spirits of newly dead Wari'. As Santo André elders described this scenario, at the moment when the male affines began to dismember the corpse, the water spirits (Towira Towira's tribe) begin to carry water to bathe the dead person's spirit. As the cutting of the corpse proceeded on earth, the bathing began in the underworld. When the cutting was finished or (there were differences of opinion on this point) when the body parts were placed on the rack to roast, the bathing reached the spirit's head, and the spirit woke up (*kerek*): "*Wak na pain ka, kerek nain kom*" [He cuts (the corpse) here; (the spirit) wakes in the water].

Does this mean that the revival of the spirit depended on the dismembering and roasting or eating of the corpse? Wari' at Santo André are unanimous in asserting that Towira Towira's act of reviving the spirit does not depend, nor did it used to depend, on what is done to the corpse. They emphasize that Towira Towira revives all spirits alike, regardless of whether their corpses are eaten, burned, buried, or ravaged by vultures. They see little connection between the manner in which a body is disposed of and what happens to its spirit. Another argument against the belief that Wari' ate their dead in order to liberate the spirit or drive away the ghost is that it fails to explain why Wari' *ate* the corpse, for everyone agrees that the spirit regained consciousness when its corpse was cut or began to be roasted, not after it was eaten.[4]

While there is little support for an instrumentalist interpretation of mortuary cannibalism as something that Wari' considered necessary in order to liberate, drive away, or revive the spirit of the deceased, they clearly did believe that eradicating the body helped the spirit adjust to its new existence in the underworld. The spirits of newly dead people, like the spirits of recently killed animals, remain emotionally attached to their former lives, and the corpse is one of the strongest links to that former life. Even if they do not conceive of the corpse as a prison from which the spirit must be liberated, nor as an insurmountable impediment to a spirit's transition to its new existence in the otherworld, Wari' nonetheless recognize that the corpse's continuing existence makes it harder for the spirit to let go of ties to its former life. They express concern about the loneliness and homesickness that the newly dead experience and see the destruction of the corpse, like the destruction of the individual's house and personal possessions, as a way to help both the dead and their bereaved kin adjust. Not finding their homes or, in the old days, not finding their bodies, human spirits have fewer reasons to want to stay on earth. Some Wari' have told me that they think it may take longer today, when bodies are buried, for spirits to come to terms with their fate of existing in the realm of the dead—but others disagree with this assumption.

Wari' consistently identify the management of emotions, not the management of ghosts, as the main reason why it is essential to destroy traces of the dead. Their explanations for mortuary cannibalism also focus not on the problem of banishing ghosts or liberating spirits, but on the problem of how to transform emotional attachments that link bereaved individuals to the recently dead.

Breaking Bonds

Especially for individuals who have lived closely with the deceased, acknowledging the fact that the relationship is ended involves letting go of old patterns of behavior linked to that relationship in order to be able to develop new patterns for living without the deceased. In many societies around the world, mourners are expected to engage in various "tie-breaking" practices, in which things that are likely to remind them of a dead individual are destroyed, thrown out, given away, or transformed (Rosenblatt, Walsh, and Jackson 1976). Changes of residence and prohibitions on using the names of the dead are other forms of tie-breaking and finalizing acts. As the authors of a cross-cultural study of grief and mourning suggested, such practices may facilitate survivors' transition and reintegration into new social roles, especially new marital relations:

> . . . [I]n a long-term relationship such as marriage, innumerable behaviors appropriate to the relationship become associated with stimuli (sights, sounds, odors, textures) in the environment of the relationship. When death . . . makes it necessary to treat the relationship as ended and to develop new patterns of behavior, these stimuli inhibit the change, because they elicit old dispositions. To facilitate change, tie-breaking practices that eliminate or alter these stimuli seem to be of great value (Rosenblatt, Walsh, and Jackson 1976:67–68).

In societies with elaborate formal tie-breaking practices, widows and widowers tend to remarry at higher rates than in societies that do not emphasize such practices. Many societies that encourage remarriage also encourage the elimination of reminders of the deceased spouse, suggesting an understanding of the idea that this may help the surviving spouse form new attachments, remarry, and begin to make a new life.[5]

In North America, even in urban contexts, where social expectations about how mourners should behave are often minimal and flexible, some tie-breaking actions nonetheless are common, such as the practice of giving away or discarding a dead person's clothing and intimate toiletry items. Even without direct social pressures to do so, bereaved individuals often consciously or unconsciously find themselves adopting certain tie-breaking practices, such as avoiding certain rooms, places, or activities that are strongly associated with their memories of the deceased.

Fears that the ghosts of the dead may return to harm living people can also function as a distancing mechanism. "Apparently ghost fear provides a tie-breaking, not through elimination of reminders of the deceased, but *through altering the image of the deceased*. . . . [G]host fear may lead the bereaved to think of the deceased as something fearful in ways that motivate cutting ties with the deceased" (Rosenblatt, Walsh, and Jackson 1976:79; emphasis added). For Wari', the creepy images of jima reinforce the idea that mourners need to dissociate themselves from thoughts of the dead. From this perspective, the Wari' assertion that destroying a dead person's possessions aims *both* to wipe out memories *and* to prevent the ghost's return looks like an expression of different facets of the same impulse to change how the living think about the dead and to create some emotional distance between them. In this vision, ghosts are not just autonomous metaphysical entities; they are manifestations of continuing and problematic linkages between the living and the dead.

Memories and Grief

Wari' echo the views of many native Amazonians when they emphasize the need for mourners eventually to set aside their thoughts about the dead. While they recognize that it is good to think about and honor the deceased in the days and months after a death, they also say one must not dwell too long or too intensely on such memories. Gradual detachment from thinking about and remembering the dead is considered a desirable social goal, for endless remembering leads to endless sorrow (*tomi' xaxa*) that endangers individual health and productivity. The negative psycho-emotional process of grieving is described by the verb *koromikat,* which refers to the experience of missing, remembering, and thinking longingly about a lost or distant kinsperson, lover, or friend. Prolonged immersion in grief becomes harmful to oneself and one's dependents, for bereaved Wari' disengage from social life and do little work. They and their families do not eat as much or as well as usual. Wari' who are in deep mourning frequently become sick and often express desires to die.

In the intimacy of Wari' communal life, each death is a major tear in the social fabric. As bereaved family members struggle with their emotions, self-destructive behaviors are not uncommon. The concept of psychologically destructive effects of endless grieving is well developed in western psychology. In "Mourning and Melancholia," Freud described the dangers of excessive, prolonged attachments to lost objects. He distinguished between the normal mourning process and melancholia, a pathological state characterized by self-reproach and self-reviling, in which the melancholy individual desires to die as punishment for the loss of the loved object. It is unclear whether the sense of guilt at the core of Freud's concept of melancholia applies to the extremes of Wari' grief. Wari' mourners' self-destructive behaviors might express self-reproach or self-recrimination, but I have no evidence of this.

Wari' see mourners' self-destructiveness as an understandable but dangerous result of intense sorrow. Bereaved people sometimes say they have seen too many loved ones die and no longer want to go on living. I have observed two such cases. The first involved a childless widow in her fifties who lived at Ribeirão. When her eleven-year-old niece (to whom she was very close) suddenly developed a high fever and died a few days later, the aunt became extremely distraught, even more dramatically bereft than the dead girl's parents. When the fire was lit to burn her niece's house and possessions, the aunt burned all of her own clothes, saying they reminded her of being with her niece. Sobbing hysterically, she had to be restrained from throwing herself into the fire as well. When I arrived a few days after the funeral, she had withdrawn into a profound apathy. Wrapped in an old blanket, she did nothing but lie on her bed or huddle next to a small fire, staring blankly into the flames. There seemed to be nothing anyone could do to bring her out of her depression, and her relatives said she had not eaten since her niece had died. As she continued to refuse food, her family did not press her but treated her gently, lowering their voices in her presence and keeping a respectful distance.

"She won't eat," said her cousin. "She's sad; she just wants to die."

"She only thinks about the ones who have died," her nephew explained. As days went by, she seemed to be wasting away before our eyes. Already thin, she began to look painfully emaciated, cheekbones protruding under hollow eyes, skin dry to the touch. Her relatives tried to comfort her, and I lamely offered candy bars, but she just stared listlessly into the fire. It seemed as if she really intended to die, as Wari' say, "of sadness."

Then a truck arrived, bringing FUNAI's regional nursing director with a supply of medicines for the village pharmacy. He ordered the woman to be evacuated immediately to the Casa do Indio clinic in Guajará-Mirim, and she passively allowed herself to be led away. When I saw her later at the clinic in town, she had regained some weight after a series of intravenous feedings but still did not talk much and spent her time sitting alone at the far end of one of the porches.

At Santo André, Manim's hard-working wife, Tocohwet Pijo', had a similar experience. For years, she had suffered from a tuberculosis infection that had proven resistant to all available pharmaceutical treatments. (Drug-resistant tuberculosis and malaria are serious health problems in the Brazilian Amazon these days.) Tocohwet Pijo' was normally active and hard working, and her tuberculosis had been in a quiescent phase in early 1987 when a twenty-year-old girl named Topa' died. Although Tocohwet Pijo' was not closely related to Topa', she continued to cry for weeks after the funeral. Her daughter, Diva, said the girl's death had reminded her mother of deaths

12. Tocohwet Pijo' was an accomplished basket maker.

in their own family, especially the loss of her granddaughter Inácia, Diva's daughter whose body had never been sent home from Rio de Janeiro.

Tocohwet Pijo' began to spend most of her days indoors, lying on her bed. She seldom spoke and declined to eat more than a few morsels of food. Perhaps because the nutritional and emotional stresses weakened her immune response, her tuberculosis flared up with a vengeance. As constant coughing racked her lungs, she grew thin. "I'm going to die soon," she told her family. In a moment of morbid humor, she told her nephews and nieces, "My lungs are full of pus (*mowi*), so they won't be able to eat my corpse!" (Recall that Wari' did not cannibalize corpses with congested lungs.) Although her family responded with concern and expressions of affection, they did not try to force Tocohwet Pijo' to eat. She might have died, but again, FUNAI medical personnel intervened and took her to the Casa do Indio for treatment.

People in all the Wari' villages tell similar stories of mourners whose self-destructive grieving caused them to "die from sadness." Wari' recognize this as an ever present possibility in the mourning process. Although they consider it fitting to mourn a lost loved one and withdraw from social interactions and productive activities for some time after a death, they also are concerned that sorrow should not overwhelm mourners to the point that it threatens their health and productivity.

Memory-Work in Mourning

The downward spiral of grief about which Wari' express concern has much in common with Freud's concept of melancholia, in which normal processes of mourning slip into an unhealthy, obsessive grief revolving around unreconciled feelings of loss. In order for bereaved individuals to be able to return to normal patterns of work and social life, they need to "work through" their loss. What Freud called the "work of mourning" is essentially memory-work. He emphasized that in order to achieve a degree of emotional detachment, mourners must deal with and transform their perceived relationship to the dead person by going through a process in which they gradually confront their memories of the deceased one by one, accept the reality that their relationship to the deceased has ended, and let go emotionally of their attachments to the object of their loss. This process of detachment, according to Freud (1981a:245), is "carried out bit by bit, at great expense of time and cathectic energy, and in the meantime the existence of the lost object is psychically prolonged." The recollection of memories of the deceased is central to the process:

> Each single one of the memories and expectations in which the libido is bound to the object is brought up and hyper-cathected. . . . Each single one of the memories and situations of expectancy which demonstrate the libido's attachment to the lost object is met by the verdict of reality that the object no longer exists; and the ego . . . is persuaded by the sum of the narcissistic satisfactions it derives from being alive to sever its attachment to the object that has been abolished (Freud 1981a:245, 255).

Freud did not elaborate much more on how detachment develops out of the experience of remembering, but in an analysis of Javanese death customs, James Siegel (1983) suggested that an act of intentionally *re*-remembering can transform the original memory by overlaying it with a new memory: the memory of the *act* of remembering. He observed that "[b]y remembering a second time, it is possible to attach oneself to (hypercathect) the second memory, and relinquish the first. The second account establishes the memory qua memory or image, set apart therefore from any association with the content of other thoughts" (Siegel 1983:5).

In many lowland South American societies, bereaved individuals are expected to observe an extended period of seclusion or semiseclusion during which they spend time remembering and honoring the dead person and the events of his or her life. This intense remembering is supposed to be finite: at a certain point, mourners are expected to set aside their memories and forget about the dead person. This pan-Amazonian emphasis on "remember-ing to forget" (Taylor 1993) exemplifies the process that Debbora Battaglia (1991:3) has called "forgetting as a willed transformation of memory."

Wari' also see memory-work as the core of the work of mourning. They say that as time passes, bereaved individuals gradually must stop thinking so much about the dead person. This is partly a matter of setting aside one's memories and partly a matter of developing new images of the deceased to substitute for or overlay old memory-images. To accomplish this, Wari' em-phasize that, first of all, it is helpful to eradicate all material traces of the deceased's former presence, because these call up the dead person's image in the minds of those who knew him or her. They say that with fewer re-minders surrounding them, family members gradually begin to think less often of the dead and eventually should feel less sorrow.

Burning and Sweeping

Wari' emphasize vision and hearing as primary sources of knowledge and stimuli to memory. The sight of material objects and the sound of a dead person's name evoke memories, and they consider it essential to destroy or transform all such tangible reminders. In addition to burning the house and personal possessions of the deceased, close family members perform a ritual for transforming memories called *ton ho'*, "sweeping."[6] For several months after the death, adult consanguines of the deceased (especially senior rela-tives of the same sex as the deceased) make a series of trips to the forest to seek out every place associated with the dead person's memory: the spot where a hunter made a blind to wait for deer, places where a woman fished or felled a fruit tree, a favorite log where the dead person liked to sit. At each spot, they cut the vegetation in a wide circle. After it has dried, they return to burn the brush and sweep over the burned circle, thereby changing the appearance of the last earthly places where memories of the deceased might cling. Wari' who have done this say that while they perform these ac-tions, they cry and keen and think intensely about their lost relative. As they confront each place and the memories associated with it, they spend some time lingering over these memories, recalling and honoring the person's life. Each act of remembering is followed by an act of obliteration that radically alters the associated space. Afterwards, Wari' say, the burning and sweep-ing have changed the place so that "it is new, different." The memories and sentiments associated with the place change, so "there is not much sadness there."

Wari' say that in the past—until the 1960s or early 1970s—the ton ho' ritual was performed with more formality than it is today. These days, mourners who ton ho' simply go quietly to the forest and carry out the ritual. Other people learn of their actions when they encounter the altered landscape. Several months after Topa' died, I was walking with Quimoin and her sister Nacom on the main path between Santo André and Hon Xitot when we entered a large, open area that looked totally unfamiliar. Sunlight slanted through a scattering of trees standing amid charred remnants of logs. Young grasses and shrubs were flourishing everywhere, filling the clearing with a soft, brilliant green. I stopped in confusion, sure we had taken a wrong turn, for I knew I had never seen this sunlit clearing any of the dozens of times I had walked this path before.

"Come on, don't stop here! Let's go!" Nacom admonished. "Don't you know this place, Beth?"

"Where are we?" I asked, but neither woman would answer. As we walked on, they glanced nervously behind and to the side. Nacom whispered, "That's where they burned it; over there is where our brother-in-law saw the log." Finally, I figured it out: this was where Topa' had died. Hurrying through the forest with her grandmother, trying to catch up with a group of women and girls who were going off to gather fruit, Topa' had tripped on a log, fallen unconscious, and begun hemorrhaging. The clearing looked unfamiliar because it was newly made. Her father had performed ton ho' here, burning the log where his daughter fell and a ring of the surrounding forest.

Wari' suspect jima of lingering anyplace someone has died, but Nacom and Quimoin were especially nervous about this spot. A week earlier, the young husband of Topa''s sister had been walking through this clearing when he saw a long log floating through the air toward him as if it were being carried by an invisible person. Everyone knew it was the ghost (*jima*) of Topa' herself.

The effect that ton ho' had on the way Nacom and Quimoin responded to this spot in the forest was typical of other places where similar burnings had been carried out. The ritual burning and sweeping does not completely wipe out the association between the place and memories of the deceased individual, for when Wari' see such a place, they recognize that it has been burned intentionally, and they remember who has done it and why. What the transformation does is add more layers of images and associations on top of, or alongside, the thoughts of the dead person that the place evokes. Instead of seeing this place in the forest and thinking only about what happened to Topa' there, Nacom and Quimoin saw the new clearing, the altered space, and thought also about how her family had burned the spot and swept over it in order to forget her. The sight conveyed a message about her relatives' efforts to cope with their loss. After Topa"s brother-in-law encountered the ghostly floating log, that story became another prominent memory attached to the place. As Quimoin and Nacom walked through the clearing, fear of her ghost seemed to have edged out or overlaid thoughts about Topa' herself.

Before the contact, the attempt to destroy and transform tangible elements associated with the dead extended to destroying and transforming the corpse itself. Given the strength of Wari' ideas about the body's social meanings, it is understandable that a corpse is the most powerful reminder of all,[7] the visible embodiment of who the dead individual was in life. Replete with all the substances and experiences that the individual shared with others, the body is a tangible connection between the deceased and his or her close kin. As long as the corpse persists, it is a focus for bereft survivors' thoughts and actions. As a man from Rio Negro-Ocaia told Vilaça (1992:265), "If we bury, we think about where he [the deceased] walked, where he worked; we think about his skin being there in the earth still. With the fire it is good, it finishes all the body, we don't think more." In traditional funerals, mourners' dramatic expressions of identification with the dead person's body were followed by a dramatic sundering of these bonds, beginning with the dismemberment of the corpse.

The relationships, connections, and sentiments that corpses embody do not dissolve automatically at death but persist and must be addressed. In order to transform and silence the emotional attachments that link living people to their memories of the dead, and the spirits of the dead to their former lives, Wari' felt it necessary to destroy the body along with other traces of the dead person's life. Dismembering and roasting or burning the corpse set into motion a process of disassembling physical objectifications of the individual's social identity and social relations, a process ultimately intended to help the living feel differently about their loss.

Decomposing and Recomposing Images of the Dead in Lowland South America

The ways in which Wari' respond to death and cope with its aftermath have much in common with the practices of many other lowland South American peoples who also emphasize the need to distance the dead from the living and change mourners' memories. Avoiding the name, burning the house, and destroying or giving away the property of the dead are widespread practices among Amazonian Indians. In a brilliant essay on South American conceptions of personhood and death, Anne Christine Taylor noted that this eradication of visual and verbal traces is an attack on the features that constituted the uniqueness of the deceased, the features that gave the dead person a specific place in the network of human relationships. "Far from stressing continuity with the ancestors and enshrining their memory in names, epics or monuments, lowland Amerindians expend considerable time and ingenuity in losing their dead, forgetting their names and deeds and emphasizing their remoteness from the world of the living" (Taylor 1993:653). What Amazonian Indians tend to emphasize is the obliteration of the dead person as an *individual*. In the minds of the living, the deceased gradually moves from being remembered as a specific member of human society to being conceived in generic terms, as part of an amorphous community of ancestors.

The corpse is the most tangible evidence of who the dead individual was in life, but even after the corpse has been disposed of, the body continues to be a focus for remembering,[8] for mourners' images of the deceased are encapsulated most directly in visual memories of the person's physical appearance. When corpses are buried intact, there is little to differentiate them from visual memory-images of how the person looked when alive. As Taylor notes, "If biological death is not enough to separate the living from the dead, it is primarily because the dead are remembered, and remembered visually as living beings with a specific appearance" (1993:655) Given the felt need to transform mourners' experiences of remembering, it is not surprising that many lowland South American peoples emphasize how the bodies of the dead change their form so that they no longer look like they did when they were alive.

Native Amazonian societies take several distinct approaches to transforming mourners' memory-images of the dead. One approach is to emphasize how the physical appearance of an individual's spirit changes after death so that the spirit no longer looks like the person mourners knew. Another approach is to confront mourners with explicit images of how the corpse changes as it decays. Some native Amazonian cultures seem to have a near obsession with emphasizing images of rotting corpses and recounting the details of their progressive disintegration, their stench, and their pollution. A number of groups that bury corpses (and thus save mourners from having to see the actual process of decomposition) nonetheless evoke graphically detailed images of the process of their decay. Funeral oratory and mourning songs are full of references to flesh decaying, body fluids dry-ing up, and corpses being reduced to skeletons. Taylor (1993:665) explains that among the Jivaro of eastern Ecuador, mourning chants and songs begin by stressing the separation of the dead from the living and the progressive dissolution of the dead person's social identity and social ties, with the loss of his or her name and ability to see and hear. From these affirmations of the depersonalization of the deceased, mourners move into a "soul song," in which the dead person's physical appearance "is gradually ground into oblivion, through an obsessive and very graphic description of the rotting of the flesh and particularly of the face." Jivaroan mourners are bombarded with affirmations of the radical change in the dead person's identity, which is most explicitly evident in his or her altered visual appearance.

In some other South American societies, death practices force living people into direct encounters with signs of the corpse's decay, by allowing the corpse to rot while still exposed, or by disinterring the remains after the flesh has rotted. An even more direct way to modify mourners' images of the corpse is to dismember and burn, cook, or eat it before their eyes. In lowland South America, cannibalism and cremation tended to be public events witnessed by most members of a community, including especially the dead person's close relatives. In precontact Wari' funerals, from the moment the corpse left its relatives' arms, the family saw it progressively lose its individuality as it was butchered, cooked, and consumed in the generic manner in which all Wari' corpses were treated, regardless of distinctions of gender, age, or status.

Why Eat Rather Than Burn?

Ideas about human bodies, spirits, memory, and mourning explain why Wari' consider it essential to erase material traces of the dead, an imperative that used to include destroying the corpse. What these ideas do not explain is why Wari' preferred to destroy corpses by *eating* them. After all, burning is another way to eradicate remains, and Wari' considered cremation as effective as cannibalism in this regard. Yet they preferred to eat corpses rather than burn them whenever possible. Why did Wari' favor cannibalism over cremation? One might speculate that cannibalism was more effective in attenuating emotional attachments because it fragmented and dispersed the bodily remains in ways that cremation did not. When Wari' cremated a corpse, they did not scatter the ashes but buried them together beneath the floor of the house where the funeral was held. When the corpse was eaten, the uneaten body parts and funeral paraphernalia also were burned and buried in the floor, but the body parts that had been eaten were carried away in different directions in the bodies of the multiple individuals who had consumed them. However, this does not seem to be the way Wari' think about cannibalism, and I have never heard them mention the idea that living people carry bits of dead people in their bodies. They talk about cannibalism as a way to destroy the corpse, not to divide and disperse it.

A step toward a more illuminating understanding of why Wari' preferred to eat their dead is the recognition that cannibalism carried meanings that cremation did not. Burning evokes little more than loss and destruction, whereas eating evokes complex meanings related to food, especially meat, and the social relations (among individuals and families and between humans and animals) that produce food. If strands of cultural ideas about the body, memory, and emotion were the warp in the fabric of Wari' ritual responses to death, strands of ideas about animals and eating were the weft that, interwoven with these concepts, created the distinctive pattern of their practice of funerary cannibalism.

PART IV

EAT AND
BE EATEN

CHAPTER NINE

PREDATOR AND PREY

The distinct and respectful manner in which Wari' handled corpses at funerals emphasized the understanding that the human flesh was not ordinary meat. At the same time, dismembering, roasting, and eating the corpse obviously resembled the preparation and consumption of game. This ambiguity —the dissonance of the corpse that simultaneously was and was not like animal meat—was an ambiguity that gave the act of eating the dead much of its symbolic power. Wari' relate to animals in a multitude of ways, and identifying the corpse with aspects of animalness opened up a plethora of potential meanings to which mourners might respond in reorienting themselves and coming to terms with the new situation after a death.

"Eating is for animals," outsiders told the Wari' after the contact. "People are not animals; people are not meat to be eaten." In western thought, much of the revulsion that cannibalism provokes is a reaction against its apparent blurring of distinctions between humans and animals by treating human substance like animal meat. Equating a dead person's body with meat is likely to seem grossly insulting to the deceased, for most westerners think of animals as inferior and subordinate to people. In English, to treat someone "like a piece of meat" is a debasing objectification of the other.

Wari' cannibalism also carried a message of objectification, for it externalized the dead, graphically marking their new position outside the collectivity of living people. In the Wari' language, *karawa* (animal, meat) is a category that contrasts with *wari'* ("we," person, human being) (see Vilaça 1992). *Karawa* does not refer only to animals; in various contexts Wari' may apply the word *karawa* to almost any nonhuman (that is, non-Wari') thing, being, or entity. *Karawa* is not *wari'*. Treating the corpse *ak karawa*, "like meat," thus made a powerful statement about the status of the deceased. No longer *wari'*, no longer part of the collective "we," the dead were differentiated from living people, their bodies now like meat eaten by a community of living meat eaters to which the dead no longer belonged.

This is a point where Wari' exo- and endocannibalism converged. In eating both their enemies and their fellow Wari', they marked the distance and relation between themselves and the humans they ate as being analogous to the distance and relation between people and the animals they eat. Exocannibalism was accompanied by gestures that made this equation with animals an expression of contempt for a foreigner defined as a nonperson. Endocannibalism was performed with very different gestures, in which the animal analogy was neither dehumanizing nor degrading, but an evocation of positive images of eating and sharing meat.

Distance and difference were not the only meanings endocannibalism evoked, for Wari' do not think of eating as just the consumption of an object. They express a constant awareness that food is a product of social relations with others who gather, grow, kill, cook, and distribute it. Meat eating involves relations, not just with other people, but also with the animals that are killed and eaten. Wari' think of many of the animals they eat as powerful, wily, immortal spirits. Slaughtering and consuming them is not so much an act of human mastery over the nonhuman as a transaction that is an exchange in an ongoing dynamic of rivalry and exchanges between hunters and hunted.

Symbolically equating the dead with animals did not imply degradation of the deceased as it would in a society like my own, where most people consider animals a lower form of life. Wari' do not think of animals as subordinate to humans. Rather, they imagine that humans and certain animal spirits (the species called *jami karawa*) have the capacity to relate to each other more or less as equals, as antagonists who sometimes cooperate in wary partnership. This is possible because jami karawa are really human beings, in the sense that these animals' spirits are human, *wari'*. Because such animal spirits are human, Wari' believe they can deal with them much as they deal with other people.

Reciprocity is an organizing principle of Wari' social life, and one form it takes is reciprocal predation, an exchange in which participants kill and consume each other, alternately trading roles as predator and prey. One expression of this concept is the idea that certain diseases are the flip side of hunting: the major animals that Wari' hunt and eat have spirits that hunt and eat Wari', causing people to get sick and die. Reciprocal predation is also a theme in the intergroup parties of hüroroin and hütop, in which hosts symbolically kill and revive their guests, who may return the favor in another party later.

Reciprocal predation is central to Wari' concepts of death, for at the moment when a person dies, his or her spirit is said to be ritually "killed" (rendered unconscious in itam) at the underwater hüroroin party hosted by Towira Towira and the water spirits, who include the Wari' ancestors. These roles reverse when the underworld spirits, incarnated as white-lipped peccaries, come out of the water to be hunted by living Wari'. Dynamics of reciprocal predation thus organize Wari' cosmology in multiple levels of relationships: among Wari' subgroups, between humans and animal spirits, and between the living and the dead. The consumption of the dead at funerals encapsulated a vision of the human position in this cosmology, the destiny to be both meat eater and meat.

At the core of Wari' understandings of life and death is the recognition that predation is seldom a one-way street. Rather, to be a predator, one sometimes also must be prey. Members of a group that kills and consumes members of another group will be killed and consumed by that other group if they have an ongoing relationship. The work of culture, as it was created by Wari' culture heroes and as it is perpetuated in the institutions and cosmological dynamics they established, is to channel some relations to predatory outsiders (be they carnivorous spirits or potentially hostile neighbors) into social exchange arrangements in which Wari' have the opportunity to be predators and not just prey.

A good starting point for an exploration of ideas about animals, predation, and reciprocity is the story that explains when and why the Wari' ancestors began to practice endocannibalism. Appendix A presents one version of this origin myth.[1] This tale links mortuary cannibalism's origin to the beginnings of true Wari' culture, when their ancestors acquired fire and became farmers and hunters. The story has two parts that mirror each other with parallel tales of how a selfish, antisocial individual hoarded fire until she or he was tricked by wily Wari', who stole it. In both cases, gaining possession of the fire and the ability to cook food meant that Wari' would themselves be eaten. In the first part of the story, fire belonged to an elderly woman who was both a jaguar and a barbaric cannibal who preyed on her own Wari' kin and ate them raw. When people stole her fire, they were able to cook and eat birds, but jaguars (which eat people) and other carnivores were unleashed into the world. The second part of the story explains how a selfish Wari' man named Pinom captured the fire and kept it to himself until a shaman (in the guise of a frog) stole some embers and shared the fire with other Wari'. Once they had fire, Wari' could clear fields, grow and cook corn, and kill and cook animals. Yet, consistent with the tendency toward mutualism in their social arrangements, after they became meat eaters, Wari' were obliged to be cooked and eaten themselves when they died.

It was Pinom who started the practice of endocannibalism. Angry at the theft of his fire, he swore at the Wari', saying, "Now you will have to roast your children!"

From the Jaguar-Cannibal's Fire

This story presents the mythic origin of Wari' endocannibalism, which came with the acquisition of fire. The tale of how the shaman-frog stole fire from selfish Pinom reprises the pattern in the first story, in which bird-boys stole fire from their selfish grandmother, the jaguar-cannibal-crone. In both cases, Wari' used trickery to get fire so they could cook and live as civilized people, and as a consequence, something fundamental changed in their world. Just when the people who had climbed into the sky acquired the fire that would allow them to cook and eat animals, jaguars and other carnivores came into existence. When Wari' gained the means to prey on animals, animals began to prey on people. And when the frog-shaman stole Pinom's fire and Wari' began to cook and eat corn and meat, they had to begin to roast their own dead. In Jimon Maram's version of this story, which is the version presented in Appendix A, Pinom tells the Wari' to roast their children but says nothing about eating them or about what to do with adult corpses. However, Jimon Maram and other Wari' with whom I have talked interpreted Pinom's statement as a general injunction to practice endocannibalism after the death of anyone, not just children. This is clearer in another storyteller's version, in which Pinom's last words are, "You will die! Your children will die a lot! You will eat yourselves; you will roast yourselves!" The point is the reflexivity implied in the possession of fire, the fact that it put Wari' in the position of being able to kill as well as be killed, being able to cook but also be cooked.

Wari' do not see Pinom's words as some terrible curse, nor do they think of cannibalism as a horrible punishment meted out in retribution for their ancestors' thievery. No one regards the mythic precannibalistic existence as a better life. On the contrary, before their ancestors had fire, they were helpless victims, exploited and preyed upon by the avaricious jaguar-cannibal-grandmother who devoured children raw. Possessing fire empowered Wari' in multiple ways, liberating them to become predators themselves, hunters of animals and eaters of meat, which they consider the best of all foods.

The story is also about the Wari' people's empowerment as farmers, for with fire, they could clear fields (by the slash-and-burn method) and grow crops and cook plant foods. Before they had fire, Wari' had no crops and subsisted mostly on raw forest foods—palm hearts, nuts, and fruits. Fire made them civilized farmers and eaters of corn, which Wari' regard as the most nourishing plant food, essential for creating strong, healthy bodies and equally essential to the rituals and parties that structure relations among members of different groups.

Fire also empowered Wari' in their relations to enemy outsiders, wijam. Though the story of Pinom concerns only the origin of the practice of eating their own dead, not the practice of eating enemies, Wari' see the ritual control of fire in relation to the spirits of destructive natural forces as empowering them in killing and eating enemies as well. As described in Chapter 2, when a group of warriors set out to attack an enemy, the expedition's ritual leader carried a special bundle of slow-smoldering firebrands (muruhut). During the warriors' journey toward their encounter with the enemy, the fire bearer had to treat this fire bundle with utmost care and observe a stringent set of behavioral restrictions, for if he touched water or handled the firebrands disrespectfully, violent storm spirits (topo) would emerge from the water and assault the war party. To be in the forest during such a storm is always dangerous, but for warriors, it was calamitous, for a topo storm was a sign that their enemy-killing venture would fail and that the war party had to turn around and go home.

If all went well, when the war party found an enemy to attack, the ritual leader who carried the firebrands untied the bundle (bound with the type of liana used at funerals to tie the corpse-roasting firewood) and gave each warrior a smoldering brand to carry in a small basket on his back.[2] The ritual leader then chose the moment to attack, shot the first arrow, and was honored as the "true" killer of the enemy. When the warriors regrouped after the attack, they recombined their firebrands to kindle a cooking fire to roast the enemy's body parts so others could eat them later. Thus, Wari' identified the ritual control of fire as fundamental to collective human agency in warfare, just as the myth of Pinom identified the domestic control of fire as fundamental to the life-sustaining productive activities of farming, hunting, and cooking.

* * *

Wari' with whom I have discussed the story of Pinom have considered it transparently logical that gaining fire and the ability to cook meant that people would be cooked and eaten themselves. An echo of the equanimity with which my informants seemed to regard this connection can be heard at the end of the story, when Pinom tells the people, "Now you will have to eat your children." The Wari' shaman does not protest or complain. Instead, with quintessentially Wari' attitude, he points out to Pinom, "You, too. You will roast *your* children, too."

Although the story of Pinom presents the mythic explanation for when and why Wari' began to practice endocannibalism, individual Wari' do not seem to connect it to their own motives for engaging in cannibalism. Of the dozens of elders whom I have asked, "Why did you eat the dead?," not one has mentioned Pinom. "It's only a story," said Jimon Maram when I asked him directly. Tokorom Mip agreed: "It doesn't tell why *we* ate the body."

At the level of cultural ideas and symbols, the story of Pinom and the jaguar-cannibal's fire is yet another reflection of the patterns of predation and reciprocity that permeate Wari' cosmology, rituals, social arrangements, and eschatology. Another area in which mutual predation is a prominent theme is Wari' ideas about human relations to two major categories of spirits: the animal spirits called *jami karawa* and the water spirits of the underworld (*jami kom*), which also can become animals. Wari' imagine the worlds of both kinds of spirits as parallel universes that mirror certain features of Wari' society. All these spirits are thought to be essentially human, and they relate to living people in some of the same ways that Wari' subgroups relate to one another, with an awareness of the potential for both antagonism and cooperation. In the mirror of their imaginings about animals' spirits, Wari' see their own self-images. As people who pride themselves on being hunters and, in the past, warriors par excellence, Wari', not surprisingly, perceive some of the most vivid reflections of their own humanity in images of the jaguar.

Jaguar Reflections

The Wari' word for jaguar, *kopakao'*, probably derives from *ko' pa' kao,* "one who kills to eat." As the most powerful predator of the Amazonian forest, the jaguar embodies the dangerous, unpredictable, and deadly forces that exist outside society and beyond human control. At the same time, the jaguar is also human and highly social. Jaguars are said to live in villages under the water, and some Wari' tell of having seen a jaguar dive into a river and not resurface, having gone down to its underwater home.

Jaguars are linked to mortuary cannibalism in several ways. In the story about Pinom, mortuary cannibalism began when Wari' acquired the fire that originally belonged to the crone from whose burning body jaguars and other carnivores emerged. Jaguars also are said to be the only animal that practices mortuary cannibalism. According to Santo André villagers, jaguar funerals are just like precontact Wari' funerals, except that, as far as they know, jaguar mourners eat only the head and burn the rest of the corpse. They say they know this as a result of something that happened in the Negro-Ocaia area many years ago. As Quimoin Oro Eo told this story, a kinsman of hers named Oro Jein Oro Nao' was in the forest when a jaguar attacked and killed him. Men from Oro Jein's village found his corpse and tracked down the jaguar who had killed him. After shooting it, they took the jaguar's head as a trophy, which they placed in the men's house (*kaxa'*) in their village.

At Oro Jein's funeral, his relatives and friends were crying over his corpse, when they looked up and were startled to see the dead jaguar's relatives (who looked like regular people) walking into the village. The jaguar-people went to the kaxa' where their jaguar kinsman's head lay and held a funeral of their own, in which they ate some of the head. The air was filled with crying and keening pouring from the two funerals simultaneously. Both Oro Jein's corpse and the other remains of the jaguar's head were cremated. (Oro Iram, who was listening to Quimoin tell this story, explained that people did not eat Oro Jein's corpse because his flesh was completely rotten by the time they found his body.) After the jaguar mourners finished crying and eating, they left quietly and went back to the forest.

The close identification that Wari' perceive between themselves and jaguars is most explicit in the idea that human and jaguar perspectives on reality are mirror images of each other. Wari', of course, perceive themselves as people and see jaguars as animals. For their part, however, jaguars perceive themselves as people and see Wari' as jaguars. Wari' like to illustrate this reversal by describing what happens when a jaguar attacks a person. An ordinary person (that is, someone who is not a shaman) sees the jaguar as a feline with claws and teeth, walking on all fours. The jaguar, however, sees himself as a man walking upright and carrying a bow and arrows, for his claws are the bow, and his teeth are the arrows. When this jaguar-hunter meets a person, to the jaguar's eyes, the person looks like a jaguar, so he shoots it. An ordinary person observing this attack would see a beast ripping into human flesh and eating it raw. But from the jaguar's own perspective, he has used a knife to butcher the carcass, and he carries the meat home in a basket for his wife to roast. Besides seeing Wari' as jaguars, jaguars also may see Wari' as *wijam,* human enemies. After a jaguar kills a person, the jaguar-warrior lies in a hammock in ritual seclusion, like Wari' warriors did after killing enemies, and drinks sweet corn chicha that his wife prepares. What looks and tastes like chicha to the jaguar-warrior is really his victim's blood.

Wari' ideas about parallels between humans and animals are more elaborate with regard to jaguars than with regard to any other species except white-lipped peccaries. Wari' see jaguars in their own image and see themselves in the jaguar. In hunting, in warfare, and in the rites of mortuary cannibalism, they have identified with the predatory powers that sprang from the original jaguar-cannibal's fire.

The Humanity of Animal Spirits

The jaguar belongs to, and in some ways is the essence of, the category of animal spirits called *jami karawa.* Like jaguars, all jami karawa perceive themselves as people and tend to see Wari' as animals. The primary species that Wari' classify as jami karawa include jaguars, brocket deer (*Mazama americana* and *M. rondoni*), white-lipped peccaries (*Tayassu pecari*), collared peccaries (*Tayassu tajacu*), capuchin monkeys (*Cebus* sp.), tapirs (*Tapirus* sp.), fish, bees, snakes, and a carnivore called *orotapan,* which I cannot identify with a single species.[3] Wari' identify *orotapan* variously: as fox, wolf, or *cachorro da mata,* "forest dog."

The source of a jami karawa animal's humanity is annatto, the fruit whose seeds are ground to make the red body paint that is a symbolic marker of human (Wari') identity. All jami karawa carry annatto in their bodies, along with the fruit of the babassú palm, which yields a body oil that is mixed with annatto to make the paint. A spirit that has annatto is human and has transformative powers. So closely is annatto identified with a spirit's ability to jamu (in the sense of manifesting itself in human form) that when I asked shamans whether certain species do or do not jamu, they often responded by saying, "No, that animal has no annatto," or, "Yes, it carries annatto in its body."

Only shamans, with their special powers of vision, are able to see and communicate with jami karawa in their true human forms. Conversely, the only Wari' whom such animals readily perceive as human beings are shamans. Several shamans explained that, when they walk alone in the forest, animal spirits look like people who speak the Wari' language and converse with them. The most powerful shamans, like Maxun Kwarain, may see all jami karawa as Wari', but most shamans say they perceive as human only the particular species with which they themselves are identified.

Wari' believe that jami karawa live in communities like precontact Wari' villages, with family dwellings and a men's house. Some species have fields where they grow crops; others hunt and roast their food. Some are fond of singing and dancing. Although different species live in separate villages and have distinct food preferences and other customs, all are part of one society in which the various species are analogous to Wari' subgroups. Some people even talk about animal groups using the *oro-* prefix that designates a collectivity such as a Wari' subgroup or a foreign population: they speak of Oro Min' (Tapir People), Oro Komem (Deer People), Oro Kataxik (Collared Peccary People), and so on. Wari' imagine the various species interacting much as Wari' subgroups do: intermarrying, throwing parties for one another, and punishing adultery with mixita fights. (Spots on a deer's hide are said to be marks from such beatings.)

When members of different species marry, one spouse changes its species to match its partner, for species identities are fluid and interchangeable among jami karawa. As people at Santo André explained it, fish spirits can become white-lipped peccaries or orotapan, and orotapan can become white-lipped peccaries or fish. Jaguars, orotapan, and fish can change at will into deer, collared peccaries, or capuchin monkeys, and vice versa.[4] White-lipped peccaries have an odd link to jaguars: it seems that, in the past, jaguars were also called *mijak,* although today *mijak* refers to white-lipped peccaries.[5] Bees originated as jaguars too, for a story tells us that honey came into being when a jaguar leapt high onto a tree trunk and turned into a hive of *xinto,* the most powerful medicinal honey. Among jami karawa species, only snakes are not identified with jaguars, for snakes are unique in that they are the vengeful spirits of Wari' who died of snakebite.[6]

The notion that animals can change their species identities at will appeals to Wari' imaginations. A number of individuals appreciatively explained that a spirit that wants to eat fruit becomes a deer, then changes into a jaguar when it wants to eat fish. The only limit to such transformations is that jami karawa can become only other jami karawa species; they cannot become non-jami karawa species, nor can they become inanimate objects. This fluidity of identity begs the question of what meaning species identity has if it can be acquired and discarded so easily. The answer is that species identity has limited significance, for Wari' see physical bodies as temporary incarnations through which spirits perceive and act in the material world. While incarnated in a particular body, an individual spirit acts from the perspective of that animal's attributes, but since a spirit can change its external identity by changing its bodily form, species distinctions are little more than metaphysical cosmetics.

Wari' shamans can change their identities, too. When I first met the Lage shaman Timain Oro Mon, for example, he was a fish shaman. When I saw him two months later, he had become a jaguar shaman because, he said, he got tired of being a fish. "I didn't get full eating," Timain explained, because fish eat only a few foods. As a jaguar spirit, he ate lots of meat, and his belly was full when he returned from his nighttime journeys.

Perspectivism and Human-Animal Relations

A fascination with the creative power of shifts and reversals of perspective, especially shifts between human and animal identities and points of view, is a fundamental principle in many lowland South American cultures. Viveiros de Castro (1996, 1998) calls this orientation "perspectivism." Sylvia Caiuby's (1997) study explores the way the Bororo of Mato Grosso form self-images based on how they imagine that others perceive them. In this "play of mirrors," others serve as a mirror into which Bororo society looks to find an image of itself, in a complex process of reflection and self-reflection.

Among the Wari', the play of mirrors takes many forms, especially in relation to animals. In another expression of the pattern in which predators and prey switch positions, jami karawa cause sickness and death by hunting humans in the same way that Wari' hunt jami karawa. When jami karawa attack a person's spirit, they shoot magical arrows that cause sickness, pain, and fever and interfere with blood circulation. Shamans often extract from their patients' bodies bits of wood or reed which they say are spirits' arrow tips. Like human hunters, jami karawa who wish to kill aim at the heart, where the wound makes blood collect and thicken in the chest. When an animal spirit attacker removes the heart of its human victim's spirit and carries it away to eat, the person's physical body dies. Some Wari' imagine that animal spirits eat the heart raw, while others think they roast it.

Alternatively, jami karawa may attack in their animal forms, especially when their motive is not to kill but to recover annatto or other magical fruits that the person has swallowed. A hunter who kills a jami karawa animal is supposed to ask a shaman to remove any magical fruits the carcass contains, but nowadays, hunters seldom bother to do so. If someone swallows its invisible fruits, the animal's spirit may enter the person's body and begin to eat his or her innards in order to recover its fruits. As long as the spirit stays in the outer flesh, the person will just be sick; but if the attack progresses to the heart, the person dies. As evidence that animal spirits eat their victims' internal organs, Wari' point out that, in the past, when they cut open corpses in preparation for cannibalism, the liver and other internal organs often appeared to be all chewed up, pocked with tooth marks. This is interesting from a medical standpoint, since ascites, a liver disease that can be caused by intense or repeated bouts of malaria and other infections, leaves a pockmark pattern on the liver.

In English, there is a saying "You are what you eat," but Wari' might turn this around to say that you become what eats *you*. When an animal spirit enters someone's body and begins to eat it, the victim's human spirit may begin to turn into an animal of the same species. Some shamans claim to have seen patients' spirits in the process of acquiring animal features, such as a tail or fur. Sick adults and children sometimes moan or grunt in ways that resemble animal sounds, and their care givers interpret these vocalizations as alarming evidence that the animalization of the patients' spirits is underway. Elders say that, in the past, sick people's expressions of animalization were more common and dramatic than they are today.

By the time the victim of such an animal spirit attack dies, the person's spirit-body has become an animal carcass, which the attacking spirit carries off to eat. This animalization does not seem to affect the ultimate destiny of the person's spirit, for most Wari' agree that, like other ordinary Wari', the victim's spirit, in its true human form, goes to the underwater realm of the dead. The fine points of metaphysics about which I pestered them (with questions such as, when the victim of such an attack dies, does he or she have one spirit or two, human or animal?) do not seem to concern Wari' much. What does concern them is the question of why animal spirits attack and what can be done about it.

Wari' believe that when jami karawa attack people, they do so because the animal spirit misperceives the person as an animal of its own kind. One well-known example is the story of the uncanny experience of a man named Tokwan who lived in the Negro-Ocaia area before the contact. Tokwan was a deer spirit shaman, and one day he went to visit his friend, a male deer spirit (*jamikon kotowa*). To Tokwan's eyes, the deer and his family looked like people. The deer husband had just come home from hunting, and game was roasting on the hearth. His wife served Tokwan a dark, sweet beverage made of the purple fruit that deer spirits carry in their bodies.

At first glance, Tokwan thought the roasting meat was venison, but when he took a closer look with his shamanic vision, he saw that it was really a Wari' man he knew who lived in a different village. From the deer spirits' perspective, they—the deer spirits and Tokwan, the deer shaman—were human beings, and the dead man's corpse was venison.

When Tokwan returned home, he told the people in his village that the man was dead. Not long afterwards, a messenger arrived bringing news of the man's death and a summons to his funeral.

When jami karawa attack people and make them sick, they do so because they see Wari' as enemies or animals, as different from themselves. If a core dynamic of Wari' cosmology is the equivalence and reversibility of human and animal identities, its core irony is that people and animals ordinarily are unable to perceive their common identity. Embodiment separates them with a veil of illusion, so that people ordinarily perceive animals only as animals, while animals see themselves as human and people as animals or enemies. This illusion is fundamental to Wari' existence; without differentiation between people and animals, there could be no hunting or fishing. The downside is that animal spirits attack and kill human beings with disease.

If the dynamic of lethal reciprocity is inalterable, Wari' nonetheless can attempt to prevent, divert, or combat specific attacks by animal spirits. This is the job of shamans, who can mediate between people and animal spirits because an animal spirit recognizes a shaman as a human being and forms a relationship with him. Since animals attack when they see ordinary people as animals, one of a shaman's most effective strategies is to try to persuade an animal spirit attacker that its victim is human, not animal or enemy prey. Shamans have some leverage with their companion species because of the kinlike bonds they share. Shamans say they usually address their animal spirit companion as *aji'*, "elder brother," a term Wari' men use in various contexts to express amicable intentions toward one another. The bond between a shaman and his animal spirit companion means that when such an animal spirit makes someone sick, a shaman whose spirit is of the same species as the attacker has the best chance of persuading it to desist by telling the attacking spirit that its victim is Wari', a human being like itself. Alternatively, a shaman may act in his own animal spirit form to combat certain other species. For example, a jaguar shaman can expect to win a fight against a fish spirit, for jaguars eat fish.

When animal spirits recognize Wari' as people like themselves, they tend to treat them kindly. Though it may seem paradoxical, jaguars and anacondas (*Eurectes murinus,* the giant water snake that kills its prey by coiling around it), which are the two species that kill people most dramatically, are thought to be the most helpful spirits. Both are said to have great powers for healing and to be willing to travel long distances to assist a shaman in curing. Anacondas, however, are seldom seen these days, and shamans rarely talk about them. Jaguars and white-lipped peccaries dominate contemporary discourses about shamanism, and the kinship bonds that shamans share with these and other animal spirits are the primary source of their power to heal.

Carnivores and Cannibals

If jami karawa are really human, then when Wari' eat animals of these species, they engage in a kind of cannibalism—albeit cannibalism masked by the outward bodily differences between people and animals and balanced by the fact that jami karawa hunt and eat Wari' in return. Far from considering cannibalism deviant or inferior as a mode of consumption, the pattern of precontact Wari' food practices implicitly suggests that cannibalism based in a relationship of reciprocity is the only proper form of meat eating. This is not a principle that I have heard Wari' state directly; I came to see the connection only when I began to unravel the puzzle of which species Wari' do and do not categorize as jami karawa.

There are many animals in their environment that the people of Santo André do not consider jami karawa, including anteaters, armadillos, spider monkeys (*Ateles* sp.) and several other monkey species, caiman, paca, agouti, capybara, and all species of birds. The question of why some animals, and not others, are thought to have human spirits perplexed me for a long time. Wari' were no help in answering it; they say they simply know which animals have human spirits and which do not. A partial solution appeared when I looked at how jami karawa species fit into precontact patterns of predation and realized that jami karawa comprise two kinds of animals. Some are predators or venomous animals: jaguars, orotapan, and snakes. Wari' believe these animals kill people, and hunters will kill them on sight. The other, nonpredator jami karawa species—deer, peccaries, capuchin monkeys, and tapirs—are (with one exception discussed below) all of the mammals that the precontact Wari' considered good and completely safe to eat. These species are hunters' preferred prey, and they also are the spirits that prey on Wari' and cause disease and death.

Wari' categorize animals according to how safe they are to eat. *'Iri karawa* (real animals) are the primary edible species, whose meat anyone can eat.

Almost all Wari' agree that deer, peccaries, tapirs, capuchin monkeys, and spider monkeys are 'iri karawa.[7] Animals that Wari' consider inedible or unhealthy to eat are called *kaji karawa* (strange animals or bad animals). Animals that people at Santo André deem inedible include jaguarundi, ocelot, otter, porcupine, tree squirrel, opossum, rat, bat, freshwater dolphin, caiman, and raptorial birds (hawks, owls, and vultures). Animals considered edible but not healthy to eat include armadillos (*Priodontes giganteus* and two *Dasypus* species), three-toed sloth (*Bradypus tridactylus*), agouti (*Dasyprocta agouti*), agouti paca (*Agouti paca*), capybara (*Hydrochoerus hydrochaeris*), coati (*Nasua nasua*), and titi monkey (*Callicebus torquatus*). Wari' believe that these species' flesh, blood, or fat can stunt the growth of children and cause illness or deformity in adults. Anyone in a state of growth or procreation should not eat these meats; they are safe only for the elderly or (in the case of a few species) for unmarried adolescents. Before the contact, Wari' seem to have followed these food rules fairly closely, but these days, many families eat kaji karawa (especially paca and agouti) even though they admit there is some risk in doing so. Regardless of how lax they are about food rules these days, most Wari' still think of the primary 'iri karawa—deer, peccaries, tapirs, capuchin monkeys, and spider monkeys—as the only "real" animals that one ideally ought to eat.

How does being good to eat relate to having a human spirit? Comparing the list of 'iri karawa mammals and the list of jami karawa mammals reveals that all but one of the good-to-eat mammals have human spirits, while none of the more unhealthy species (kaji karawa) has human spirits. Safe, nourishing meat comes only from animals with human spirits; the meat of animals that lack human spirits is dangerous to eat. In other words, cannibalism—humans consuming humans—is the most proper form of meat eating.

If cannibalism is the ideal form of carnivorousness, it is not a cannibalism that asserts one group's dominance over the other, but a cannibalism of mutualism. The animals Wari' consider best to kill and eat are the same ones that attack and eat Wari' in illness, though they also create shamans to cure such afflictions. The relationship between people and these animal spirits is a give-and-take dynamic of eating and being eaten.

* * *

Spider monkeys are the glaring exception to the preference for eating animals with human spirits. Wari' unanimously agree that spider monkeys are 'iri karawa, a preferred game animal whose meat is fine for everyone to eat. Yet unlike the other good-to-eat mammals, spider monkeys are not jami karawa. They do not have human spirits, do not create shamans, and do not cause illness.

This anomaly may relate to the fact that, although spider monkeys are not human spirits, they are distant relatives of the Wari'. According to a well-known story, long ago, all spider monkeys were male. Wanting a wife, one spider monkey persuaded some Wari' men to let him marry their sister. Eventually, this woman turned into a spider monkey herself, and today's spider monkeys are her descendants—which makes them related to Wari' by marriage. Relations between families of affines are supposed to be based on reciprocity: ideally there should be more marriages between the families involved, but at a minimum, affines should give one another meat once in a while. Spider monkeys cannot give people spouses, but they do provide meat by allowing Wari' to hunt them freely without retaliation. The spider monkey's anomalous position as the only 'iri karawa that is not jami karawa— that is, as the only preferred game whose spirit does not attack people— thus fits a logic of affinal relations. It also fits the logic of endocannibalism: spider monkeys are affines, and thus it is proper to eat them.

The principles underlying Wari' categorizations of animal foods suggest that ideally one ought to eat only those with whom one has established an exchange relationship. Social exchange is sustainable only on the basis of reciprocity; thus, one will be eaten by those whom one eats. To live as a fully civilized human being is to act as both predator and prey, eater and eaten, in a cosmic dynamic set in motion when the mythic Wari' ancestors captured the jaguar's fire, from which culture and cannibalism were born.

The Underworld Society of Animals and Ancestors

The human destiny to be prey as well as predator is enacted at the moment of death, when a person's spirit is "killed" at the underworld's hüroroin party. This ritual killing and subsequent revival of the spirit initiate the newly dead individual into the underworld society, from which he or she eventually will emerge as a peccary to be hunted and eaten by living Wari'.

The Wari' ancestors' villages are located under the deep waters of the larger rivers. Each subgroup has its own underworld village, located near the area where the group lived before the contact. The villages of dead Oro Mon are under the Lage River; the Oro Eo ancestors' villages are in the upper Negro River; and so on. Santo André villagers who are descended from the Dois Irmãos population say that their ancestors' homes are beneath the main channel of the Pacaas Novos River and in some of its deep flooded inlets, which local Brazilians call *bahias*.[8]

When Wari' die, their spirits go to live in the underwater village where their close dead relatives dwell. These communities resemble precontact Wari' settlements, with houses and fields where the ancestors grow corn and other crops. People work, but life is easy, food is abundant, and the ancestors feast on garden produce and wild fruits and nuts. One of the biggest differences from mortal life is that there is no hunting or fishing in the world of the dead, because there are no animals. The animals that make their homes beneath the water—fish, white-lipped peccaries, jaguars, and tapirs—look like human beings when they are underwater.

The story of Jao Panajü tells of a time when all animals disappeared from the earth, finally emerging from the water (*paxikom*) when Wari' summoned them to attend a festival (Vilaça 1989: Appendix III). Today, Wari' still see the water as home to the most powerful animals. The underwater world is simultaneously a source of animal fertility and the source of human death.

Throughout much of Amazonia, ancestors are thought to live in a sort of parallel social world, a society that exists outside the world of the living and differs from it in key respects. As Taylor (1993) has noted, there is an emphasis on the essential foreignness or otherness of the ancestors, who often are conceived as a sort of neighboring tribe or species. Sometimes this social difference is expressed in metaphors of enmity, with the ancestors being seen as hostile, predatory, and even cannibalistic. Sometimes it is expressed in an emphasis on the positive social features that differentiate the ancestors' world from that of the living.

Manuela Carneiro da Cunha (1981) has noted that native Amazonian visions of the world of the dead are a "free field of fabulation," where human imaginations may construct images of possible societies untroubled by the everyday realities that plague the living. The world of the ancestors often appears as a kind of utopia where hunger, disease, deformity, aging, and social strife are abolished. For some lowland South American peoples, the afterlife is a world without marriage or affines, where everyone is blood kin and thus exempt from obligations to in-laws and from the conflicts affinal relations can generate.[9] For Wari', however, death does not abolish marriage and affinity, for their ancestors may remarry and even give birth to new spirit children. Instead, what is strikingly absent in Wari' visions of the afterlife is the distinction between humans and animals, the illusion of bodily differences that masks their common humanity. The world of the dead is a purely human world in which all spirits have human form. Without animals, there is no hunting of animals, and since there are no animal spirits, there is also no illness.

Water Spirits

When someone is dying, his or her spirit is said to leave the body and walk along a long path that leads below the water to the realm of the dead. There, the spirit is greeted by the leader of the underworld, a giant man named Towira Towira. His influence over the movements of the underworld spirits that appear as fish and white-lipped peccaries resembles the power of the Masters of Animals figures that control animal fertility and the movements of game in a number of other Amazonian societies.[10]

Wari' images of Towira Towira emphasize sexual and fertility-related attributes. *Towira* means "testicle," and the character's doubled name commemorates the huge size of his genitalia, which hang below his knees. Towira Towira's wife, who seems to have no name, is also a giant, with pendulous breasts and exaggerated female sexual organs. Although Towira Towira and his wife look human, they are not Wari' ancestors. Rather, they are *xikun wari'*, "other people," a term Wari' use these days to describe Indians from other tribes. Towira Towira's speech is said to be intelligible to Wari', but some elders recall words from his language that are not in the Wari' vocabulary.

When human spirits arrive in his underwater village, Towira Towira greets them as his guests, and his wife offers fermented corn chicha. If a spirit drinks this beer, the physical body he or she left behind on earth dies, while underwater, the person's spirit falls into itam, the state of rigid unconsciousness equated with death.[11] In earthly hüroroin, when a guest falls unconscious, the party's main host may cry, "I've killed my prey!" Thus, Wari' envision death as an act of ritual predation in which a human spirit is symbolically killed in a festival hosted by the spirits of the underworld.

The spirits of Wari' ancestors live in their own villages, apart from Towira Towira's group, but they belong to the larger underworld society of which he is the leader. As time passes, the spirits of Wari' ancestors seem to lose their individuality and gradually blend into the amorphous category of generic underworld spirits. Wari' use the term *jami kom*, "water spirits," to refer to all members of the underworld society, including both their own ancestors and the nonancestral beings from Towira Towira's group. The ancestral and nonancestral spirits act together in some contexts and separately in others, and they have distinct powers and relationships to living people.

When jami kom leave the water, they take on the bodies of animals. The Wari' ancestors can become only white-lipped peccaries, but the non-ancestral water spirits can assume several forms: they can become white-lipped peccaries or orotapan, but most often they appear as fish.

Wari' think of white-lipped peccaries mostly as the spirits of their own ancestors. The ancestor-peccaries are a generally positive force, for they bring meat, help shamans heal, and do little harm. Theoretically, white-lipped peccary spirits can cause illness, but in practice, Wari' seldom blame them for specific illnesses. Many have told me that ancestor-peccary spirits make people sick only in order to create shamans, and that on the rare occasions when they kill people, they do so out of love. In particular, these deaths are said to happen if parents mistreat or neglect a small child. Such mistreatment may anger the child's dead grandparent so that he or she causes the child to become sick and die, thereby allowing the child's spirit to live with more caring kin in the underworld. In general, Wari' think of the ancestor-peccaries' relations to living people as being based not on hostility but on affection and nostalgia.

The nonancestral water spirits who can appear as fish play a different role. Wari' regard them with suspicion and ambivalence, for although these spirits can provide fish for people to eat, they cause a great deal of illness and death. The nonancestral water spirits are, in fact, the ultimate source of human death, for no matter what illness, accident, or trauma makes a person's spirit leave its physical body and journey to the underworld, it is Towira Towira's beer that definitively kills the human body.

Fish spirits are regarded as the most malicious and devious of all jami karawa. Wari' imagine them as sly predators, always on the lookout for an opportunity to attack. Fish spirits are especially dangerous in large numbers, such as the schools of small fish that sometimes suddenly appear in the flooded forest during the rainy season. People at Santo André recall an incident in which an adult brother and sister went to the forest together and found a spot teeming with fish. After killing many fish and carrying them home, both got sick with fever and died on the same day. People say that after such an attack, it will be many years before fish return to the same place.

In the first days and weeks after a death, a newly dead individual's lonesome spirit may ask fish spirits to try to capture a loved one. Fearing such an occurrence, the relatives of a recently deceased girl said they would not fish much for several weeks, nor even spend much time near the river, because they were afraid of being attacked by fish spirits sent by the dead girl.

The antagonism inherent in Wari' relations to the nonancestral water spirits contrasts markedly with the cooperation they enjoy with the water spirits who are their own ancestors. The presence of their kin in the underworld opens the possibility for people to have some influence with the more hostile water spirits that control human death and the movements of white-lipped peccaries and fish.

* * *

If the dead are to become fully integrated into the underworld society, and if their bereft kin are to eventually accept this transformation, there must be some distance and differentiation created between the dead and the living. One way this distance develops is through distortions of perspective that resemble the perceptual reversals prevalent between Wari' and jami karawa animals, who perceive themselves as people and see people as animals. As described in Chapter 5, Wari' say that when the spirit of a newly dead individual awakens from itam, the lonely, disoriented spirit walks back to the surface of the earth but finds itself unable to communicate or interact with people there. The spirit's faculties of sight and hearing are distorted, so that instead of hearing its family's lamentations of grief and loss, it hears cries of "We don't like you! Go away!" Instead of perceiving its family's expressions of love and longing, the spirit sees them waving fighting sticks, threatening to beat the spirit. Instead of perceiving its kin as loving consanguines, the spirit sees them acting like angry affines, ready to fight.

Death creates perceptual barriers that place the living and the dead in emotional opposition to one another, so that sentiments of love and longing are misperceived as hate and rejection.[12] Living mourners' perceptions of the dead also are distorted. Instead of perceiving a homesick spirit longing for their love, mourners see the frightening ghost called *jima*. The ambivalence of mourners' relationships to the dead—the simultaneous impulse to cling to them and to push them away—is represented in this pairing of negative and positive images of the deceased: as the repulsive ghost who threatens its kin with death, and as the perfected spirit who one day will become a peccary that brings food to its living loved ones.

The Transformed Ancestors

In the world of the dead, all the ancestors are healthier and more beautiful than they were in life. Everyone's spirit-body is perfect: strong, vigorous, and in the prime of life. The elderly become young again, children mature into strong young adults, the sick are healed, and deformities, disabilities, and blemishes disappear. With illness, aging, and imperfection abolished, the spirits of the dead look different than they did when they were alive. Taylor (1993:655) sees cultural emphases on the transformed visual appearances of the dead as another dimension of the pan-Amazonian focus on altering mourners' relations to the dead by presenting new visual images to those who think about them. She points out that since mourners cannot actually see the made-over dead, such new images must always remain rather imprecise and generic, and the vagueness of imagery contributes to a process of deindividualizing the deceased.

For Wari', white-lipped peccaries are the primary new form that living people eventually come to associate with the dead. Though some like to talk about their ancestors' lives as peccaries, the peccaries themselves are a very generic image with little individuality. Again, as Taylor suggests, the cultural emphasis on how an ancestor's visual appearance changes seems to be part of the process of depersonalizing images of the deceased, a transformation that may encourage mourners to recognize that the dead individual has become something different, foreign and amorphous.

In view of the pan-Amazonian emphasis on eradicating individuality and separating the dead from the living, it seems somewhat contradictory that many native Amazonians also stress the idea that the ancestral society has ongoing interactions with communities of living people. Throughout Amazonia, such interactions are commonly conceived as a sort of partnership or alliance between the dead and the living that is sustained by relations of reciprocity, a give-and-take between the two worlds (Taylor 1993:654–655). This is part of a pattern that is characteristic of many lowland South American cultures, in which the notion of "society" includes communities of the dead and cosmology cannot be separated from social organization (Viveiros de Castro 1992:26–27). The society of living people and the society of their ancestors often behave almost like two halves of a moiety system engaged in continual interactions and exchanges with each other.

For Wari', the most important manifestation of such partnership is the idea that the ancestor-peccaries return to earth to feed their living kin. Wari' envision their interactions with underworld spirits as modeled after the loosely reciprocal parties exchanged among groups of living Wari'.[13] In earthly parties, the guests who are "killed" at one party ideally reciprocate with a party of their own at which they, in turn, "kill" members of the group that hosted the earlier party. Similar exchanges take place between living Wari' and the underworld spirits. At death, Towira Towira "kills" the Wari' person's spirit, who is a guest at the water spirits' hüroroin party. Roles reverse when the water spirits leave the water and become peccaries, who perform in the role of guests, singing tamara and dancing before being killed by Wari' hunters. Thus, Wari' see human death and the hunting of white-lipped peccaries as complementary events, two poles in a dynamic of mutual predation between living people and water spirits. Both sides benefit from this arrangement: Wari' acquire meat and fish to eat, and the water spirits acquire new human spirits to join their society.

Funerals and the Powers of Predation

At one level, the act of eating the corpse at a funeral indicated that the deceased was no longer fully human and was in transition to a new identity as part of the animal world. At the same time, however, numerous aspects of the funeral rites emphasized the dead person's humanity and connections to living people. This emphasis was expressed through painting the corpse with annatto (a marker of human identity), through invoking kin terms in keening and singing eulogies about the dead person's life and deeds, and through the relatives' embracing of the corpse and expressions of self-identification with the deceased. Even as they began to cut the corpse and treat it like meat, Wari' marked it as different from other meat by allowing it to rot and initially refusing to eat it. The message was clear: this was a *human* body that was being eaten, not an animal carcass.

When the affines finally accepted the flesh and ate it, they thus placed themselves in the position of carnivores eating flesh marked explicitly as human, wari'. How did Wari' conceptualize this self-identification with predators? Ideas about power and agency in predatory relationships seem central to their understanding of this role. Precontact funerals abounded in references to the aspects of hunting, meat eating, warfare, and exocannibalism in which the power to act as a predator derived from the ritual regulation of relations to powerful spirit forces outside or on the margins of Wari' society.

The funeral fire itself originated in the story of Pinom and the jaguar-cannibal-crone from whose fire Wari' acquired the civilizing capacities for agriculture, cooking, hunting, and endocannibalism. The scarlet macaw feathers that decorated the funeral firewood and roasting rack evoked the story of Hujin, in which scarlet macaws emerged from the bodies of the leader of the underworld and his son (in their white-lipped peccary forms) when Wari' killed them. This mythic event initiated the arrangement in which human death and the hunting of white-lipped peccaries are framed as aspects of the parties exchanged between Wari' and the underworld spirits.

Other funeral elements linked endocannibalism to warfare and the killing of enemies. The decorated firewood bundle used for roasting the corpse was tied with makuri xe', the same liana used by war parties to roast enemy body parts and to tie the special firebrands that ensured warriors' success by maintaining proper relations to the destructive storm spirits that dwell under the water. Another link to warfare appears in the belief that the dead person's spirit is transformed in a process analogous to the transformation of a warrior after he kills an enemy. Wari' say that the swelling and bloating of the corpse is the visible sign that the person's spirit is undergoing a transformation like the swelling of the belly of an enemy killer in ritual seclusion. The spirits of the newly dead also become killers. In the underworld, when Towira Towira's beer "kills" a human spirit and it enters itam, its spirit-essence is said to leave its spirit-body. Some say the spirit goes off to kill enemies. Others say the spirit just eats fruit and kills and eats birds. Either way, the dead person's spirit (which has been slain as "prey" at Towira Towira's hüroroin party) acts as a predator. (At earthly hüroroin parties, the spirits of men in itam are said to leave their bodies to go in search of enemies or birds to kill.) For the spirit of a newly deceased individual, this transformation to predator begins at the moment of death, when it enters itam, and is completed when the spirit is revived, which was thought to happen at the same time as the cutting and cooking of the corpse.

About three days after death, Towira Towira and the other water spirits awaken the dead person's spirit in the same way party hosts awaken their guests from itam, with a warm water bath that makes them 'e' wa, "come back to life." Wari' also give warm water baths to newborns, sick people, and warriors returning from killing an enemy. Particularly for babies and warriors, such baths mark acceptance or (re-)integration into sociality. In hüroroin parties, the bathing and revival of male guests is followed by an exuberant celebration in which the men from both communities join together, arms around one another's shoulders, in a raucous song-and-dance that temporarily dissolves the ritualized oppositions between their two groups. In the underworld, Towira Towira integrates the revived spirit into the underwater society by painting it with genipap, the black paint that marks social transitions. From this point forward, the individual belongs to the underwater community.

Warriors emerged from their belly-swelling transformation with new vitality, health, growth, strength, beauty, and longevity. Wari' consider this the highest state of perfection that mortals can attain. After death, when all Wari'—females and males, children and adults—are empowered to act as predators, human spirits experience a similar transformation, in which they transcend the limitations of mortal existence and become perfected immortals, exempt from disease, debility, deformity, aging, and ugliness.

The perceived parallel between the revitalizing transformations of enemy killers and of the spirits of the dead is another conceptual link between exo- and endocannibalism in the Wari' worldview. Just as the transformative agent in exocannibalism was not the enemy flesh that was eaten but the enemy blood and spirit that the killer absorbed, the transformative agent in endocannibalism was not the flesh that was eaten but the ritual processes of the underwater hüroroin party, with its elements reminiscent of the ritual process that transformed and empowered the killers of enemies.

Death and rebirth, mortality and fertility, predation and generativity are richly interwoven in the imagery and ritual practices surrounding funerals and enemy killing. Wari' call the underwater realm *paxikom,* which is also the word for "womb." Other fertility imagery is evident in Towira Towira's huge genitals and his wife's pendulous breasts. In the enemy killer's transformation, the Wari' (like a number of other lowland South American peoples) see analogies between the warrior's state and the female reproductive processes of menstruation or pregnancy (see Conklin in press). Just as the transformation of warriors constituted a kind of perfecting rebirth that empowered men and enhanced their productivity and ability to take care of their communities, the perfecting transformation and rebirth of the spirits of the dead empowers them to maintain the life-supporting, food-giving relations between the ancestor-animals and living Wari' communities.

The various symbols evoked in precontact funerals—the stories of Pinom and Hujin, the ritual control of fire in warfare, the notion of death as a hüroroin party, and the analogy between transformations of enemy killers and transformations of spirits of the dead—all refer to contexts in which Wari' believe their people have developed spiritual capacities and arrangements that empower them to kill and eat outsiders (animals, enemies, water spirits) and not just be killed and eaten by them. Productive relationships are generated by crossing, transcending, and reversing boundaries, including especially the boundaries between predator and prey. Human agency is generated and enhanced through participation in, and transformations of, the powers of predatory others unlike oneself. Empowerment comes from appropriating the jaguar-cannibal's fire, absorbing enemy blood and spirit, and using the rituals of social reciprocity and intergroup parties to turn potential aggression into mutually beneficial, life-sustaining exchanges with other groups. Yet, empowering as these cultural forms are, they never establish domination over the other. The flow of social life is generated through exchange. To be a predator, one must sometimes be prey.

* * *

"Eating is for animals. . . . [P]eople are not meat to be eaten," missionaries tried to convince the Wari'. For Wari', however, the magic and power of human existence derive from the commonality of human and animal identities, from the movements between the worlds of people and animals created through participation in both sides of the dynamic of eating and being eaten.

CHAPTER TEN

HUNTING
THE ANCESTORS

Death imposes an irreversible distance between the living and the dead, a divide across which the two groups perceive each other only dimly and with distortion. Only after both the dead and the living have accepted the finality of the changes death has wrought and have become reconciled to their new lives can they once again approach each other in forms that each can perceive clearly. Wari' say it takes a long time for dead people's spirits to adjust to their new existences because they miss their living relatives. Only after a spirit has become fully integrated into the ancestral society will he or she join the other ancestors when they emerge from the water as white-lipped peccaries and visit living Wari'. Some months or years after a death, a shaman usually tells a bereaved family that their relative's spirit has appeared as a peccary, and this is taken as tangible evidence that the individual is completely integrated into the ancestors' society. For many Wari', especially women, images of white-lipped peccaries come to dominate their thoughts about dead relatives, for this is the only form in which ancestors can interact with living people in a nonthreatening way.

When an ancestor's spirit emerges from the water in a peccary body, the ancestor-peccary approaches a hunter who is a close relative and presents itself to be shot, thus ensuring that some of its meat will go to feed the relatives whom the ancestor remembers and for whom the ancestor cares. Being shot does not harm the ancestral spirit, for spirits never die. When a peccary is shot, its spirit leaves its animal body and returns to the water. The

*13. Torein, with a
white-lipped peccary.*

next time the individual comes out of the water, he or she will incarnate in another peccary body.

With their special powers of vision, Wari' shamans can look at a dead peccary and identify the ancestral spirit inside. Before butchering a peccary, hunters are supposed to ask a shaman to look at the carcass and ascertain its identity. Shamans almost always identify a peccary spirit as a close consanguine, or sometimes a close affine, of the man who shot it. Usually, the peccaries that hunters kill are people who have died within fairly recent memory.

Wari' see nothing strange about hunting their own ancestors, as I learned from a conversation I overheard one afternoon at Santo André the day after two white-lipped peccaries had been killed. The shaman, Maxun Kwarain, was chatting with a young widower named Jimon O', whose wife had died in childbirth two years earlier. Although the young man was no longer mourning publicly, he clearly still missed his wife and had not remarried, despite the fact that, as a single father, he was struggling to care for two small sons.

Maxun Kwarain told Jimon O' that he had talked to the roasting peccaries and that one turned out to be Jimon O''s dead wife.

"Is that so?" the young man responded nonchalantly. "Is it all right in the water?"

"She's fine," the shaman assured him. "With the peccaries, she took another husband and has a peccary baby now."

"That's nice," was the young man's only comment.

Eavesdropping nearby while eating a mango, I nearly choked. "Jimon O'!" I exclaimed. "Doesn't that make you *sad?* Aren't you sad that your wife's cousin killed her yesterday and you ate her today?!"

Jimon O' looked puzzled at my outburst. "No," he replied. "Why should I be sad? They just killed her body. She isn't angry. Her children are eating meat. It doesn't hurt her; she'll just have another body. Why should I be sad? The ancestors are happy that we have meat to eat."

To Wari', the idea that some of the animals they eat are their own relatives is neither morbid nor repulsive. They see the peccaries' gift of their own flesh as a natural extension of the food giving that is the essence of family life. While alive, Wari' give of their bodies to nourish family members through breast milk, semen, and the foods that their physical labor produces. Death disrupts these flows of nurturance, but ancestors who still remember and care may return periodically to feed their living kin with their own bodies, transformed into the white-lipped peccary meat that Wari' consider the most nourishing of all meats.

Each death of a Wari' individual creates a new ancestor, and each newly made ancestor has emotional ties to living people. Over the years, as the dead grow accustomed to existence in the underworld, their memories of their former lives grow dim, and their nostalgia and concern for those left behind become less intense. Individual ancestors gradually seem to forget about their living kin, much as living Wari' gradually stop thinking so much about their dead. In the underworld, it is the newcomers who have the strongest ties to living Wari'. They are the ones who still remember their families and are remembered by them, and they are most likely to direct the peccary herd to the hunting territories of their living relatives. When the ancestors incarnate as peccaries, it is these recently deceased individuals who are most inclined to present themselves for their kinsmen to shoot. Thus, each death renews a Wari' community's ties to the underworld spirits, reinforcing and perpetuating this meat-giving relationship. Jimon O''s dead wife could no longer hold her young sons in her arms, but even from beyond the grave, she could feed them and let her family know that she still cared.

"Pigs" from the Ancestors

White-lipped peccaries are unique among the fauna of the Amazonian rain-forest, for they are the only terrestrial mammals that travel in herds. White-lipped peccary herds may number a hundred or more animals, so it is not surprising that many native Amazonians think of them as social groups of human or protohuman beings. Wari' see the peccary herd as a group of their ancestors coming to visit. Like visitors who put on musical performances for their hosts, the peccaries sing tamara music and dance. When Wari' shoot peccaries, the killing is analogous to the moment when hosts at hüroroin and hütop parties "kill" male guests by pressing beer upon them until they lose consciousness in itam.

The shaman Maxun Kwarain, who had the spirit of a white-lipped peccary, often talked about how he dream-journeyed through the forest and spent the night singing and dancing with the peccaries. On several occasions, he sent children to find me in the morning and tell me to go see him. Each time I arrived at his house, he would hold up his hands to show how his fingers formed a V shape like a peccary hoof and his palms were covered with tiny scratches. "See how my hands are all cut up from running through the forest?" he would say. "I sang tamara with the white-lipped peccary spirits last night." One morning he showed me some leaves of a type said to be a favorite food among the peccaries, leaves that grew far away in the forest at a place to which his spirit, but not his crippled legs, could carry him.

The Shaman, the Skeptic, and the Social Scientist

Wari' trace the beginnings of their partnership with the water spirits to events in a myth they call "Hujin" or "Orotapan." The story has many versions, but the one that means the most to me, the one presented in Appendix B, is the version Maxun Kwarain told one night in 1987, at the very end of my first two years of fieldwork. Something that happened in connection with that night of storytelling revealed an unexpected dimension of Wari' cosmology and made me reflect on my own worldview. To put this event in context, I need to say a little more about three of the people who were involved: Maxun Kwarain, Jimon Maram, and myself.

In 1987, Maxun Kwarain was one of the oldest living Wari', and along with Manim, he was widely credited with knowing more about Wari' history, lore, and music than anyone else from the Dois Irmãos group. His reputation as the most powerful shaman reflected the fact that he was the only shaman associated with two animal spirits: jaguar and white-lipped peccary. However, the respect that his shamanic abilities commanded was diluted by his perpetual begging, for he was crippled and unable to hunt or garden, so he constantly asked for food and other goods from anyone he thought might give him something. I worked with him a great deal, and although we enjoyed each other's company and senses of humor, ours was never a completely easy relationship. Maxun Kwarain delighted in teasing me as if I were a granddaughter, but he also pestered me with constant demands for trade goods. The information he shared often came in long, convoluted stories or cryptic references that he would refuse to explain until I had begged and pleaded. His stories, especially about his own life, were rife with contradictions that guaranteed I would spend hours questioning him. There also was period during which he became intensely engaged with his peccary spirit and took to going out at night in a peccary mode, grunting as he dragged himself through the sleeping village. Wari' children found it creepy, and so did I. On more than one occasion, I was awake late at night, relishing the little private time I could have to myself. As I lay under my mosquito net reading by candlelight, my reverie would be shattered by an outburst of heavy snuffling right outside my door, which never closed all the way. This was altogether too weird, and my only way of coping was to quickly blow out the candle and lie there thinking dark thoughts about a certain individual who took too much pleasure in messing with my mind.

Most Wari' respected Maxun Kwarain's shamanic abilities, but a vocal minority rejected shamanism altogether. Some of the nonbelievers were converts to the Protestant faith introduced by the New Tribes missionaries. Others rejected both Christianity and shamanism. "Maxun Kwarain talks garbage" was one man's statement on the subject. "He's my uncle, but I won't let him lay a hand on my kids," said another man.

Jimon Maram's skepticism about shamanism and the spirit beliefs that went with it was based in his Christianity. For years, he has been one of Santo André's sincerest and most faithful converts. In the 1980s, he served as the village pastor, leading services at a tiny open-air church on the edge of the forest, where his family and a few others gathered on Sunday mornings. During the first half year I lived at Santo André, I avoided associating much with him or his family, partly because I felt it was essential to communicate that, although I was North American, my work was different from the missionaries' work.

14. In preparation for the hüroroin party they hosted for visitors from Rio Negro-Ocaia in 1986, men from Santo André cut a hollow tree trunk to make a giant beer barrel, which they then had to roll several miles through the forest.

It was on Easter Sunday in 1986 that I first realized there was more complexity in Jimon Maram than I had assumed. A family had invited my husband and me to stay with them at their house by the gardens at Hon Xitot. As we left Santo André in midmorning to hike to Hon Xitot, we passed the little open-air church and noticed that it was deserted. About five kilometers into the forest, we came upon Jimon Maram in the middle of a group of men who were drenched in sweat and covered with thousands of bees. They were scraping out the inside of a huge cross-section of a tree (which was partially hollow and contained a bee hive) to make a beer barrel for the hüroroin party that Santo André was preparing to throw for people from Rio Negro-Ocaia.

The Protestant missionaries condemn hüroroin on the grounds that it involves alcohol and sexual parodies and is a venue for promiscuity and adultery. Yet here was the village pastor hard at work making a giant beer barrel on Easter Sunday.

"My relatives asked me to help," he explained rather sheepishly.

Jimon Maram's attitude toward the upcoming party seemed just as contradictory. He lectured me repeatedly about the beer drinking and other sinful behavior that would take place at the party, but he contributed more corn than anyone else for making the beer. His wife, Quimoin, and their teen-aged daughters spent hours grinding corn to brew the beer. Those days before the party were when I first got to know Quimoin and fell in love with her voice. She often sang and hummed while she worked: high, sweet, slow, repetitious melodies that seemed to drift to the treetops, weaving a spell through the clearing around her house. I found myself dropping by on the pretext of helping her daughters grind corn, just to hear her sing.

She's the best singer in the village, people said.

"Where did you learn to sing so well?" I once asked.

Quimoin hesitated, but her husband said, "Go ahead; tell her."

Then Quimoin explained that when she was a girl growing up in the Negro-Ocaia area, she was sitting by a lake in the forest one day, when she heard music, faint and far away. The music gradually grew louder, and she realized it was coming from under the water. She looked into the lake and saw people holding a party below. They were jami kom, water spirits, whom she identified as Wari' ancestors. It was from them that she learned to sing.

"Other Wari' haven't heard the water spirits' music. That's why Quimoin is the best singer," bragged Jimon Maram, visibly proud of his wife. Yet a couple of months earlier, when Manim had taken a group of singers upriver to perform at Rio Negro-Ocaia, Jimon Maram had refused to let Quimoin go along. As the time for the hüroroin approached, he announced that no one in his family was going to participate. When the party began, Jimon Maram stayed on the sidelines at first. He had forbidden his children to join the other young people in serving beer to the male visitors, but in the end, the older ones joined the fun anyway. On the first afternoon, FUNAI staff organized a soccer game, and the hüroroin activities came to a halt. As I sat on the sidelines with a group of Wari' spectators watching the match, I saw Jimon Maram headed our way, his face full of anger.

"They're messing up everything!" he exploded.

"Who is?" I sighed, bracing myself for yet another tirade about sin, sex, and inebriation.

"This soccer match—it's messing up the party! Our ancestors didn't play soccer!" With that, he stormed off in disgust.

Santo André lost the match, but everyone except Jimon Maram seemed to enjoy the game. When it was over, the party started up again where it had left off. The drumming, joking, singing, and dancing lasted two full days.

A week later, I went downriver in a boat piloted by Jimon Maram. When we stopped at Tanajura, one of the missionaries greeted us. "So how was the hüroroin party last week?" she asked him.

"The soccer match was great!" Jimon Maram replied. "Our team lost, but everybody had fun at the game." It was all I could do to bite my tongue.

Yet as I got to know him better, I came to understand Jimon Maram, not as a hypocrite, but as an intelligent man trying to find a path between two competing systems that both held value for him: the new Christianity and his people's traditions. In the beginning, I naively assumed he would know little about Wari' traditions. When I finally got to know him, however, I discovered that the ambition that motivated him to work so hard at everything he did inspired him to want to command as much authoritative cultural knowledge as possible: to learn everything the missionaries had to teach, and also to be an expert on Wari' lore and history. Of all the middle-aged men at Santo André, he spent by far the most time talking to elders about the past. Though he personally rejected certain beliefs and practices as incompatible with his Christian faith, he proved to have keen insights into Wari' cosmology and traditional beliefs.

For Jimon Maram's wife, the clash between these two belief systems did not seem as problematic. Quimoin prayed in church and tried to live by the Christians' moral teachings, but she didn't seem to worry that her songs came from a pagan underworld that the missionaries equated with hell. The beauty she had experienced beside the lake was utterly real to her, and she glowed when she spoke of it.

Jimon Maram, however, was a different story. He had not shared Quimoin's transcendent experience of the world of spirits. He was more of an intellectual, and he wanted a logical system of ideas that fit together without contradictions. Having accepted certain Christian truths as his own, he intended to affirm only those Wari' beliefs that did not conflict with them. Rejecting shamanism and the spirit beliefs on which it is based was not just knee-jerk evangelical fundamentalism; he sincerely felt that such beliefs hurt people. To believe in such spirits, he told me many times, is to live in fear. Every time someone kills a deer, people have to worry that its spirit will take revenge. When the sky darkens and wild winds flatten the forest canopy, people huddle inside their houses, afraid of storm spirits scattering sickness over the village. To Jimon Maram, it was all superstition. He prided himself on his rationalism: "If you don't believe in spirits, they can't hurt you" was one of his favorite sayings.

I was much like Jimon Maram, for my rationalism also exempted me from the mystical anxieties that are undercurrents in the lives of many Wari'. I spent nearly two years working with Maxun Kwarain and other shamans, filling notebook after notebook with the ideas they explained. As an ethnographer, I worked from the position of relativism that is our stock-in-trade: I treated their beliefs respectfully and never voiced a doubt about the ultimate reality of what they described. But as a scientifically minded westerner, I always saw the concepts they explained as *their* belief system, not as a description of how the universe really works. I never lost sleep wondering whether the spirit of the fish I ate for dinner might retaliate, or whether jaguar-shamans actually fly, or whether dead people really come back as peccaries. And I certainly did not imagine that Wari' magic could really work.

Maxun Kwarain had not given me much reason to think otherwise. A shaman's "x-ray" vision is supposed to let him see illness agents inside someone's body. But when he treated my fever, I heard him whisper to a boy, "What's she been eating?" "Fish," the lad whispered back. Maxun Kwarain solemnly ran his hands over my arms, stared intently, and announced, "Fish bones; I see fish bones in your body causing this fever." He extracted the bones, but of course, only he could see them. My fever did go away, but most illnesses are self-limiting, and I probably would have recovered anyway.

Then, at the end of the first two years I spent with the Wari', something happened that opened a crack in my metaphysical certainties. It was the end of May in 1987, when I was about to go home to the United States. My decision to leave was motivated by hunger, pure and simple. I had spent every penny of my grant money and was counting on being able to sell my camera in Guajará-Mirim in order to buy a ticket to Rio de Janeiro. In the meantime, I had used up my store-bought provisions, and when I ate, it was through the kindness of friends. Quimoin was especially good about looking out for me, sharing fish and sweet potatoes even when her own family did not have much extra. I was not the only one who was anxious about food. Fish and game had been unusually scarce, and the peccary herd had not been seen in months. Everyone was a bit on edge. I felt like a burden on my friends and knew it was time to go.

On the Friday before my last weekend at Santo André, I asked Maxun Kwarain to make one last tape recording, of the story about Hujin and Orotapan. He agreed but told me to come back after dark. This seemed odd, for we usually worked by daylight. When I arrived that evening with flashlight and tape recorder in hand, I discovered that he had invited about a dozen people, including Quimoin and Jimon Maram, to hear him tell the story. The night was cool, and we sat outdoors on palm-leaf mats, huddling close together around a low fire as the shaman told this story of how the special relationship between Wari' and the spirits of the underworld began.

The Story of Hujin and Orotapan

This story tells of a Wari' man named Hujin who fell into the water and was eaten by the leader of the underworld, a giant who appeared first as an orotapan carnivore and later as a white-lipped peccary. (In some versions, it is the spirits of Wari' ancestors who collectively fall upon Hujin and eat him.) In the beginning, Orotapan dominated Hujin and treated him as prey. Eventually, a shaman reached into the water and rescued Hujin, but Hujin was obliged to go back underwater every day to be eaten again.

Hujin finally liberated himself by winning a song-making contest with Orotapan, who had at this point turned into the giant peccary named Wem Parom. In this contest, Hujin's mastery of music making transformed his people's relations to the spirits of the underwater domain. By triumphing at song making, which Wari' consider the highest of cultural arts, Hujin freed himself from the role of being merely the water spirits' prey and showed that Wari' were worthy of being treated as equals and becoming partners in an exchange relationship. Hujin invited the water spirits to visit, and this established the intergroup parties in which hosts and visitors trade roles as predators and prey. As partners in this exchange relationship, Wari' would now be able to kill water spirits when they appeared as peccaries and fish, but they also learned that after they died, they themselves would become peccaries and be hunted and eaten by living people. This was the origin of the special relationship between Wari' society and the society of ancestors and animal spirits.

Wari' refer to the songs from the musical duel between Hujin and Wem Parom as the "Orotapan" music. These songs are special, for although I did not know it that Friday night, the music is said to have the power to summon the water spirits to appear, as white-lipped peccaries or fish, to feed Wari'.

Maxun Kwarain was an accomplished singer and one of the few elders who knew the entire cycle of songs associated with this myth. When he reached the part of the story in which Hujin and Wem Parom/Orotapan have their musical duel, he sang some of the songs. The melodies were hauntingly beautiful and different from any Wari' music I had heard. Everyone seemed enchanted, and some children who had never heard the songs asked him to teach us the words. He did, and we sang together around the fire, shoulders touching and swaying as our voices traced the graceful melodies again and again. After the shaman finished the story, we got up and left without speaking, walking home through the dark, silent village wrapped in an intimacy woven of melody and myth.

* * *

Early the next morning, the white-lipped peccary herd came. They appeared first to Jimon Maram, the skeptic, which in retrospect seemed deliciously ironic.

Jimon Maram had risen at dawn to walk to his fields at Hon Xitot. Just outside the village, a peccary darted across the path in front of him. He shot it and raced home to alert the other hunters. Within a matter of minutes, nine peccaries had been shot: the most game ever killed in one day in the two years I had lived at Santo André. With nine peccaries to eat, the community was suddenly meat rich, and everyone canceled their other plans and stayed home to feast on the kill. After weeks of scarcity, we basked in the glow of collective contentment that came on those rare occasions when there was an abundance of meat for everyone.

Quimoin's six-year-old daughter came to invite me to eat with them. As I walked up the path toward their house, I found Jimon Maram sitting alone on a log staring at the ground.

"Hey, you killed meat today!" I greeted him. "What luck!"

His face was glum and his demeanor oddly subdued. "Maybe it wasn't luck," he said slowly. "Maxun Kwarain says the peccaries came because we sang Orotapan's songs last night. He says our music called them from the water."

"I don't understand," I said.

"That's how it was in the old days," he explained. "When Wari' were hungry and wanted to eat meat, they sang the songs that belong to Hujin and Orotapan. Then the peccaries came to bring meat."

"You have to sing with respect," he emphasized, perking up a bit as he moved into his role as my teacher. "It's like a ceremony. You can't mess around [waraju] with Orotapan's music, or the peccaries won't come."

Like a ceremony? I recalled the special feeling of the night before, the sense of communion as we sang together. It had felt . . . well, almost sacred.

Light began to dawn as I realized that this partnership the Wari' think they have with the water spirits must be far more concrete than I had imagined. Singing the songs from the story of Orotapan, invoking the mythic contest between their people and the forces of the underworld, invites the underworld spirits to come and be killed and eaten. For people who value meat and fish so highly and place a premium on relationships that enhance food security, this ability to summon animal prey would be tremendously empowering.

Alongside my wonder at this new ethnographic insight was the galling realization that in all these months of conversation after conversation about peccaries, water spirits, ancestors, animals, and shamanism, no one had seen fit to tell me about a belief and a ritual that must be (or must once have been?) a tenet of their religion and cosmology, a linchpin in their confidence in a special relationship with the nonhuman world. I was finding out about it—and on my next-to-last day in the field, no less!—only because the peccaries did, in fact, show up when we sang those songs.

"I can't believe they came!" I exclaimed in amazement.

"Me neither," Jimon the preacher muttered gloomily.

Quimoin came down the path looking for us. "Come on; let's eat!" she called.

"Later!" I yelled back, turning away. "I've got to talk to Maxun Kwarain!"

I found the shaman munching contentedly on a roasted peccary haunch.[1] There was a twinkle in his eye and, I thought, more than a hint of smug vindication. I glared at him. You old goat, I wanted to say. After all these months of butting heads—my quest for facts versus your convoluted stories; my rationality versus your cranky mysticism. You know I never believed in your spirits or your magic. And now, just as I'm about to leave, this happens.

"You did this on purpose, didn't you?" I blurted out.

The old shaman just grinned and kept on chewing.

* * *

Some of my resolutely positivist-minded colleagues think I should not have included this incident in this book, for they say I betray a regrettable lapse of scientific objectivity when I admit to a moment of wondering whether our singing really did bring the peccaries. Such magic does not exist; people cannot use music to influence wild animals' movements. As a scholar who would like to maintain her credibility, I will of course say the following if asked about this incident: it was just a coincidence that the peccaries happened to appear the morning after we sang the songs that are supposed to summon them. But what I really learned that day at Santo André was a different lesson, about how an event like this can confirm a cultural vision of reality, so that an emotionally powerful experience interpreted in terms of a particular set of assumptions about how the universe works seems to validate that cosmology.

When Wari' talk about the ancestor-peccaries and the times when the herd has brought meat, they express a sense of awe and appreciation that I understood better after that Saturday morning. The preceding weeks had been the first time in my life that I had come anywhere near to experiencing the edge of hunger and the anxiety about getting food that are facts of life for too many of the world's people. During the weeks when I had no food of my own, no money, and little to trade, I gained an intimate understanding of the emotional impact of receiving a gift of food and of the importance of knowing that there are others on whom one can count for help.

I was not alone in my insecurity. No one in the community was starving or malnourished, or even really hungry, but everyone was concerned that the hunting and fishing had been so unproductive. Then one evening, some of us happened to sing the peccary-summoning songs, and the herd happened to appear at dawn. In the atmosphere of collective well-being that followed, when bellies were full of succulent roast pork and everyone was relaxing and feasting, I felt not at all inspired to argue about cause and effect with the shaman who claimed that Wari' magic had brought us this bounty of meat.

Ecology and Eschatology

Wari' believe that the music created in the culture hero Hujin's mythic contest with the predatory Wem Parom/Orotapan gives them a means to summon animals to be killed. The songs can call either the Wari' ancestors, who appear as peccaries, or the nonancestral water spirits, who usually appear as fish but may also accompany the ancestor-peccaries. Older people at Santo André say that, in the past, they often sang "Orotapan" the night before a big hunt or a collective fishing expedition, but people seldom do so anymore. No one could or would explain why the practice of this ritual had declined. Some mystery seemed to surround the Orotapan music, and I managed to learn only a little more about it. Vilaça's informants at Rio Negro-Ocaia claimed to have forgotten how to sing these songs, but the long-time administrator of the Sagarana community (which I have not visited) said that Wari' there still sing "Orotapan" fairly often. He said they sing these songs late at night, when a collective hunt or fishing expedition is planned for the next morning. He commented that Wari' always sing "Orotapan" solemnly, with a seeming reverence that contrasts markedly with the joking and horseplay that characterize other musical performances.

From an ecological perspective, it is interesting to note that these songs summon white-lipped peccaries and fish, for they are the animals that contribute the most protein to Wari' diets, a dietary pattern reported in a number of other native Amazonian populations as well (Kiltie 1980:541; and see Donkin 1985). The most dramatic quantities of animal food that a Wari' household or community can hope to obtain in a single day usually come from white-lipped peccaries or fish, for these are the only fauna routinely encountered in dense concentrations. As the only Amazonian herd animal, white-lipped peccaries can yield the most meat in return for the least expenditure of time and effort, since, in contrast to more solitary animals, the peccary herd offers numerous targets, and hunters commonly kill several animals each time the herd appears. Only the huge tapir yields more meat per animal, but tapirs are scarce and easily overhunted. Most Wari' communities see a tapir kill only once or twice a year, at most, so peccaries and fish are clearly the most significant sources of meat.

Fish resemble white-lipped peccaries in that they may appear in dense concentrations, in the huge schools that sometimes materialize in the flooded forest. Fish kills can be impressive. Two teenagers once returned from a five-hour fishing expedition with 284 good-sized fish, which they had caught by hand or killed with machetes in a temporary pool that they described as simply teeming with trapped fish.

Besides their high potential food yield, peccary herds and schools of fish are also similar in that they are not easy to locate. White-lipped peccaries are mostly herbivorous, and in order to get enough forage, the herd roams over an extensive territory. Wari' describe white-lipped peccaries as constantly on the move, stopping only briefly to graze and then moving on to another area. Hunters never know when or where they will appear, for the herd can vanish for weeks, or months, on end and then suddenly come thundering by. Wari' say that in the past, white-lipped peccary shamans dreamed of the herd's location and directed hunters to it (Everett and Kern 1997:495–496). Ordinarily, hunters do not set out specifically in search of the herd, but they respond quickly whenever it appears. A peccary sighting sparks an outburst of excitement like nothing else in Wari' village life. The man who first encounters the herd shoots what he can and then hastens to tell other hunters, who grab their weapons and rush off in pursuit.

15. In Wem Quirió's drawing, a hunter and his family give presents to the spirit of a white-lipped peccary he has shot. On the left, two women bring a pot of chicha to offer to the spirit. The hunter stands in the center, with a carrying basket adorned with a scarlet macaw feather on his back and a small clay pot in his hands. This ancestor-peccary spirit is receiving a basket, feathers for body decorations, bows and arrows, and a metal ax, which would have been stolen from a Brazilian homestead. Elders who looked at this drawing criticized the fact that people are wearing feathers on their heads, a practice that normally would have been reserved for special occasions. Wem Quirió replied that he knew this but put them in anyway because he liked the way they looked.

When Wari' go fishing, they usually manage to kill some fish, but it is harder to predict where big schools will appear. Sometimes a shallow stream or pool proves to be so full of fish that a few individuals can kill hundreds in a few hours. Other times, people walk long distances to spots that look promising but return empty handed.

In view of their common characteristics of a high potential food yield and a high degree of uncertainty about procuring them, it is not surprising that white-lipped peccaries and fish are prominent in Wari' rituals and cosmology. Wari' place great value on food (particularly meat) and the relationships through which food is produced and shared, and their religious imagery focuses on the spirits that influence the productivity of food-procuring activities. In a world populated by animal spirits that see Wari' as animals or enemies and attack almost at whim, the ancestor-peccaries are a different sort of being, with a uniquely positive relationship to living people. It is empowering for Wari' to feel they have a kind of partnership with peccaries and, to a lesser extent, with fish. This sense of empowerment is dramatically reinforced on occasions when peccaries or fish appear to respond to ritual actions, such as the singing of "Orotapan," as they did that Saturday morning in 1987.

Gifts for the Ancestors

As part of the reciprocity on which their relations to the underworld spirits are based, Wari' give gifts to the spirits of the white-lipped peccaries they kill. This practice of gift giving was at one time more elaborate and universal, but since the contact, some hunters have stopped giving gifts altogether, and others do so in a more informal manner than before.

In the traditional gift-giving rituals, before butchering a white-lipped peccary, the hunter and his family place the carcass on a mat and arrange desirable goods around it. Before the contact, these presents were items such as bows and arrows, clay pots, baskets, metal tools, and chicha. These days, gifts for peccaries often include commercial goods such as shotguns, aluminum pots, clothing, and cigarettes. When I watched Alfredo, a man in his late twenties, arrange gifts around a peccary he had killed, he casually placed a machete and a new pair of sandals next to the carcass, and his wife brought a pot of fresh chicha. The hunter is supposed to tell the peccary spirit to carry the spirits of the gifts to the underworld and tell the other spirits there that Wari' are generous and will give presents to them, too, when they come out of the water to be hunted. In this instance, Alfredo simply muttered, "Good; go on," removed the gifts, and set to work butchering the carcass.

Giving presents to peccaries is consistent with the notion that the peccaries come to be killed like guests at a party. Before the contact, at the end of parties attended by guests from a distant community, the hosts often gave the visitors (who had played the role of "prey") small gifts of food, body oil, or stone tools. This giving of presents expressed and reinforced the amicable relationship between the two groups. Similarly, Wari' hope the gifts they give to peccary spirits will promote friendly relations and encourage the peccaries to come again to be hunted.

Reciprocity in relations between humans and animals is a common theme in indigenous cultures, especially among native peoples of the Americas. In myths about the origin of cannibalism told by native peoples on North America's northwest coast, the idea that cannibalism is linked to a dialectic of reciprocal polarity between humans and animals is a recurrent theme (Sanday 1986:38–39). In lowland South America, many native peoples conceive of relationships between people and animals as cycles of reciprocal exchange and transformation (cf. Reichel-Dolmatoff 1971). Sometimes such human-animal exchanges are linked to cannibal imagery. One of the most striking examples comes from anthropologist Donald Pollock's work among the Kulina of Acre, Brazil. Pollock (1993) describes how Kulina conceptions of death revolve around multiple permutations of a cannibalistic dynamic between the living and the dead, people and peccaries. The Kulina believe that when a dying individual's soul arrives in the underworld, the Kulina ancestors, who have become white-lipped peccaries, fall upon the newly arrived soul and eat it. When the ancestor-peccaries leave the water, Kulina hunters kill them. Absorbed into the bodies of living Kulina, the ancestor-peccaries' flesh forms the new souls of Kulina babies. At death, each Kulina soul will be consumed by the ancestor-peccaries, completing the cycle in which life is regenerated through cannibalistic exchanges of reciprocal predation between living people and their ancestors.

The cosmological cycle of exchanges between peccaries and humans that Wari' envision does not seem to include a counterpart to the Kulina belief that babies' souls are formed from peccary meat. In the Wari' system, peccary meat sustains life in a nutritive sense, as the supremely healthful food that Wari' can summon in times of need. There is nothing especially unusual about Wari' visions of cyclic human-animal exchanges, for permutations of similar ideas are found in other Amazonian societies. What is distinctive about the Wari' system is the way such ideas were linked to the actual practice of funerary cannibalism. Wari' consumed their dead twice over: first as human corpses, and later as peccary meat.

Emotional Ecologies

It is as white-lipped peccary spirits (*jami mijak*) that Wari' most commonly speak of their dead, and images of the peccaries dominate imaginings about the afterlife. The idea of ancestors becoming peccaries is a generally positive image, for along with the promise of meat, it provides a possibility for ongoing relations with dead loved ones. Wari' see the ancestor-peccaries' willingness to give their bodies to feed their living relatives as a concrete expression of affection and concern for those left behind. There are several stories of dying individuals who promised to send the peccaries to their families after they died. The most dramatic account I heard concerned the mother of Alfredo Oro Nao', who died in the 1970s. Alfredo claimed that as she lay on her deathbed, his mother told him she would send the herd three days after she died. True to her promise, on the third night after her death, the peccaries thundered into the village in a wild stampede of dozens of animals, some of which ran right under the houses. "Women were screaming; children were crying and climbing into the rafters!" Alfredo reported. "All the men grabbed their shotguns, their bows and arrows. There was *lots* of meat; everyone ate meat; everyone's belly was full after my mother sent the white-lipped peccary spirits."

Most deaths are not followed by such drama, but any white-lipped peccary kill is likely to be interpreted as a visit from a specific ancestor. Regardless of whose ancestor the peccary is said to be, it is likely to remind many Wari', especially the recently bereaved, of deaths in their own families. On several occasions, I saw older women break into tears at the sight of a peccary carcass and begin to keen. Wari' say such reactions were more common in the past. Von Graeve (1989) reported that in the early 1970s, Wari' keened over the carcasses of game, crying for the animal's spirit. But my informants said they cry, not for the animal itself, but because the sight of the dead animal reminds them of relatives who have passed away.

Elderly people, especially elderly women, seem to derive some comfort from the idea that their lost kin become living animals. As the elderly feel their own deaths approaching, and as the number of loved ones they have lost grows, some begin to talk more and more about white-lipped peccaries. Though Wari' generally avoid talking about their dreams, several elders told me about having dreamed of running with the peccary herd in a joyful reunion with their kin. Such dreams are said to portend the dreamer's approaching death, and while it would be alarming for a young person to have such dreams, for the elderly, it is seen as a natural part of the transition from this life to the next.

An Oro Waram Xijein woman who died some years ago was an extreme example of how older people's thoughts and emotions may come to focus on peccaries. During one of my stays at Ribeirão, a young woman decided I needed a Wari' name. She chose the name Moroxin, which had belonged to a grandmother whom she said she had loved very much. I felt honored but then rather disconcerted, for it turned out that this Moroxin was famous for having gone completely crazy (*tamanain*) in her dotage. Not only did she dream about peccaries and talk about them constantly; she thought she already *was* a peccary. She would run off to the forest alone, staying away for days on end while her family searched for her. Eventually, her granddaughter said, they resorted to tethering the old woman to the house with a liana around her waist so she could not run away with the herd.

The Wari' relationship to the ancestor-peccaries is a life-supporting part-

nership that provides food and a comforting promise of continuing relations with dead kin in this life and beyond. Wari' dread their own deaths
and the deaths of those they care about, but they also recognize that death
is a productive event that strengthens ties between the human and nonhuman worlds. In anthropology, Durkheimian perspectives that focus on
social solidarity have emphasized the idea that death creates a rupture in
the social fabric that must be repaired. Wari' are acutely aware of death's
disruptive impact, but like many other native Amazonians, they see death
not just as a discontinuity but also as a transformation essential for the continuation of social life (Graham 1995, Viveiros de Castro 1992:255). In their
vision of this interdependence between life and death, ancestors are integral
to human society, and since death creates ancestors, death, by extension, is
necessary for the continuation of life. Human death becomes a source of
generativity, for each death renews ties between living people and the spirits
of the underworld, revitalizing their life-supporting relationship. Building
on this imagery to help bereaved individuals come to accept a loved one's
passing as part of larger cosmic processes of regeneration was part of the
"work of culture" that Wari' mourning rites aimed to accomplish.

CHAPTER ELEVEN

TRANSFORMING
GRIEF

The short path that led from the house where I had once lived to Manim's house was a path I had walked hundreds of times, but suddenly I was lost. Nothing looked the same. It was 1991, and I had just returned to Santo André after having been away for four years. Most of the village looked largely the same; some homes had been enlarged, and some new houses had been built for young couples who had become parents. But the big, old mud-brick house where Manim and Tocohwet Pijo' had lived with their two sons, their daughter Diva, Diva's two sons, her daughter Elsa, Elsa's baby, and a gaggle of chickens and ducks—the house where Diva had cried over the battered suitcase and the envelope of glossy photographs of her daughter's grave in Rio de Janeiro—that house was nowhere to be seen. I stopped in confusion; this part of the village looked completely different. Then I realized: of course, that was the intent—that everything should look different now.

The drug-resistant tuberculosis from which Tocohwet Pijo' had suffered for so many years had claimed her life the year before. Her husband, Manim, and the rest of the family must have burned the house, changed the paths, altered the look of the surroundings. Keep the ghost at bay; eliminate any reminders that might provoke sadness. Of all the people at Santo André, Manim would be most careful to do what was proper and eradicate every trace of his wife's former presence. Still, it was disconcerting to confront such a total alteration of a space that once had been so familiar.

Then a voice called out, "You've come!" and I was grounded once more. It was Elsa, a bit older but beautiful still, with a new baby on her hip and her daughter Inácia (named after Elsa's dead sister), now a luminous six-year-old, trailing behind. Elsa's mother, Diva, appeared in the doorway of a thatched house so new that the wooden beams were still a pale tan, not yet weathered to gray. The smile on her face matched my own.

"Hey, you came back!" Diva cried as we hugged.

Then both women grew somber. "Do you know?" Elsa began.

"I know," I said, glad to be able to save her from having to say the words. "I remember our elder sister who is gone. I'm sad; there is much sadness here." Unlike the first time I had shared these women's grief, this time I knew what to do. Leaning on each other's shoulders, we bowed our heads and remembered Tocohwet Pijo'.

After tears had welled for a moment, Elsa asked the inevitable next question: "And you, Beth? Is everything all right with you?"

"No, it's not all right," I had to say. "My younger brother died; I miss him very much." Then, because they didn't know, I had to recite the painful details. I had been through this speech many times in the States, but this was different. Elsa and Diva actually seemed to be listening to what I said, absorbing the words. They reached out to touch my shoulder, and we cried together.

At home, it had been difficult to talk to anyone, even close friends, about my brother's death. It seemed as though they wanted to block the information, deny the reality of the event. People would grasp for something comforting to say, but the effect was to make his death seem exceptional, an aberration. Death is not part of the normal, natural order of things—this was the message communicated by people's discomfort. When I talked about losing him, I felt guilty, as if being the bearer of bad news were shameful, contaminating.

However understandable it may be that privileged North Americans react as they do in the face of death, the effect is to deny legitimacy to the feelings of those who mourn. My own society offered little public space for expressing grief or acknowledging bereavement. Standing here, in front of this newly built house in an Indian village at the edge of the rainforest, with two women I hadn't seen in four years, it was suddenly all right to simply lean against each other and cry.

The "welcome of tears" is common among native peoples throughout the Brazilian Amazon. When someone has been away and then returns, the first information exchanged is news about who has died in the interim. In some native South American societies, the welcome of tears is an elaborate ritual greeting, with loud keening by groups of women, speeches expressing sorrow, and demonstrative crying that goes on for a long time. Among the

Wari', the greeting is much more low-key: a question is put immediately to the newcomer, an answer is given, news is shared about deaths in the community, and quiet tears or expressions of sympathy are exchanged.

The native Amazonian welcome of tears is a conventional social gesture. Surely Diva and Elsa were affected no more deeply (and probably much less so) by the news of my brother's death than were my close friends in the United States. But the existence of this custom among the Wari'—their expectation that the impact of a specific death should be acknowledged publicly and that mourners should be given a public space in which to express their grief—created a social dynamic very different from the pressures I felt at home to hide signs of sorrow. The conventionality of Wari' gestures of mourning has another effect as well: it reinforces the *social* aspect of the experience of bereavement by affirming that the sorrow and dislocation a bereft individual feels are emotions that others also have felt and with which they can identify. The postures and movements and melodies of Wari' mourning are always the same. The act of performing them thus links one individual's experience of a specific loved one's death to a long chain stretching back in time through countless prior moments when other Wari' made the same gestures, keened the same melodies. In the U.S., the lack of agreed-upon social forms for the behavior of mourners and those with whom they interact makes grief an isolating experience. Among the Wari', the conventionality of the responses to mourning carries a message of belonging that is a counterweight to the isolation of loss.

Yet grief itself is inevitably isolating. "Where's your father?" I asked Diva after we had shared our news. She gestured toward another brand-new house behind hers. It looked deserted. The door was closed; there was no cooking fire, no kids or tools or chickens, not a trace of domestic activity in the clean-swept dirt yard.

"Manim, are you here?" I called out anyway and was surprised to hear his voice respond from inside the silent house. Then I glimpsed him through a half-open window, lying rigid on his back on a bark-covered log bed. He got up slowly; evidently his arthritis was still giving him problems.

"Were you sleeping?" I asked as I entered his house. It was a startling contrast to the home where his family had formerly lived amidst jumbled piles of clothing and blankets and a chaotic clutter of possessions. This new house was bare and spotless, with a perfectly swept dirt floor, a bed, and a home-made bench along one wall. Everything still smelled of freshly cut wood. A mosquito net tied up over the bed, a couple of neatly folded blankets, a tiny pile of clothing, a machete hanging by the door, a couple of old coffee cans on a shelf: these were the sum total of Manim's current possessions.

"I was just lying down," Manim said. "That's how I am: I lie down, lie down every day. I stay in my house; I remember [*koromikat*]; I remember a lot. This is our custom [*je' kwerexi'*, "thus is our flesh"]." Then he added, darkly, "I don't go out to play around [*waraju*]; I'm not like *some* people." Glowering, he gestured pointedly with his chin in the direction of a neighboring house. "Not like *some* Wari', who go out and play and don't show respect [*respeitar*]!"

So this much at least had not changed. Ever the moralist, Manim's eternal complaint was about the laxity of others, the slippage of community norms in the years since the contact.

"When we Wari' miss someone, we stay in the house; we think about the one who is gone. I remember a lot; there is sadness in my heart," he said. "That's why I stay here [inside]."

I expressed sympathy, spoke of missing his wife, and told him about my brother's death. We sat in silence for a few moments. Then I remembered a question that had been bothering me for a long time. At home in California two years earlier, there had been a period of several weeks during which I dreamed about white-lipped peccaries every night. The dreams always came just before dawn, weird images of being in the midst of dozens of moving animal bodies, surrounded by sounds of snuffling and the vibrations of hooves pounding the earth. Nothing else ever happened in these dreams, but the images of restless peccary bodies were somehow profoundly disturbing. At the time, I had dismissed them as a meaningless remnant of imagery from the dissertation I was writing. Although I knew that Wari' say peccary dreams foretell the dreamer's death, I felt perfectly healthy and had no intention of dying. The dreams eventually went away, but soon afterwards came my brother's unexpected death. I asked Manim what he made of this.

"When somebody dreams about the white-lipped peccaries, it's not just the one who dreams who is going to die," he said. "When the peccaries come, they can carry away your relative, too. So, Beth, your brother went off with the peccary spirits?"

This suggestion was more than I could handle at that moment. To change the subject, I mentioned the event that had taken place just before I left Santo André four years earlier, when we sang the "Orotapan" songs and the peccaries showed up the next morning. Manim had been away from the village at the time, and I had never had a chance to talk to him about it.

"Yes, I heard about that," he said and smiled for the first time. "That's how it was in the old days, when we lived in the forest [before the contact]. All the Wari' sang 'Orotapan'; they sang and sang at night. The day came, and people said, 'Here come the white-lipped peccaries!' Wari' killed them; there was lots of meat. Lots of meat! Wari' sang 'Orotapan,' and the peccaries came."

"Fish, too?" I asked.

"Fish, too," Manim nodded. "We sang 'Orotapan'; here came the fish spirits. Wari' killed lots of fish!"

Do people still sing the "Orotapan" songs? I asked. No, he said; they had not done so for a long time.

"Why not?" I asked.

"Who knows?" he shrugged. Then he returned to the subject of water spirits. "Fish spirits are not good; they don't like Wari'; they kill Wari' a lot. White-lipped peccaries are good. A person dies; his spirit goes to the water. He stays there, he stays there, then the peccary spirit comes back. 'Here come the white-lipped peccaries!' Wari' say. [Then] Wari' kill lots of peccaries; they eat lots of meat!"

Manim's enthusiasm about peccaries led him to draw a connection to funerary cannibalism. "In the old days," he said, "when we made the big fire and placed the body there, it was as if the one who had died became a white-lipped peccary ['ak ka mijak pin na]." Switching to Portuguese for emphasis, he repeated, "Parece queixada: It appeared to be peccary."

Eating the Dead

The transformation of images of the dead that Manim described was another meaning that lay at the heart of Wari' funerary cannibalism: when the corpse was roasted, it was "as if the one who had died became a white-lipped peccary." The cooking and eating of the corpse, prepared as if it were game, blurred the distinction between human and animal, highlighting the fundamental ambiguity of death: the fact that the dead are simultaneously part of us (wari') and foreign to us (karawa). It is difficult to imagine a more powerful representation of Wari' ideas about the way death moves an individual out of the social collectivity and into a foreign domain, from which he or she will return as meat to feed the living.

Peccary imagery eventually comes to dominate Wari' relations to their ancestors in the years following a death. Wari' do not think or talk about their dead as generic animals; I have never heard anyone call the dead karawa. Rather, except for shamans (whose spirits become the particular animals from which the individual shamans derived their powers), the spirits of dead Wari' participate in the animal world specifically as white-lipped peccaries. Jami mijak, "white-lipped peccary spirits," is one of the most common terms by which Wari' refer to their ancestors. For individuals who, like Manim, saw the eventual transformation from human to peccary implied in the sight of the roasting corpse, this link between the two contexts in which Wari' ate their dead (at funerals and later as animal meat) connected death to a set of positive ideas and religious concepts.

The cultural frameworks that many peoples, including many native Amazonians, have developed to facilitate the process of mourning often interpret human death as part of larger cosmic processes. Regardless of the immediate circumstances surrounding a particular person's demise, Wari' eschatology interprets the event in terms of the generic scenario in which every death is another episode in the endless cycle of interactions and exchanges between the societies of living people and animals/water spirits. The idea that the dead continue to provide food for and interact with their living kin may have the psychological effect of softening the sense of loss felt by those left behind, for the notion that the dead will be rejuvenated as peccaries is a promise that life and some nurturant relationships will continue even after death. Cross-culturally, ideas about the continuity of life after death have been widely recognized as psychologically helpful for bereaved individuals trying to cope with the loss of a loved one (Lifton 1979). The Wari' ancestor-peccaries embody the additional promise that the dead do not completely abandon their families but may continue to care for them.

This speaks to anxieties at the heart of Wari' family and communal life: insecurities about the loss of social support and concerns about getting food, especially meat. The death of a family member is not just an emotional trauma; it also has implications for subsistence and other practical aspects of living. An adult's death directly reduces food production for his or her family, while a child's death diminishes the family's future prospects and the network of affinal ties that would have been extended or strengthened by the child's eventual marriage and offspring. Regardless of whether a specific death has much immediate impact on subsistence, every death reminds Wari' of the fragility of social bonds and brings into play fears about losing the support of the others with whom their lives are intertwined.

The white-lipped peccaries offer some compensation for the losses death imposes, for the ancestors and their fellow water spirits can be called upon to bring meat or fish. The kinship ties that, during life, linked an individual to specific relatives are transformed, after death, into a general enhancement of life-supporting relations between Wari' communities and some of the animals they eat. The peccary-ancestors exemplify the notion of the "life-giving death" that is a theme in many religions (de Coppett 1982), the idea that out of death comes a renewal of fertility and generativity, of the resources or relationships that support human life. Symbols of regeneration are prominent in death rituals throughout the world, but the nature of what is symbolically regenerated varies, reflecting differences in societies' priorities. "If death is often associated with a renewal of fertility, that which is renewed may either be the fecundity of people, or of animals and crops, or of all three," observed Maurice Bloch and Jonathan Parry (1982:7). "In most cases what would seem to be revitalized in funerary practices is that resource which is *culturally conceived* to be most essential to the reproduction of the social order" (emphasis in the original). For Wari', the reproduction of their social order depends especially on relations to kin, affines, and animals. These are the specific relationships that their death rituals reaffirmed.

In the trajectory of Wari' mourning, bereaved individuals are supposed to gradually let go of their old relationship to the deceased and accept a new, more impersonal situation in which the lost relative comes to be seen as one among many ancestor-peccaries who occasionally return to feed living Wari'. In precontact funerals, the cannibalized corpse—the human body treated like meat—was both an icon and an instrument of these metaphysical and emotional transformations. Just as mourners at funerals pile on top of one another with the weight of the corpse on top, the beliefs and ritual acts that surrounded precontact funerals piled layer upon layer of potential meanings—about bodies and relationships, memories and emotions, food and animals—under the symbolic weight of the corpse that was roasted and eaten.

Hwet Mao': Coming Out of Mourning

Wari' see the months following a death as a period of adjustment for both bereaved relatives and the dead person's spirit. While the bereaved are gradually coming to terms with their new lives without the deceased, the dead person's spirit is gradually getting used to its new existence in the underworld. For both parties, a successful transition depends on achieving some degree of emotional detachment so that they dwell less in memories of what has been lost and focus more on the present and future.

Wari' traditionally brought the last phase of mourning to an end with a ritual hunt and feast called *hwet mao'* (to come out, reappear) that marked bereaved family members' emergence from formal mourning and return to full engagement in community life. In the Dois Irmãos region, the practice of this ritual has faded since the late 1960s, becoming more private and less elaborate. Families continue to mark the end of mourning by going out to hunt together, but they do not stay away as long as people did in the past, and there is no community-wide celebration when they return. Still, whenever bereaved individuals decide to return to public life and behave in a more animated fashion, people say, *"Hwet mao' pin na wari'"* [The person has come out].

The period of public mourning, during which close relatives of the deceased define themselves as being in a state of active grieving, has no set limit. A number of elders expressed the opinion that it is appropriate for mourning to last about a year, until the return of the season during which the person died. But they also emphasized that the decision about when to stop mourning is a personal one. Even within a family, some individuals may continue to grieve intensely long after others in the household have ceased.

Mourning is a time of attenuated sociality and disengagement from many productive activities. Wari' mourners spend a great deal of time in their houses, and they do not interact much with people outside the circle of close kin. Though there is no rule against eating meat or fish, mourners perform less work and hunt and fish less than usual, so they seldom have much meat to eat. Hwet mao' traditionally marked the end of these mourning behaviors with a return to hunting, meat eating, and singing.

Hwet mao' hunts commonly took place several months after the dead person's close senior kin had completed the ton ho' ritual in which they honored memories of the dead and then burned and swept over places associated with them. When several members of the dead person's family (including especially the senior man who had directed the funeral) felt that it was time for mourning to end, family members left the village for an extended hunting trip. They might invite other hunters to join them, and any women and children who wanted to go along might accompany the hunters. The hunting party always included consanguines (*'iri nari*) of the dead person but might include affines (*nari paxi*), as well.

According to Santo André elders, the hunting party was ideally supposed to leave the village when the moon was new and return at the second full moon afterwards, which meant that the hunt would last about six weeks. By setting a date for their return, hunters ensured that the women who stayed in the village could know when to have corn chicha and pamonha ready for the feast. Holding the party at the full moon also is consistent with the notion of finalizing the mourners' dissociation from the dead, for ghosts (*jima*) do not come out when the moon is full.

As they left the village, the hunting party sang a little tamara music, marking the first time they had sung since the death. Their journey often took them deep into the forest to places where game could be expected to be abundant. In the Dois Irmãos region, many hwet mao' hunting parties went to the swampy area of lakes and seasonally flooded forest that lies between the Dois Irmãos and Mamoré Rivers. Since Wari' did not farm or locate villages there before the contact, this area seems to have served as a sort of de facto game reserve, where hunters could expect to find abundant prey.

On a hwet mao' hunt, the hunters tried to kill as much game as possible—any kind of mammal or bird considered good to eat. The members of the hunting party did not consume much of the meat, eating only the liver and other edible internal organs, which are perishable and also considered especially good for building blood and restoring vitality. They built a huge roasting rack and preserved the meat by smoking it continuously for weeks over a slow, smoldering fire. When people talk about hwet mao' hunts, they emphasize this image of a huge roasting rack piled high with smoked animal carcasses.

Although the hunters killed many species of game, Wari' always mention spider monkeys and white-lipped peccaries first when describing the animals killed on such hunts. They seem to consider these species especially appropriate prey for hwet mao' hunts. Spider monkeys (who are mythic descendants of a Wari' woman) and white-lipped peccaries (who are Wari' ancestors) are similar in that these are the species with which Wari' feel they have the most positive relations. The peccary herd's appearance might be taken as a sign that the dead relative's spirit had brought or sent the herd, but this interpretation does not seem to have been necessary to the hunt's success. The focus was on killing mass quantities of game in general, on piling up an overwhelming bounty of meat. In other contexts, the amount of meat contributed by one peccary seems significant, but in the profusion of game accumulated on hwet mao' hunts, a single peccary carcass would not stand out. This may have reinforced, in yet another way, the transition away from focusing on the individuality of the deceased. Hwet mao' dramatized the many kinds of animals in the forest and the abundance of the animal world, of which the mounds of game on the giant roasting rack were tangible evidence.

At the appointed full moon, the hunting party returned home, ideally timing their arrival to occur at the time of day when the kinsperson they were mourning had died. Before entering the village, the group stopped at a nearby stream to bathe and paint themselves with genipap and annatto. This was the first time they had used body paint since the death, and it signaled their readiness to return to communal life.

Carrying their game-laden baskets on their backs, the hunting party made a ritual entrance into the village, humming loudly to announce their arrival, and set the baskets of meat on the ground in front of their homes. The animal flesh was explicitly identified with the dead person. Standing over the baskets of meat, they sang kin terms for the deceased one last time, using the same words they had used in death keening. After this final act of honoring the dead person's memory, the senior man who was directing the ritual announced, "Sadness has ended; now happiness begins," inverting the pronouncement with which he had begun the funeral. In the feast that followed, the meat was shared with everyone present and eaten along with pieces of the pamonha prepared in advance by women in the village. Everyone joined in singing tamara music, and women sang *i jain je e'* songs (women's music sung at hüroroin parties).

"Meat takes away sadness," Wari' say when they explain how this feast brought the end of formal mourning for those who took part in the hunt. The return to consuming large quantities of meat marked the mourners' reengagement with social commitments and with the giving of aid, for after months of depending on others to some extent for food and support, the dead person's family now presented great quantities of meat to the whole community. The ritual process that had begun with the funeral, at which affines forced themselves to consume bits of the often inedible human flesh presented by the consanguines, ended with this feast, at which consanguines and affines joined together in eating large quantities of succulent animal meat provided by the dead person's family.

Taken as a whole, the sequence of Wari' mourning rites—disposing of the corpse, burning the deceased's house and possessions, burning and sweeping over each place associated with memories of the dead person, and the final collective hunt and feast—constituted a rite of passage that aimed to accomplish the two primary objectives commonly found in death rites everywhere: to remove the deceased from the world of the living to the symbolic world of the dead, and to facilitate survivors' acceptance of the death and the consequent alteration of social relations (Bloch and Parry 1982:4, Rosenblatt, Walsh, and Jackson 1976:87). The series of Wari' death rituals constructed these transformations around the fertile complexity of meanings attached to two prime symbols: the human body and human relations to animals. Maurice Bloch (1992) has argued that throughout the world, many religious and political rituals revolve around the theme of transforming individuals from prey (victims) to predators (hunters/killers). Bloch sees the ritual movement from prey to predator as an affirmation of human transcendence over the forces of death, a denial of the transience of life and social institutions. He suggests that rituals achieve this transformation by symbolically sacrificing the participants with acts of violence, so that they can partake of the power of immortal forces that lie outside human society and then be "reborn" as predators rather than as prey.

A plethora of Wari' myths, rituals, and cultural images illuminates the dynamic in which the move from prey to predator is achieved through the generative processes of ritual and social exchange. This dynamic appears most explicitly in the cultural scenario in which the spirit of a newly deceased individual is received into the underworld, is killed as prey, becomes a predator, and is remade as a perfected, immortal being. Among the Wari', however, ritual movements are seldom one-way. Consistent with the patterns of equivalency, reciprocity, and reversals of perspective that permeate Wari' cosmology and social arrangements, predators are also prey, and after death, human meat eaters become meat to be eaten.

To Feed and Be Fed

At the heart of Wari' death and mourning rites are concerns with the social and ecological relations in which they perceive their security and productivity to be grounded: the nurturant exchanges of which family life consists, the commitments among affines, and the special relations Wari' feel they have to certain animals they kill and eat. Their social and ritual responses to death emphasize creating, affirming, and reinforcing the networks of social relations through which food and other forms of support are produced and circulated among people and between people and animals. Meat eating is not just an expression of predatory relations to animals or enemies outside Wari' society. It also relates to feeding others and being fed by them.

More than any other event or activity, death puts social commitments on public display. During funerals, the dead person's close kin ('iri nari) come together and act as a group. Regardless of whatever resentments they may have harbored toward one another before the death, family members affirm their solidarity as they sit together holding the corpse, crying and keening and making collective decisions about how to conduct the funeral. After a funeral, the dependencies that characterize Wari' kin relations are dramatically evident when the dead person's immediate family is left with no house, no food, and almost no possessions. The family usually goes to live with relatives elsewhere, upon whom they depend for food and care during the weeks of deepest mourning. A death in the family activates the support of one's kin with an intensity like few other events in Wari' life.

Death also activates the support of affines, for funerals showcase affinal commitments. Close affines perform the considerable work necessary to carry out a funeral and watch out for the well-being of the grieving family. All the nari paxi present at a funeral "help" the bereaved family by crying with them for hours on end. When Wari' talk about affines' roles at funerals, they emphasize that affines help the dead person's family do the things that must be done that the iri' nari could not do on their own. They respond to the bereaved family from an emotional position compounded of empathy, attentiveness, and requisite detachment. Regardless of how sad or upset individual affines may feel, they are expected to constrain their emotions so they can focus on performing the tasks necessary to support the bereaved consanguines. Building on Viveiros de Castro's insights about native lowland South American "perspectivism," Vilaça (2000:94) has suggested that affines and other nonrelatives have a perspective in regard to the deceased individual that differs from the consanguines' perspective. "Kinsfolk continued to see the loved one in the corpse . . . and for this reason were unable to eat the body, while non-kin perceived clearly that they were no longer confronted with a human being, *wari'*. The service which they rendered to the deceased's kin . . . was that of forcing the kin to share their vision: the corpse was no longer a person." They accomplished this by cutting, roasting, and eating the corpse, "as if edibility was the only irrefutable proof of non-humanity."

Wari' interpret the act of eating the dead in the funeral ritual as an act of compassion for the bereaved and for the dead themselves. The nari paxi expressed compassion in two major ways: by demonstrating empathy in identifying with the bereaved family members' suffering (expressed most directly in crying with them), and by giving help (with the eating of the corpse being the most tangible form of help given by the group of nonkin as a whole). In precontact funerals, the conventions for giving and receiving the flesh that the nari paxi cut up, roasted, and ate constructed these acts around the analogy of food sharing on the part of the dead person's close kin, who urged the others to eat. The nari paxi hung back, insisting that they could not eat because they were too sad, in a ritualized refusal that again affirmed their identification with the bereaved kin. When the nari paxi finally accepted the flesh to eat, the way they handled it suggests another analogy as well, for it resembles interactions between hosts and guests at tamara parties, where guests sing and dance and receive from their hosts bits of food speared on thin sticks. The analogy is telling, for in many ways, the eating of the corpse was a performance put on for the benefit of those who watched.

Dismembering and Remembering

The imperative that Wari' feel to distance, destroy, and transform their dead is closely tied to the themes explored in Part III of this study: the recognition of the human body's role in composing persons and social relationships and the body's centrality in memory and mourning. As a primary site where identities are formed and interpersonal bonds created, sustained, and experienced, the human body is a focus of the physical and emotional ties that link the living and the dead. It also is a site that can be acted upon in an effort to loosen and transform those ties, a site where old memories can be overlaid with new ones and new relations to the dead can begin to take shape. Precontact Wari' death rites posited a transformation of psycho-spiritual bonds between the living and the dead through simultaneous transformations of two "bodies": the corpse and the dead person's immaterial spirit-body. Implicit in the physical transformation of the corpse was a message about the metaphysical transformation of the individual's other "body," the spirit that becomes a perfected, immortal being and eventually will be re-embodied as a living animal. By eradicating and altering material traces of the dead person's presence among the living, including the body itself, the sequence of death rites aimed to move mourners through a progressive transformation of emotional attachments. This psychological transformation was paralleled and facilitated by the progressive accumulation over time of new memory-images of the dead person transformed from human into animal, from living meat eater into a giver of meat eaten by the living.

Mourners' public expressions of loss peaked at the moment Wari' describe as most emotionally difficult in a precontact funeral: the moment when the corpse was taken from its relatives' arms to be dismembered before their eyes. As noted earlier, in lowland South America, the preparation and consumption of the corpse seems to have almost always taken place in full view of the dead person's closest relatives, whether or not they themselves took part in eating it. These close family members were the ones most deeply affected by the death and thus most likely to experience the persistent memory-attachments that many native South Americans consider problematic and in need of management through ritual. As relatives watched the dismemberment and consumption of the corpse, the sight must surely have impressed itself on their memories of the deceased, leaving them with new and different images of the individual.

Wari' recognize this transformation. After one has watched a corpse be dismembered and eaten, several elders have told me, one does not think about that person in quite the same way: "It [the memory] is different." Alongside recollections of how the person looked in life stand images of the person's body being dismembered and eaten. These must have been highly charged, powerful, ambivalent images.

The emphasis Wari' place on vision and the impact of visual reminders suggests that the experience of *seeing* the corpse be cut up and consumed may have been a central component of mortuary cannibalism's subjective impact. When Wari' explain their insistence that all close kin arrive at the funeral before the family disposes of the body, they often say that all the relatives must *see* the body (and, by extension, see what is done with it). To be told what has happened is not enough; one should be there to see it for oneself. In cases in which a close relative was unable to attend the funeral, sometimes one of the nari paxi would save a piece of the roasted flesh and consume it later, before the eyes of the person who had been unable to see the corpse itself and see what was done with it (Vilaça 2000:93, 97).

Psychologists recognize that the sight of a corpse—especially the corpse of a close relative or friend—can leave a deep impression. For some, the sight may be traumatic, and the experience of viewing or touching the corpse may affect how they think about the dead person afterwards. An example comes from Geoffrey Gorer's work with bereaved individuals in Britain. Gorer (1965:7) described an Englishwoman who had lost both of her parents, who "said that she thought that the really important difference between her grief for her father and that for her mother was that she had seen her father in the coffin and never seen her mother cold, and, as a result, she felt that the funeral was a farce, and that her mother is not really dead. She remembers her mother as a live woman, her father as a dead man."

"When the body was eaten, we did not remember or long for [*koromikat*] the dead person much" is the truism Wari' elders repeat over and over. Destroying the corpse by eating or burning it erased the most tangible focus for thinking about the deceased. The sight of the corpse being eaten conveyed an inescapably blunt message about the individual's new status as one who was no longer part of the collectivity of living people and who was in transition to a new existence in the world of animals and ancestors. Precisely because it was so graphic, the experience of watching the corpse being cut up, cooked, and eaten must have imprinted deeply in individuals' memories and thoughts about the deceased.

Pierre Bourdieu (1977) and Paul Connerton (1989) have emphasized the importance of bodily experiences and postures in creating and conveying memories. Wari' mourners' sensory experiences with the corpse are not just visual, but also intimately tactile and olfactory. Close kin embrace the cold, intact corpse for hours. In precontact funerals, they received the roasted body parts and, using their hands and moving slowly and deliberately, they separated the flesh from the bones. The sensory memories of this experience must have stayed with them for a long time.

The sensory aspect of funerals that Wari' talk about most is the smell, the way the stench of rotten flesh penetrated the skin and hair of everyone at the funeral. For people who consider cleanliness so important and place a priority on surrounding themselves with good, pleasant smells, this voluntary immersion in decay and pollution may have reinforced, at yet another level of primal embodied experience, the radical disjuncture, the absolute break in continuity, that death imposed on their relations to the deceased.

The transformation of memories and emotions that was a main objective of the social process of Wari' mourning involved first eradicating and altering tangible reminders, including the corpse, and then developing new images of and relations to the deceased as a member of the world of animals and ancestors. The detachment and emotional resolution sought in the mourning process came not from completely forgetting about the dead, but from coming to relate to them in more impersonal terms, as participants in the ongoing cycles of generative exchanges—between humans and animals, predators and prey, the living and the ancestors—that are the organizing dynamics of the Wari' universe. In a multitude of ways, Wari' practices facilitated this transformation by projecting imageries, enacting rituals, and providing forms of social support affirming the idea that the nurturant arrangements that create and sustain Wari' bodies, persons, families, and society continue even in the face of death. In enacting the idea that the dead feed the living, the series of mourning rituals that began with the eating of the corpse and ended with the feast on animal meat evoked the theme of connections between death and the regeneration of life that has run through the death rites of many cultures since time immemorial. Tracing the ideas behind Wari' cannibalism may seem like an excursion into exotic territory, but the path leads back to near-universal human concerns.

* * *

The Wari' case speaks to an issue that lies at the interface between symbolic and psychological interpretations of cannibalism: the question of how cultural representations articulate with individual emotions and experiences. The sentiments at the heart of Wari' funerary cannibalism were neither the aggressive, antisocial, resentful impulses nor the desires for identification

and incorporation that most western models of cannibalism have emphasized. Rather, Wari' endocannibalism and the social practices surrounding
it responded to emotions of grief and anxieties about the rupture of family
relationships and the disruption created by a group member's demise. Eating the dead reflected a felt imperative to negate that destabilizing loss and
turn it into something more positive. By drawing on cultural ideas about the
social, psychological, and moral meanings associated with human bodies,
animals, predation, and food, Wari' constructed a powerful, multifaceted
set of images and rituals to shape and guide mourners' behavior and emotional experiences.

Did this cultural framework really help bereaved individuals cope with
their grief? It is impossible to know for sure, for an answer to this question would require a retrospective assessment of individual psychological
experiences decades after the last Wari' corpse was consumed. Ultimately,
all we can know is that Wari' elders are unanimous in affirming that the
ritual process that included eating their dead did make it easier to find some
emotional peace.

Trying to understand cannibalism from Wari' points of view involves
crossing conceptual boundaries to look at social life through the lenses of
different cultural assumptions—a shift in perspective not unlike the Wari'
shaman's engagement with his animal companion, or the human spirit's
journey to and from the underworld. In confronting questions about life
and death and the nature of humanity, Wari' have found prime spaces for
reflection in their images of the worlds of animals, spirits, and foreigners.
In the past five centuries of outsiders' encounters with indigenous South
Americans, the worlds of native peoples, and ideas about their practices of
cannibalism, have often played similar roles, providing counterimages and
perspectives that outsiders have used to define themselves, reflect upon the
wisdom of different ways of living, and ask what it means to be human.
These questions come to the fore anew in exploring what cannibalism meant
to the Wari' and why they felt it to be the most compassionate way to treat
a loved one's body. Their experiences challenge us to reflect upon our own
ways of responding to death and to consider the forms of support we do
and do not offer in the human search for social, symbolic, and emotional
resources for dealing with the problem of bereavement and consuming grief.

AFTERWORD

My brother, to whom this book is dedicated, died on the day I completed the final draft of the study in which I first tried to come to terms with the ethnographic material from which this book has evolved. Jim was my *xa,* younger sibling: flesh of my flesh, the one I carried on my hip, as Wari' would say. When the news of his death arrived, every fiber in my being resisted. The impulse for denial came from deeper than I knew possible. "*No,*" was my first response. "This isn't happening. My brother is *not* dead."

But he was gone: my brilliant, handsome, Eagle Scout brother. His passing left a hole in the universe. Five days later, our family gathered in a cemetery in southwestern Iowa on a hill surrounded by lush green corn fields planted by our cousins, who look after the cemetery. Rows of graceful old cedars shelter five generations of our ancestors, including eleven sets of grandparents from both sides of my family. As I touched my brother's cold, hard flesh for the last time, our sister, sitting beside him, was carrying in her womb the first member of our next generation. Uncle Jim would have adored his nephews.

At the funeral, our elder brother told a story that ended with the blessing "May a thousand eagles spit in your eye." On Jim's tombstone we engraved a scene in memory of the Pacific Northwest mountains where he had spent so much time hiking. Though Wari' find some of my people's ways of dealing with death distasteful, I think they would like this scene of an eagle soaring above a forest where a deer grazes in peace, no hunter in sight.

Koromikat tamana inem, xa.

THE STORY OF MORTUARY
CANNIBALISM'S ORIGIN

Of the many versions of this story, I have chosen to present the one Jimon Maram told one night when I was staying with him and his family at their house near their maize fields at Hon Xitot. After we finished eating that evening, Quimoin lit a chunk of resin and set it to burn on a thick green leaf, and its flickering flame cast shadows on the faces of the children who lay down to listen. The house had no walls, and as a huge full moon rose over the forest, brilliant light and sharp shadows spilled into the surrounding clearing while we listened to the story of how cannibalism and culture began.

* * *

There was an old woman who was the only person who had fire. To get fire from her, Wari' had to gather lots of firewood and give her presents of fish. If anyone tried to steal her fire, she caught them and ate them raw, like a jaguar eats its prey.

This woman had two grandsons; she was the boys' *pa'*, their mothers' mother. The boys' mothers went to catch fish to trade for fire. The boys stayed home, and their mothers told them not to go to their grandmother's house. When the mothers returned, they gave the fish to the old woman, who let them use her fire temporarily. The old woman ate the fish raw, too.

The boys were thinking about how good it would be to be able to roast food. Without fire for cooking, no one could eat fish or meat. People tried to cook food by putting it in the sun, but it just got hot and rotted. The people were unhappy, but they were afraid of the old woman and did not know how to kill her.

The boys had an idea. They built a platform high in the treetops, the kind that hunters use as a blind to wait for birds and monkeys to shoot. A thick liana hung from the platform. The boys told the women to make a lot of maize meal (*kuwata*). They filled a big basket with the meal, and many Wari' climbed up the vine into the treetops. All the people climbed up to a land in the sky where there is water, honey, and game. They went away to escape the old woman.

Then the boys climbed into the hunting blind and called the old woman. She sat on the ground below, waiting for them to kill a bird for her to eat. She ate many birds; she ate them raw and liked to eat lots of blood. The old woman sat below and criticized the boys' efforts. "You missed the bird! It got away!" she screamed.

Her grandsons told a bird to lead the old woman far away. The bird flew close to her, almost touching the ground. The boys called, "Get it, grandma! Catch it! You missed it!" The bird flew farther away. The old woman ran after it. "You missed it!" yelled the boys. The bird flew on, leading the old woman farther and farther away.

The boys heard their grandmother's voice in the distance, fading away as she ran after the bird. They climbed down and went home. The older boy told the younger one to roast another bird they had killed on their grandmother's fire. They cooked it, ate quickly, and started to climb up the liana.

Halfway up, the boys saw the old woman coming after them. She was angry; she wanted to eat them. The old woman started climbing the liana. She got close to the younger brother, for he was tired and could not go on. He said, "I will become a woodpecker, elder brother!" His brother told him to keep climbing. But the younger brother turned into a bird and flew away, so the elder brother turned into a bird, too. They flew to their father's house in the sky.

The boys went to Pinom, the man who was the leader of the group and the "owner" of the liana. They told Pinom that the old woman was coming. Then they went to look for a fish to cut the liana. First they tried a tucunaré fish, but it had no teeth. Then they tried another fish, but it, too, had no teeth. Finally, they tried a big, light-colored piranha with sharp teeth. The piranha began to cut the liana. "Stand back, people!" cried the piranha.

The old woman was getting close. At the last moment, the piranha cut through the vine. The old woman fell far, far down to the ground. She landed in her own fire, and her body began to burn. Out of her burning body came jaguars, ocelots, jaguarundis, and orotapan. [In some versions of this story, other carnivores—tayras, weasels, and coati—also emerge from this old woman's burning body.]

"And that," explained Jimon Maram, "is why there are jaguars on earth." Then he continued with the story:

The Wari' were very happy that the old woman was dead. They got ready to descend from the sky, but the liana was gone. They went looking for fruit trees in the land in the sky. They found a fruit called *kahowip* and roasted and ate it. They tossed the seeds to earth so kahowip trees would grow below, so the people would be able to jump down into the treetops.

Then they searched for bees to get beeswax. Everyone decided what kind of animal he or she wanted to be. Some rolled the wax into long tails and put them on. The capuchin monkey had a very long tail. The spider monkey had a shorter tail, but it was still good enough to wrap around a tree branch. Lots of Wari' had decided to be monkeys. They had become monkeys completely, and everyone was practicing jumping.

The capuchin monkey was proud of his long tail. He sat in the men's house (kaxa') showing it off. The spider monkey was envious. He sneaked up behind the capuchin, grabbed the capuchin's long tail, and traded it for his own, shorter tail. This is why the capuchin monkey has a short tail, while the spider monkey has a nice, long tail.

The capuchin monkey was very angry, and he cursed at the spider monkey. The spider monkey got angry and said, "Now when people shoot you, capuchin, you will fall to the ground." This is why capuchin monkeys fall to the ground when they are shot, while spider monkeys remain perched in the trees.

The capuchin found a way to get back at the spider monkey. Hiding one of his fingers, the capuchin showed that he had only four fingers. He tricked the spider monkey into taking off one of his own fingers, so that he was left with only four.

The kahowip trees were ripening on earth below, and everyone got ready to descend. All of the Wari' had become animals. There were lots of monkeys of all different species. There were also tapirs, deer, turtles, armadillos, and birds—all kinds of animals.

The trees had grown up from the earth below, and the fruit was ripe. The animal-people said, "Let's go!" They started to jump down into the top branches of the trees. The squirrel monkey was the first to jump. The squirrel monkey carries its baby on its back, and the squirrel monkey husband told his wife to hold on tight to their baby. He got ready to jump. "Stand back a little!" he warned. The squirrel monkey went out on the end of a very thin branch. He jumped and landed on the top of the fruit tree below. He ate the fruit. His wife and baby jumped also, but their landing broke the tree branches. They showed the broken branches to the other monkeys in the sky.

There were other kahowip trees, and the other monkeys jumped down on them. Then the other animals jumped. The people who had become birds came down, too. Everybody descended from the sky. The kahowip trees were all smashed up.

It was then that they realized they had left the fire behind in the land in the sky. They wanted to roast and eat fruit, but they had no fire.

Two boy orphans were still up in the sky; they had not jumped down yet. They were trying to decide what kind of birds to be. They talked to many different kinds of tinamous. They tried all of the birds' songs but did not like any of them enough. Then they found the partridge; they decided to become partridges because they have the prettiest song. The boys made beaks for themselves out of beeswax. Then they swallowed some embers from the fire and started to fly toward earth.

The monkeys and other animals who had already jumped down had become human again, but they had no fire. They called to the boys who were partridges, calling them to bring the fire. But the boys were still birds, and they were eating fruit. They flew away. Only when they were full of fruit would they become Wari' again.

The people wanted to kill the birds to get the fire. Pinom, the man who was their leader, said he would do it. He called the bird-boys by imitating the partridge's song. Pinom killed the two bird-boys, cut them open, and found the fire in their bellies. Then Pinom swallowed the fire himself.

The boys came back to life. They were completely human again. The boys told the others that Pinom had swallowed the fire. Pinom was keeping the fire to himself. When he got possession of it, he became selfish.

The Wari' were suffering without fire. They killed game, made pamonha, and tried to roast food in the sun. It didn't work; the food just spoiled. Only Pinom and his family ate well. Pinom roasted meat and fish and cooked pamonha and chicha. He made his fires in secret, hidden from the others. He always doused the fire with water so no one else would get it.

Wari' talked about how to get fire from Pinom. A shaman said that he would do it. He turned into a large frog. There was a Brazil nut tree by the water's edge. Pinom climbed it to get Brazil nuts and gathered lots of firewood to roast the nuts. The shaman-frog hid, watching and waiting. Pinom made his fire. He lit the fire by farting. The shaman-frog was hidden, watching. A spark flew toward him, and he swallowed it. Pinom saw this happen and chased the shaman-frog. The shaman-frog went hopping toward the water and dove in.

Pinom began to fling water out of the stream in order to catch the frog. He left his fire burning untended. Frantically, Pinom cut open tadpoles, frogs, and fish, but he found there was nothing inside any of them. The shaman-frog had escaped with the fire.

Pinom had left his Brazil nuts roasting in the fire. He looked up and saw the shaman on the path, lighting a fire by farting. Pinom was angry. He went back to the village and saw that the shaman had already given fire to all the people.

Pinom was very angry. He swore at the Wari', saying: "Now you will have to roast your children! I won't feel sorry for you all. I'm angry at you!"

The shaman replied, "You, too. You will roast your children, too. You will burn all your children."

"And that," Jimon Maram concluded, "is why we used to roast ourselves. That is why we ate ourselves."

TIIE STORY OF HUJIN
AND OROTAPAN

This is the story described in Chapter Ten, the story that Maxun Kwarain told the night before the peccary herd appeared. In the text, my explanatory comments appear in double brackets, [[]]. In single brackets, [], are the comments of Jimon Maram, who sat down with me the day after Maxun Kwarain told this story to work through the tape-recorded narrative and clarify various points.

* * *

Hujin was a Wari' man who was married and had a child. Hujin lived near the Negro River, and his older brother lived in a village on the other side of the river. Hujin crossed the river and had sex with his brother's wife. His brother was angry but he did not want to fight. To punish Hujin, his called him to drink chicha. He forced him to drink many pots of chicha and vomit repeatedly. [[This is the punishment meted out in hüroroin and hütop parties as retribution for ritual transgressions.]] There were many clay pots full of chicha. First Hujin drank the small pots; then he drank the big ones. [He had to vomit a lot to consume all the chicha.]

After so much drinking and vomiting, Hujin almost went into itam. However, he remained conscious and decided to go home. His nephew went along with him to see him home, but when they reached the river, Hujin said he would cross alone. He told his nephew to bathe in the river and go home.

Hujin was crossing the Negro River on a log bridge [made of tree trunks lashed together]. When he reached the middle, his eyes were rolling, and he fell off the log into the water. The water was really a village, and Hujin landed in the men's house (kaxa').

Orotapan came. He was a giant carnivore. Orotapan ate Hujin. He ate all of his flesh but saved the bones.

Then Orotapan made new flesh appear on Hujin's bones. He threw the bones in the air, and they came down whole, making a new body for Hujin. Orotapan ate Hujin again. Again he tossed Hujin's bones in the air to recreate his flesh and eat him again. The fourth time that Orotapan tossed Hujin's bones in the air, Hujin disappeared. A Wari' shaman had reached into the water, caught Hujin, and pulled him out.

Hujin went home to his own house. He felt terrible. He had a headache and wrapped a vine tightly around his head [[a headache remedy]]. He was hoarse and could not talk. He felt very cold and said, "Light the fire!" The others asked whether he had drunk his brother's chicha, and he said yes.

Early the next day, Hujin went back into the water. He landed in the men's house, and a woman came to give him chicha. [Jimon Maram commented at this point that "Hujin discovered Towira Towira," the water spirit leader whose wife offers chicha to the spirits of Wari' on the verge of death.]

Every morning, Hujin returned to visit Orotapan underwater. While he was gone, the sun did not shine on earth. Dark storms (*topo*) swept the earth. There were cold, raging winds and lots of rain.

Wari' men asked Hujin where he went every morning, since he never returned with any game. Hujin's throat was getting better, and he could talk, so he replied, "Because Orotapan ate me; that's why there is no sun."

Hujin went back under the water and saw Wem Parom. [[Orotapan is also Wem Parom, a giant white-lipped peccary. He is the leader who is always in the middle of the peccary herd and of schools of fish. Wem Parom is the master of music, and he makes latex-covered drums (*towa*) of all sizes. From him, the Wari' learned the art of making music and drums.]]

The peccary leader, Wem Parom, sang a song. Hujin responded by making a beautiful song of his own. He sang about Orotapan's association with the wind raging on earth above. Wem Parom was surprised and asked where Hujin had learned that song. Hujin said he made it himself. Then Wem Parom sang a song. Hujin responded with another song, about Orotapan's throat being spotted like a jaguar's. Wem Parom responded with a song about eating Hujin. Their song-making duel went on and on. [These days, only a few elderly Wari' know all these songs. This contest between Hujin and Orotapan was the origin of music among the Wari'.]

If Hujin had lost this contest, Orotapan would have eaten him.

All the water spirits came out of the water onto the land in the bodies of white-lipped peccaries. They came to sing and had many drums. Wem Parom stood in the middle of the line of dancers, beating a big drum. The other peccaries had smaller drums. [The peccary dancers formed a long line as dancers do in a hütop party.] While the peccaries were singing and dancing, a little armadillo scratched at Wem Parom's foot as he was beating his drum. Wem Parom felt it and was irritated. He started stamping his foot and dropped his drum [which spoiled his performance]. Wem Parom looked down and saw the little armadillo. He was angry and blamed Hujin, saying, "You did this!" Hujin replied that he did not.

[With that interruption, Wem Parom lost the contest.]

Hujin tried to placate the other peccaries. He said to them, "You all are young. Wem Parom is very old and will die soon." Wem Parom agreed, and that was the end of the fight between him and Hujin. [[By winning the song-making contest, Hujin stopped being just the prey of the water spirits and was recognized as their equal, able to develop an exchange relationship with them.]]

Wem Parom sent his son to get Brazil nuts from Hujin's people. [This gift of food marked the establishment of friendly relations.] Hujin carried the Brazil nuts to his house, and Wem Parom's son went along. Wem Parom's son looked human, but when they got close to Hujin's house, he turned into a small fish. Hujin wrapped Wem Parom's fish-son in palm leaves so other people would not see him.

Hujin told his relatives he was going to give corn beer to the fish-son of Wem Parom. He took him into his house, which was screened off so no one could see he was a fish. Hujin gave Wem Parom's fish-son lots of beer. Wem Parom's fish-son drank and vomited and drank and vomited it all [as guests do at hüroroin and hütop parties].

Hujin told the other Wari' to get Brazil nuts and pamonha [[unleavened corn bread]] and put this food on the path outside the village. He carried Wem Parom's fish-son, wrapped in leaves, out of the village. Wem Parom's fish-son turned back into his human form. He took the food and left.

Hujin knew the water spirits were coming. He told the other men to make many new arrows, and he told the women to make lots of beer. He said, "Tomorrow the white-lipped peccaries will come."

Hujin told all the women to leave the village. Only the men stayed. He told them to stay up on the sleeping platform and not step on the ground. They had lots of beer and Brazil nuts ready for the water spirits.

The white-lipped peccaries came with Wem Parom. The peccaries drank all of the beer and ran around breaking the pots. [This was like a hüroroin party, at which male guests storm the hosts' village, acting the part of wind spirits that destroy houses.]

The Wari' men shot the peccaries in the heart. Hujin told them to shoot Wem Parom and his son. The Wari' killed them, and from their bodies emerged scarlet macaws and two types of parrots. The macaws flew around the village and flew away. Hujin told the other peccaries that they could leave.

Hujin explained the peccaries to the Wari'. He explained which of the peccary visitors were Wari' ancestors and which were Wem Parom's people [[nonancestral water spirits]]. [This was the first time Wari' learned who the peccaries really were.] Hujin told the Wari' that now they knew that when they died, they themselves would become white-lipped peccaries.

Hujin looked at the slain peccaries and told the Wari' which ones were their ancestors. The people began to cry. This was the first time they knew what happens to human spirits after death. Hujin told the Wari' that they must respect the scarlet macaw because it belongs to Orotapan.

Hujin continued going to visit Orotapan underwater every morning. He never stayed home. His older brother missed him and was sad. His brother thought maybe he should go into the water himself so he could see more of his brother, Hujin. He made preparations to kill himself, gathering everything needed for a funeral: a roasting rack, a decorated firewood bundle, mats to lie on, and leaf wrappers to roast his internal organs. When everything was ready, he lay down on the mat and said goodbye to the others. He stabbed himself in the neck with a sharp new arrow point and died. The Wari' cut him up.

Hujin came out of the water and saw the smoke from far away. He rushed to the place and saw his brother's corpse already being roasted. The others said that it was Hujin's fault for not staying home more. Hujin hurried to the water to follow his brother's spirit, but his brother's spirit had gone ahead. Hujin searched through many houses and villages of the ancestors under the water. He found his brother and addressed him angrily, saying, "It is not a good place here; it is not a beautiful place underwater."

His brother told Hujin to bring the brother's wife to join him underwater. He told Hujin to tell her that his brother wanted his cotton for spinning. Hujin did as his brother asked. The wife said the cotton was in the rafters. Hujin looked but could not find it. His brother's wife reached up into the rafters, and a poisonous spider bit her. Hujin ran to the water to tell his brother that his wife had been bitten. He saw that her spirit was already there with her husband. Her spirit had traveled fast.

On another day, Hujin's brother sent him to get resin (*katokwan*, used for making arrows) from the brother's second wife. As she was searching for the resin in the rafters, a scorpion bit her. Her spirit went to the water and joined her husband, too. Hujin's brother told Hujin to take care of the brother's son. Hujin promised that he would.

Hujin's own wife got pregnant, and their child was born as a fish. [This was because Hujin had been eaten by the water spirit, Orotapan, who can become a fish.] Hujin took his fish-son to the water and turned him loose. Orotapan ate Hujin again, and Hujin turned into a fish. He could be fish or human. Three or four more times, Hujin's wife gave birth to a fish. Each time, Hujin put the fish-child in the water. The last time that Hujin had a son born as a fish, Hujin killed and cleaned his fish-son and roasted him in leaves. He said, "I'm going to eat my son and die in order to be with my sons and my brother." Hujin ate his fish-son and got terrible stomach pains and died. He ate his son and died.

NOTES

Introduction

1. The word *wari'* ends in a glottal stop, a quick cut-off of the final sound indicated by the apostrophe at the end of the word. As in all words in the Wari' language, the stress is on the final syllable. The term *wari'* is the first-person plural pronoun: it means "we," people. "Pakaa Nova" is a name of uncertain origin; variant spellings include Pacaas Novos, Pacaa Nova, Pakaa Novo, and Pakahanova. I use the denomination "Wari'" in deference to the sentiment of many individuals who dislike being called "Pakaa Nova."

2. The theme of dying individuals' horror at the idea of burial and a preference for their corpses to be eaten, cremated, or allowed to rot above ground has been reported in other South American societies, including the Arawakan-speaking Matsigenka (Shepard n.d.) and Panoan speakers (Dole 1974:307, Erikson 1986:198) in western Amazonia and the Guayakí in Paraguay (P. Clastres 1974:319), as well as among war captives taken by the Tupinambá of coastal Brazil (Viveiros de Castro 1992:289–90).

3. For overviews and summaries of reports of mortuary cannibalism in lowland South America, see Dole (1974), Métraux (1947:22–25, 1949), Sullivan (1988:512–524, 665–668, 856–862), and Zerries (1960). The quality and reliability of data must be evaluated in each individual case.

4. In the Ucayali River region of southeastern Peru and in the adjoining Brazilian territory of Acre, a number of peoples who spoke Panoan languages reportedly practiced endocannibalism (see Dole 1974, Kensinger 1995, McCallum 1996b). In eastern Bolivia (south and west of Wari' territory), endocannibalism reportedly was practiced by other Panoans and by several groups that spoke Chapakuran languages, the language family to which the Wari' language belongs (see Ryden 1942:117).

5. One common method for removing flesh from bones was to bury the corpse and exhume it later, after some or all of the flesh had rotted away. The Yanomami of northern Brazil and southern Venezuela, who are one of the few societies in which some communities still practice a form of endocannibalism, may place the corpse on a high platform in the forest and leave

it there until it rots. On Yanomami endocannibalism, see Albert (1985), Becher (1968), and Clastres and Lizot (1978).

6. Studies of endocannibalism in Melanesia include Gillison (1993), Lindenbaum (1979), and Meigs (1984). Sanday (1986) presents a comprehensive survey of cross-cultural cannibalism and anthropological theories of cannibalism. Other useful cross-cultural overviews include Arens (1979), Brown and Tuzin (1983), Harris (1977), and Sagan (1974). Ernst (1999), Goldman (1999), Kelly (1977), Knauft (1993), Rumsey (1999), A. Strathern (1982), and Zubrinich (1999) describe other forms of cannibalism in Melanesia, including the consumption of witches and enemies and ideas about the cannibalistic practices of witches and enemies.

7. For example, Peggy Sanday (1986:7) made the general statement that "[e]ndocannibalism recycles and regenerates social forces that are believed to be physically constituted in bodily substances or bones." I. M. Lewis (1986:73) wrote that "the ritual consumption of parts of the human body enables the consumer to acquire something of the body's vital energy."

8. See Acosta Saignes 1961:161–162, Dole 1974:307, Erikson 1986:198, McCallum 1996b: 70, Reichel-Dolmatoff 1971:138–139.

Chapter 1

1. On colonialist exploitation of representations of cannibalistic native peoples, see Arens (1979), Barker, Hulme, and Iversen (1998), Brown and Tuzin (1983), Goldman (1999), and Taussig (1987).

2. When the Spanish friar Bartolomé de las Casas argued against the enslavement of certain American Indian groups such as the Trinidad islanders, he based his argument not on the idea that slavery was wrong, but on the claim that these Indians had been wrongly accused of being cannibals (Whitehead 1984:72–73).

3. Whitehead (1984:82) notes that rationalizations about the legitimacy of brutality against cannibalistic peoples persisted for centuries. In the Argentine in the 18th century, Indian groups were said to be "*tan caribe*" (so Carib-like) "that they ate human flesh and were, thus, held to be in need of immediate and violent subjugation."

4. Steadman and Merbs (1982) criticize the evidence for cannibalism in the New Guinea highlands.

5. The ethnographic evidence for cannibalism is discussed in Brown and Tuzin (1983), Lindenbaum (1982), Rawson (1997), Rivière (1980), Sahlins (1979), and Sanday (1986). Gardner (1999), Goldman (1999), and Osborne (1997) provide good summaries of the current state of this controversy. Goldman (1999:18) says the evidence for the practice of cannibalism in Melanesia is so clear that "we regard Papua New Guinea as the locale that marks the tombstone for Arens' denial of cannibalism."

6. Arens (1979:36–38) initially argued that Dole's (1974) claim to have witnessed an Amahuaca mother eating the powdered bone ash of her dead child cannot be believed because Dole's meticulous account did not describe seeing the bones ground into powder. He suggested this meant Dole did not really know what was in the powder the mother consumed, and he treated this as evidence of the flimsiness of ethnographers' purported eyewitness accounts of cannibalism. Recently, Arens recanted this criticism, saying, "I now believe it was unreasonable to adopt this position" (1998:46). After acknowledging the probable reality of both the Amahuaca bone eating reported by Dole and the European practice of medicinal can-

nibalism described by Gordon-Grube (1988), Arens suggested that these were not bona fide forms of cannibalism. "I would suggest that none of the instances mentioned above should be deemed anthropophagy," he wrote, and went on to observe, "To my knowledge no one has ever suggested that Western societies, or for that matter these particular activities or groups, be understood as cannibalistic" (1998:47). However, in the preceding paragraph Arens had cited Gordon-Grube's 1988 article, which was titled "Anthropophagy in Post-Renaissance Europe: The tradition of medicinal cannibalism."

7. On Anasazi cannibalism, see White (1992), C. and J. A. Turner (1999), Darling (1998), and Kantner (1999). Pickering (1999) addresses the lack of evidence for cannibalism among Australian Aborigines, despite the One Nation Party's claim to the contrary.

8. Studies of the Tupinambá treatment of war captives include Fernandes (1963 [1949] and 1970 [1952]), H. Clastres (1972), and Viveiros de Castro (1992).

Chapter 2

1. In the nineteenth century, Chapakuran-speaking groups in Rondônia included the Torá, Jarú, Urupá, Huanyam, and Urunamacan. For an account of Chapakuran ethnohistory, see von Graeve (1989:49–50). Chapakuran speakers still living today include the Moré of eastern Bolivia, among whom the native language has almost died out, and a few Oro Win, traditional enemies of the Wari' whom FUNAI relocated to the Wari' community of Rio Negro-Ocaia and later moved to a reserve farther upstream on the Pacaas Novos River.

2. The mean annual temperature in Rondônia is 28 °C, with absolute maximums of 36–38 °C. (Millikan 1988:12). Humidity is high, and minimum temperatures always remain above freezing. The hottest months are August and September, at the peak of the dry season, but the dry season also brings sudden drops in temperature called *friagens,* in which masses of cold air sweep down off the Andes mountains into the Amazonian lowlands. Temperatures can drop to as low as 15 °C in less than an hour, bringing a chilly respite from both the heat and the biting insects, which seem to die or go dormant during cold snaps.

3. Vilaça (1996:213–223) presents multiple versions and an analysis of this myth.

4. Von Graeve (1989) traces the history of this region in western Rondônia and the hostilities between Wari' and Brazilians.

5. See Vilaça (1992:47–130) for a more detailed discussion of Wari' exocannibalism.

6. Vilaça (1996:120) has reported that some people in the Rio Negro-Ocaia community say that women ate enemy flesh and that women's expressions of desire to eat it motivated men to go out and kill enemies. My Santo André informants insist that in the Dois Irmãos region, only men ate enemy flesh.

7. At Santo André in 1987, nineteen households were composed of a single nuclear family with children, five extended-family households included a young, childless married couple living with the wife's kin, and five extended-family households included an elderly parent.

8. I loosely translate *kaxa'* as "men's house," but *kaxa'* properly refers to the sleeping/sitting platform in the men's house, not to the building itself.

9. Becker-Donner (1955) described such a sleeping platform in an uninhabited Wari' village she visited.

10. Mason (1977:85–131) categorized Wari' kin terminology as a Crow-Omaha system. Vilaça (1992) analyzed Wari' terms for consanguines and affines.

11. Papers in Kensinger (1985) highlight the importance of sibling bonds in lowland South America. As Judith Shapiro (1985:2) noted, in many native Amazonian societies, "siblingship commonly provides the dominant metaphor for solidarity and cooperation."

Chapter 3

1. In a memoir of these events, Father Gomez de Arruda recalled: "At the beginning of 1963 there was a new outbreak of influenza. . . . And the SPI did not have, they said, anything, neither medicines, nor food, to help in this decisive hour for the simple conservation of the *life of these unfortunate Indians.*—Note this well: Their hunger was so great that the Ororantien [Oro Waram Xijein, a Wari' subgroup] found themselves forced to *eat the cadaver of one of their companions.* ([This] hard reality [was] known by all the [SPI] staff of the [Ribeirão village] post.) . . . The Truth is that, without the intervention of the [Catholic] Prelacy, that crisis of influenza and misery would have done away with the last [Wari'] . . . of Ribeirão" (Gomez de Arruda n.d.:6; emphasis in the original).

2. As early as the mid-1950s, Francisco Meireles, a famous director of the regional government Indian agency (SPI), foresaw the importance of protecting Wari' territories and took steps to do so. Legal delimitation of Wari' reserves began in the mid-1970s. In 1981, rights to the reserves of Rio Negro-Ocaia, Lage, and Ribeirão were affirmed by the process of *homologacão*, the issuing of a presidential decree that is one of the final steps in the establishment of legal title on a par with the land rights of non-Indians (CEDI 1987:11, 60, 79). The legal process for the Pacaas Novos reserve (which includes Santo André) was not completed until the 1990s, because this area is on the border with Bolivia and for many years the military blocked the finalization of indigenous land rights in border areas.

Chapter 4

1. Before the contact, when bachelors lived in the communal men's house, a bachelor who got sick was carried to his mother's house, for Wari' say the men's house was a place of health, and there should be no illness there.

2. Even at the clinic or hospital in Guajará-Mirim, patients rarely stay alone. Sensitive to the value Wari' place on family care, FUNAI's nurses and administrators often encourage one or more family members to accompany patients taken to town for treatment.

3. Affines are responsible for burying the corpse among the Cashinahua (Kensinger 1995), Canela (Crocker 1993), and Xavante (Maybury-Lewis 1974:281). Among the Kagwahiv (Kracke 1978:13) and the Mundurucú (Murphy 1960:72), the dead are buried by members of the opposite moiety, the group from which members of the dead person's moiety take marriage partners.

4. Individuals "own" specific tamara songs during their lifetimes. In tamara performances, the dancers stand in a line and pass a small drum from person to person. The one who is drumming leads the others in singing his or her songs.

5. Vilaça (1992:214) records a variation in which the intestines might be given to the relatives to hold. She also reports that hair and fingernails were placed in a ceramic pot, then thrown into the fire.

6. I thank the linguist Barbara Kern for first calling this to my attention.

Chapter 5

1. Berndt (1962:269-290) presents one of the most detailed accounts of gastronomic, or dietarily motivated, cannibalism. He describes a number of societies in the eastern highlands of New Guinea where the cannibalism of both enemies and fellow group members purportedly was practiced until the mid-twentieth century. In these societies, cannibalism carried a variety of cultural meanings, including ideas about the gastronomic value of human flesh. Berndt cites an abundance of evidence to support his assertion that "[d]ead human flesh, to these people, is food, or potential food." Steadman and Merbs (1982) are highly critical of Berndt's data and interpretations and argue that there is no convincing evidence that cannibalism was practiced in New Guinea.

2. The one case of pure hunger cannibalism of which Wari' have told me was an incident of murder and surreptitious consumption that allegedly took place in the Lage area in the 1950s, during a precontact epidemic of diarrhea and dysentery that incapacitated whole communities. According to the story, amid the chaos of death and disease, an Oro Waram couple kidnapped a female toddler from the Oro Mon subgroup while the child's mother was incapacitated with dysentery. The couple allegedly took the little girl to the forest and strangled, dismembered, roasted, and ate her in secret "because they were hungry for meat." When the child's Oro Mon relatives discovered what had happened, their outrage forced the murderers to flee, though the couple returned several years later to live among their Oro Waram relatives at Lage.

I first heard this story when I was doing a survey of Lage households and arrived at the home of a middle-aged Oro Mon woman. I asked about her family, and she gave me the names of her parents and a little sister, all deceased. When I asked what her sister had died of, she replied, "[The woman's name] ate her." Thinking that I had misunderstood, I asked again, and her story spilled forth in a rush of bitter anger. She was especially resentful that the Oro Waram eventually accepted the murderers back into the community and that the couple later had the nerve to go on living in the same village with the Oro Mon relatives of the girl they had killed and eaten.

Two other women were sitting with us, and at first they hung back, listening and nodding as this woman recounted the painful details. When I questioned the veracity of her story (which was so unlike anything I had heard before), the other women joined in. "It's true!" they cried. "Everybody knows about this; ask any Wari' out there." I followed their advice and asked a number of people. All the Oro Mon with whom I spoke insisted the story was true. When I asked the alleged murderess herself, she said she remembered the little girl in question but claimed the child died of illness. When I asked the alleged murderess's Oro Waram relatives, they evaded my questions without denying the accusation. To me, this suggested that the story might be true, for why else would they not deny it? But I do not know for sure.

3. Garn and Block (1970) suggested that cannibalism has little dietary value, whereas Vayda (1970) and Walens and Wagner (1971) argued that cannibalism may have nutritional significance for populations with marginal protein intake.

4. For the debate over whether native Amazonians suffered protein shortages, see Beckerman (1979), R. Carneiro (1970), Gross (1975), Lathrap (1968), and Ross (1978). Studies in which clinical examinations or dietary intake assessments found adequate protein intake include Berlin and Markell (1977), Chagnon and Hames (1979), Dufour (1983), and Milton (1984).

5. This resonates with Hélène Clastres' and Jacques Lizot's (1978) observation about the complicated rules surrounding the Yanomami Indians' practice of eating human bone ashes: "There is an *excess* of rules . . . that perhaps is opposed to the excess of voracity of the mythic jaguar."

6. Vilaça (1992:24–34) gives a detailed account of how Wari' use kinship terminology in relations among consanguines and affines.

7. Sanday (1986:46) cited the Hua and Bimin-Kuskusmin of New Guinea, the Fijian islanders of the South Pacific, the Kwakiutl and Iroquois of North America, and the Aztecs of Mexico as examples of societies where cannibalism or cannibalistic myths or fantasies seemed to express oral-incorporative imagery and a dialectic of "a weak ego and an overpowerful maternal figure."

8. Stephen (1998) used Wari' endocannibalism as an example of her model, but she mistakenly stated that the dead person's close consanguines cut up the corpse and misinterpreted other details as well.

9. A corollary belief is that a person who has been cut to pieces and then put back together must under no circumstances drink fermented chicha. This implies that the individual will not participate in beer-drinking festivals during this period of reintegration.

Chapter 6

1. Tocohwet, Diva's aunt, once showed me a kettle that had been a present from her deceased husband, and I know a few other families who kept some small item associated with a dead relative.

2. One shaman, who lives in the Lage/Ribeirão area, explained his perceptions of the permeability of the body this way: "Look at my body," he said, demonstratively striking his upper arms and thigh. "To you it looks hard, solid, doesn't it? But when I look at a person's body, I see holes—many little holes in the skin."

3. Most elders assert that blood comes from the mother, and that men contribute nothing to the formation of fetal blood. Some Wari', especially younger people, suggest that newborns' blood also contains some paternal elements derived from semen.

4. In Wari' cosmology, annatto is a marker of humanity, of being wari'. The only animals that possess annatto are jami karawa, animals whose bodies are inhabited by a spirit that is human in form. Ordinary people cannot see spirits, but shamans see jami karawa as people who look like Wari'.

5. The bond between the shaman and his companion animal spirit is the basis of the shaman's ability to cure certain illnesses. When an illness is diagnosed as an attack by a particular kind of animal spirit, a shaman who shares kinship with that species may be summoned. The shaman can appeal to kinship bonds to persuade the animal spirit to desist, and he typically addresses the attacking animal spirit by the honorific *aji'*, "older brother." Invoking one of the strongest kinship bonds, the shaman tells the spirit that the patient is wari', "one of us," and requests or orders the spirit to leave the patient alone. The shaman has this power only because of the common identity established by the body substance he shares with the animal spirit species.

6. For many Wari' men, the restriction on killing and eating the companion animal species is a disincentive to assuming the shaman's vocation. A number of men have told me they gave up being shamans because they and their families were tired of going hungry. Maxun Kwarain

said that when he first became a white-lipped peccary shaman, his family was upset and tried to convince him to give it up. They depended on him to hunt for them, and they knew that as a peccary shaman, he would no longer kill this most productive of game animals.

7. Just as children eat with their father, the enemy spirit eats when the warrior eats. Maxun Kwarain creatively invoked this idea to justify his habit of constantly begging food. He said that the five spirit "children" inside his body (from the five Brazilian enemies that he claimed, falsely, to have killed) ate a lot, leaving him constantly hungry!

8. It takes skill to dismember a corpse respectfully and efficiently without contaminating oneself or others. Although any adult male affine could be asked to perform the dismemberment, certain men were considered especially competent and were often called upon to perform this service.

9. In 1961–62, the first contacts and the epidemics that followed started near the beginning of the dry season, the time when fields must be cleared for planting. Wari' were so sick that they planted little that year, and SPI agents' telegrams and letters from this period are full of constant pleas for food and medicines.

10. Wari' consider fighting sticks (*temem*) the only appropriate weapon to use against fellow Wari'. Blows struck with temem are supposed to draw blood only; killing with such a stick is expressly prohibited.

Chapter 7

1. On Amazonian notions of personhood, see Seeger, da Matta, and Viveiros de Castro (1979) and McCallum (1996a). The starting point for my treatment of the cultural construction of personhood is the now classic approach articulated by Mauss (1985), who contrasted individual awareness of the self with the social idea of the person. My approach to the body and its social implications has been influenced especially by the work of Battaglia (1990), M. Strathern (1988, 1992), and T. Turner (1995).

2. There is no clear consensus about where in the body the spirit resides, and some Wari' feel that the spirit does not really exist until it comes into being as an entity separate from the body. In Wari' notions of fetal development, the spirit, the head, and the eyes develop first and simultaneously. Gender differentiation comes next, with the formation of the fetus's genitals and nipples, followed by the body trunk and limbs. Imbued with a spirit, the fetus in its mother's womb is already conscious and self-aware, able to recognize its kin and feel affection for them. In beliefs about animal spirits and shamanism, slain animals' spirits retain links to their bodies as long their eyes remain in their carcasses, and altered visual perception is a primary power of the Wari' shaman.

3. The idea of a bodily image or double is central to the concept of *jami-* (spirit). Wari' use the word *jami-* for various reflections and representations: shadows, photographs, and physical traces of prior events, such as footprints (*jami kaximaxi'*, "the jami of our foot") or scars (*jaminain nan*, "the jami of the wound"). It also applies to nonvisual traces, such as the voices of people who are heard but not seen (*jami kapijaxi'*, "the jami of our mouths"). What these diverse phenomena have in common with the jami spirit that animates the individual person is that they are images or traces that represent or evoke the physical entity with which they are associated.

4. When mother and father are of the same ethnicity or subgroup, there is no question about their offspring's identity. When parents are from different groups, my Santo André informants

say that place of birth determines the child's identity: individuals affiliate with the subgroup in whose territory they are born. (Vilaça [1992:141–143] reports other opinions on this issue.) Although Wari' cite rules about determining subgroup affiliations, subgroup identities are fluid and strategic, and in different contexts individuals may identify themselves differently and cite different bases for figuring identity.

5. Non-Indians of the region hold similar beliefs.

6. In contrast to central Brazilian cultures, in which names and naming practices are highly elaborated (see Maybury-Lewis 1979), Wari' treat names more casually, and individuals change their names for a variety of reasons.

7. Although they stopped building men's houses in their villages after the contact, in the 1970s, Wari' in the Dois Irmãos area built two men's houses in secluded parts of the forest away from the settlements. The shaman, Maxun Kwarain, told people to do so because the new generation of boys growing up since the contact needed to learn about Wari' traditions. Older men, fathers, and sons held a series of all-male retreats at the men's houses. The artist Wem Quirió, who was one of the boys who participated in these retreats, remembers the experience as a time of joking, horseplay, and storytelling about life before the contact.

8. See Conklin (in press) for a detailed account and analysis of beliefs and practices associated with killing enemies.

9. Wari' ideas about the relation of changes in social status to physical transformations of blood and flesh contain many parallels to the puberty seclusion rites of the upper Xingú societies described by Viveiros de Castro, who observed:

> The corporeal changes thus produced are the cause and the instrument of transformations in terms of social identity. That means that it is not possible [to make] an ontological distinction . . . between physiological and sociological processes on the level of the individual. The corporeal changes can be considered neither as indicators nor as symbols of the changes of social identity. . . . The social does not deposit itself upon the Yawalapiti body as an inert support, it *creates* that body (Viveiros de Castro 1979:41; my translation, emphasis added).

Chapter 8

1. *Jima* is the unpossessed form of the noun *jamixi'* (our spirit). The closest English equivalent to *jima* is "ghost," but the Wari' term has a considerably wider meaning. *Jima* refers to a corpse as well as a disembodied manifestation of the spirit of a dead person. *Jima* is a generic, depersonalized concept, the only form of *jamixi'* that does not require the speaker to identify the possessor of the spirit. Wari' speak of both the collectivity of ancestors and individual ancestors as *oro-jima*.

2. Several other deaths were attributed to ancestors seeking the company of their kin, but in these cases, the ancestors were said to act not in the form of jima but as white-lipped peccaries. Soon after death, before the individual's spirit has adjusted to existence in the underworld, it also may send a fish spirit to carry away—that is, kill—a loved one.

3. Albert (1985), P. Clastres (1974:316), Dole (1974:306), Ramos (1990:196), Zerries (1960).

4. Vilaça (1989:378) also noted that the desire to dissociate body from spirit fails to explain why the Wari' preferred cannibalism over cremation, but she suggested that Wari' view the acts of cooking and eating as implicit in the act of making fire. "[F]or the Wari'," she wrote, "culi-

nary preparation (which is initiated with the cutting of the prey) and devouring are interrelated and indissociable processes. The cadaver is roasted in the fire that, in its origin, is cooking fire (see the myth of *Pinom*). In this sense the cadaver is prepared as prey and should be ingested as such" (Vilaça 1992:263). However, Wari' do make fires for many purposes other than cooking: for warmth, to drive away insects, to heat water for bathing, to burn fields, and to burn the houses and possessions of the dead and places associated with their memory. In the past, corpses that could not be eaten were cremated in a fire that was not used for cooking, and Wari' considered this as effective as cannibalism for separating the spirit from its body and from the world of the living.

5. Rosenblatt, Walsh, and Jackson (1976) found that, in societies (like that of the Wari') where tie-breaking is elaborated, there is a greater likelihood of remarriage by sororate or levirate (according to which a widow or widower marries the brother or sister of the dead spouse). They suggested that "[w]here the two people who would marry are both inhibited by reminders of the deceased, and perhaps of well-learned nonmarital responses to each other, removal of the reminders is more facilitative of marriage" (1976:76). They also found a strong positive correlation between the elaboration of ghost fears and remarriage rates, with instances of levirate and sororate more likely to be present where fears of ancestral ghosts are strong (1976:79).

6. Compare this to William Crocker's account (1993) of the ritual of remembering and honoring the deceased among the Canela of central Brazil.

7. Viveiros de Castro (1992:213) has noted Tupian notions of a connection between the persistence of a corpse's flesh and the persistence of memories linking the dead and the living.

8. Viveiros de Castro (1992:213) identifies the flesh of the corpse as "the substratum of memory" in the eschatology of the Araweté, Tupian speakers of the middle Xingú-Tocantins River region of Pará, Brazil. Araweté bury their dead, but they believe that the souls of the dead are cannibalized by the gods. As the gods devour the soul-body, they devour the individual's memory of his or her life on earth, although complete forgetting takes a period of several years. The gods then revive the soul that they have stripped to a skeleton, making the individual into a god like themselves, a god without memory.

Chapter 9

1. Vilaça (1992:237–246, 1996:224–234) presents several versions and analyses of this myth.

2. The figure of a warrior carrying firebrands in a small basket on his back evokes the image of Xaji, the quintessential warrior spirit who appears as a shooting star. Like the ritual leader of a war expedition, Xaji carries firebrands in a basket on his back that glow as he travels across the sky. Wari' say that some shooting stars fall to earth with an audible sound; when such a shooting star appears, it indicates the direction Wari' warriors should travel to kill an enemy. If the star appears to have one "leg," one enemy will be killed; two "legs" means two enemies will die.

3. Members of some subgroups, especially in the Lage/Ribeirão area, add other species to the list of jami karawa, including armadillos (especially the large species called *tatu quinze kilos* in Portuguese), agouti, paca, coati, squirrel, and caiman. There is little consensus about these other species, which rarely attack and create shamans, and they tend to be regarded as weak spirits of little consequence. The Santo André villagers who are the focus of my study reject

categorizing these other animals as legitimate jami karawa, and I follow their lead in limiting my discussion to the primary jami karawa species on which everyone agrees.

4. Tapirs live underwater, along with jaguars, fish, and white-lipped peccaries, but it is unclear whether tapirs transform themselves into other species, though they can take on the appearance of a specific living person.

5. An elderly Oro Nao' woman at Santo André first told me about the arcane usage of *mijak* as the term for jaguars. Later, I found confirmation on a word list that had been collected among the Oro Mon shortly after the contact in the early 1960s, where the Portuguese word for jaguar, *onça*, was translated as *mijak*. If an arcane name for jaguars has come to be transferred to white-lipped peccaries, it may suggest that Wari' used to think of them as having something in common. This connection is intriguing, for they are the two animals with which Wari' identify most closely and the two most directly related to endocannibalism.

6. Wari' attribute most cases of snakebite to ancestors who died of snakebite and who, having become snakes themselves, kill their kin out of desire for companionship. To dream of someone who died of snakebite is a premonition that the person's spirit, now a snake, is waiting to strike. Several Wari' reported that they or others were bitten on the day after such a dream. When a snake bites, the snake spirit is said to enter its victim's body and shoot arrows from inside, causing the bleeding sores that break out on snakebite victims' skin.

7. Especially in the Lage/Ribeirão area, some Wari' add other animals to the list of iri' karawa, including anteaters and large rodents (paca, agouti, capybara), but Santo André residents disagree.

8. Before the contact, Wari' generally did not live next to the larger rivers, so the villages of the dead were located at a distance from living people's homes. Since FUNAI has mandated that Wari' villages be located on the banks of the Pacaas Novos, Ribeirão, and Negro-Ocaia Rivers, people now live in closer proximity to the spirits of the dead. For some, this is too close for comfort. The idea of a landscape saturated with the dead became an issue in 1986, when almost the entire population of Ribeirão abandoned their village, which has been at the same site since the 1960s. The mass exodus occurred in response to the sudden death of an eleven-year-old girl who had collapsed with a raging fever that neither the FUNAI nursing assistant nor Wari' shamans were able to treat. The local FUNAI administrator had left for several days, taking the truck that was the only way to get sick people to the medical clinic in town. The villagers blamed him for the girl's death, and in the chaos of anger and fear that followed, they also came to the conclusion that Ribeirão was an unhealthy place because there were too many spirits of dead people (especially spirits of dead shamans, which are especially dangerous) lurking around the river. A consensus emerged to abandon the site, and around a hundred people packed up their belongings and trekked to a new site in the Lage reserve, which they said had good soil and was free of such spirits. By the time I arrived at Ribeirão several days later, only eight Wari' and a couple of nervous FUNAI employees remained. Ultimately, almost everyone returned, because they had gardens at Ribeirão and because FUNAI officials refused to send nurses or teachers to the new village.

9. On the absence of affinity in the afterlife, see also Viveiros de Castro (1992:294-295). Bloch and Parry (1982:27-32) discuss eschatological images of the end of affinity in the afterworld as a cross-cultural theme, with special reference to Melanesia.

10. Like Towira Towira, the Masters or Mothers of Animals and other animal protectors who appear in some other native Amazonian peoples' cosmologies are often giants who control

the fertility and movements of certain animal species. Since they can determine the success of hunting, hunters try not to offend these spirits, and some groups perform rituals to propitiate them (Descola 1996:126, Murphy 1960, Reichel-Dolmatoff 1971:80–86, Zerries 1954).

11. A few Wari' have described experiences in which, when they were sick or dreaming, their spirit traveled to the underworld, where, confronted with this life-or-death choice, they declined to drink Towira Towira's beer. One shaman described how the spirits of his deceased grandparents, aunts, uncles, and elder siblings crowded around him, urging him not to drink. "Don't take it!" his elder sister warned. "Go home! Don't die yet! Your children are crying for their father." Heeding his relatives' advice, the shaman refused the beer, turned around, and walked back to the surface of the earth to go on living.

12. Another dimension of perceptual reversals revolves around inverse correspondences between the state of the corpse and the state of the spirit. Ideally, Wari' die at home in the arms of their kin and surrounded by keening lamentations that bear witness to the dying person's social identity. But underwater at the moment of death, the individual's spirit is treated like impersonal "prey" killed by the water spirits. Three days later, this opposition reverses. Towira Towira revives the spirit and makes it whole and beautiful, marking the individual as human and social. At the funeral, this is the moment when mourners begin to cut the corpse and treat it as if it were prey.

13. Actually, it would be more accurate to say that the Wari' parties are modeled after the exchanges with the water spirits, since in the myth of Hujin, these parties originated when the underworld spirits first came out of the water to visit the Wari'.

Chapter 10

1. As a shaman with white-lipped peccary spirit, Maxun Kwarain should not have eaten peccary meat. But he also had jaguar spirit and claimed that this allowed him to eat peccary meat.

REFERENCES

Abraham, Nicholas, and Maria Torok

1994   Mourning *or* melancholia: Introjection *versus* incorporation. [Originally published in 1972.] Pp. 125–138 in *The Shell and the Kernel 1: Renewals of Psychoanalysis. Writings of Nicholas Abraham and Maria Torok,* edited by Nicholas T. Rand. Chicago: University of Chicago Press.

Acosta Saignes, Miguel

1961   El canibalismo de los caribes. In *Estudios de Etnología Antigua de Venezuela.* Caracas, Venezuela: Universidad Central de Venezuela.

Albert, Bruce

1985   Temps du Sang, Temps de Cendres. Représentation de la Maladie, Système Rituel et Espace Politique Chez les Yanomami du Sud-est (Amazonie Brésilienne). Ph.D. dissertation, Laboratoire d'Etnologie et de Sociologie Comparative, Université de Paris X, Nanterre.

Alto do Madeira

1957   [Untitled.] 4 April. Clipping in Microfilm #403 in archives of the Fundação Nacional do Indio, Brasilia.

1962   Fome e doenças diziimam índios pacaas-novos. 16 March.

Arens, William

1979   *The Man-Eating Myth: Anthropology and Anthropophagy.* New York: Oxford University Press.

1998   Rethinking anthropophagy. Pp. 39–63 in *Cannibalism and the Colonial World,* edited by Francis Barker, Peter Hulme, and Margaret Iversen. New York: Cambridge University Press.

Askenasy, Hans

1994   *Cannibalism: From Sacrifice to Survival.* Amherst, N.Y.: Prometheus Books.

Barker, Francis, Peter Hulme, and Margaret Iversen, eds.

1998   *Cannibalism and the Colonial World.* New York: Cambridge University Press.

Basso, Ellen B.

1995   *The Last Cannibals: A South American Oral History.* Austin: University of Texas Press.

Bates, H. W.
1864   *The Naturalist on the River Amazons*. 2d edition. London: John Murray.
Battaglia, Debbora
1990   *On the Bones of the Serpent: Person, Memory, and Mortality in Sabarl Island Society*. Chicago: University of Chicago Press.
1991   The body in the gift: Memory and forgetting in Sabarl mortuary exchange. *American Ethnologist* 19:3–18.
Becher, Hans
1968   Endocanibalismo yanonámi. *Actas y Memorias, XXXVII Congreso Internacional de Americanistas (1966)*, Argentina, 3:41–49.
Becker-Donner, Etta
1955   First report on a field trip to the Guaporé region (Pacaas Novos). *International Congress of Americanists* 31(1):107–111.
Beckerman, Stephen
1979   The abundance of protein in Amazonia: A reply to Gross. *American Anthropologist* 81:533–560.
Berdan, F. F.
1982   *The Aztecs of Central Mexico*. New York: Holt, Rinehart, and Winston.
Berlin, Elois Ann, and E. K. Markell
1977   An assessment of the nutritional and health status of an Aguaruna Jívaro community, Amazonas, Peru. *Ecology of Food and Nutrition* 6:69–81.
Berndt, Ronald M.
1962   *Excess and Restraint: Social Control among a New Guinea Mountain People*. Chicago: University of Chicago Press.
Bloch, Maurice
1992   *Prey into Hunter: The Politics of Religious Experience*. New York: Cambridge University Press.
Bloch, Maurice, and Jonathan Parry
1982   Introduction to *Death and the Regeneration of Life*, edited by Maurice Bloch and Jonathan Parry. New York: Cambridge University Press.
Bourdieu, Pierre
1977   *Outline of a Theory of Practice*. Translated by Richard Nice. Cambridge: Cambridge University Press.
Brown, Michael F.
1986   *Tsewa's Gift: Magic and Meaning in an Amazonian Society*. Washington, D.C.: Smithsonian Institution Press.
Brown, Paula, and Donald Tuzin, eds.
1983   *The Ethnography of Cannibalism*. Washington, D.C.: Society for Psychological Anthropology.
Caiuby, Sylvia Novaes
1997   *The Play of Mirrors: The Representation of Self Mirrored in the Other*. Translated by Izabel Murat Burbridge. Austin: University of Texas Press.
Carneiro, Robert
1970   The transition from hunting to horticulture in the Amazon basin. Vol. 3, pp. 244–248 in *Proceedings of the Eighth International Congress of Anthropological and Ethnological Sciences*. Tokyo: Science Council of Japan.

Carneiro da Cunha, Manuela

1978   Os Mortos e os Outros: Uma Análise do Sistema Funerário e da Noção de Pessoa Entre os Indios Krahó. São Paulo: Hucitec.

1981   Eschatology among the Krahó: Reflection upon society, free field of fabulation. Pp. 161 174 in Mortality and Immortality: The Anthropology and Archaeology of Death, edited by S. Humphreys and H. King. London: Academic Press.

Carneiro da Cunha, Manuela, and Eduardo B. Viveiros de Castro

1985   Vingança e temporalidade: Os tupinambás. Journal de la Société des Américanistes [Paris] 71:191-208.

CEDI (Centro Ecumênico de Documentação e Informação)

1987   Terras Indígenas No Brasil. Rio de Janeiro: CEDI, Museu Nacional/Universidade Federal do Rio de Janeiro.

Chagnon, Napoleon A., and Raymond B. Hames

1979   Protein deficiency as a cause of tribal warfare in Amazonia: New data. Science 203: 910-913.

Clastres, Hélène

1968   Rites funéraires guayakí. Journal de la Société des Américanistes 57:63-72.

1972   Les beaux-frères enemis: A propos du cannibalisme tupinamba. Nouvelle Revue de Psychanalyse 6:71-82.

Clastres, Hélène, and Jacques Lizot

1978   La part du feu: Rites et discours de la mort chez les yanomami. Libre 3:103-133.

Clastres, Pierre

1974   Guayakí cannibalism. Pp. 309-321 in Native South Americans: Ethnology of the Least Known Continent, edited by Patricia J. Lyon. Boston: Little, Brown and Company.

1998   Cannibals. Translated by Paul Auster. The Sciences 38(3):32-37.

Conklin, Beth A.

1989   Images of health, illness and death among the Wari' (Pakaas Novos) of Rondônia, Brazil. Ph.D. dissertation, Medical Anthropology Program, University of California at San Francisco and Berkeley.

1991   Umas Observações Sobre as Condições de Saúde e Nutrição Entre a População Wari' (Pakaas Novas) de Rondônia. Archives of FUNAI (Fundação Nacional do Indio), Brasília, Brazil.

1994   The politics of disease in a native Amazonian society. Paper presented at the 48th International Congress of Americanists, Sweden.

1994   O sistema médico wari'. Pp. 161-186 in Saúde e Povos Indígenas, edited by Ricardo V. Santos and Carlos E. A. Coimbra Jr. Rio de Janeiro: Editora Fiocruz.

1995   "Thus are our bodies, thus was our custom": Mortuary cannibalism in an Amazonian society. American Ethnologist 22(1):76-102.

1996a   Reflections on Amazonian anthropologies of the body. Medical Anthropology Quarterly 10(3):373-375.

1997a   Body paint, feathers, and VCRs: Aesthetics and authenticity in Amazonian activism. American Ethnologist 24(4):711-737.

1997b   Consuming images: Representations of cannibalism on the Amazonian frontier. Anthropological Quarterly 70(2):69-78.

In press Women's blood, warriors' blood, and the conquest of external vitality in Amazonia. To be published in Gender in Amazonia and Melanesia: An Exploration of the Compara-

tive Method, edited by Thomas A. Gregor and Donald Tuzin. Berkeley: University of California Press.

Conklin, Beth A., and Lynn M. Morgan

1996　Babies, bodies, and the production of personhood in North America and a native Amazonian society. *Ethos* 24(4):657–694.

Connerton, Paul

1989　*How Societies Remember.* New York: Cambridge University Press.

Correio da Manhã

1962a　Antropofagia: Ex-inspetor reviveu ritual por êle mesmo preparado. 11 January.

1962b　Não consegiu evitar que índios devorassem menina. 14 January.

1962c　Padre denuncia abandono dos índios Pacaás-Novos. 15 January.

1962d　Frade diz a governador que índios morrem na miséria. 25 January.

1962e　Morticínio. 28 January.

1962f　Vilão disputa glórias com heróis no "inferno verde." 24 February.

1962g　Frade acusa inspetor do SPI de fazer chantagem. 25 February.

Crocker, William H.

1993　Canela relationships with ghosts: This-worldly or other-worldly empowerment. *Latin American Anthropology Review* 5(2):71–78.

Cruzeiros, Os [São Paulo]

1961　Assim vivem e foram vistos na selva os indígenas Pakaa-Novas. Transcript in archives of CIMI (Conselho Missionário Indigenista), Brasília, Brazil.

1962　Pakaanovas. 23 March.

Da Matta, Roberto

1976　*Um mundo dividido: A estrutura social dos indios Apinaye'.* Petrópolis: Vozes.

1979　The Apinayé relationship system: Terminology and ideology. Pp. 83–127 in *Dialectical Societies: The Gê and Bororo of Central Brazil,* edited by David Maybury-Lewis. Cambridge, Mass.: Harvard University Press.

Darling, J. Andrew

1998　Mass inhumation and the execution of witches in the American Southwest. *American Anthropologist* 100(3):732–752.

de Carvalho, Bernardino

1962　Pakaanovas: Antropófagos da amazônia. *Os Cruzeiros* [São Paulo], 10 February 1962, pp. 118–124.

De Coppett, Daniel

1982　The life-giving death. In *Mortality and Immortality,* edited by S. Humprheys and H. King. New York: Academic Press.

Descola, Philippe

1994　*In the Society of Nature.* New York: Cambridge University Press.

1996　*The Spears of Twilight: Life and Death in the Amazonian Jungle.* Translated by Janet Lloyd. New York: New Press.

Diário de Noticias

1962　Inquérito para apurar caso dos pacaas-novos. 16 January.

Diaz del Castillo, Bernal

1956　*The Discovery and Conquest of Mexico.* Translated by A. P. Maudslay. New York: Grove Press.

Dole, Gertrude E.

1974   Endocannibalism among the Amahuaca Indians. Pp. 302–308 in *Native South Americans: Ethnology of the Least Known Continent,* edited by Patricia J. Lyon. Boston: Little, Brown and Company.

Donkin, R. A.

1985   The Peccary. *Transactions of the American Philosophical Society* 75, Part 5. Philadelphia: The American Philosophical Society.

Dornstreich, Mark D., and George E. B. Morren

1974   Does New Guinea cannibalism have nutritional value? *Human Ecology* 2(1):1–12.

Douglas, Mary

1966   *Purity and Danger.* London: Routledge and Kegan Paul.

Dufour, Darna L.

1983   Nutrition in the northwest Amazon. Pp. 329–355 in *Adaptive Responses of Native Amazonians,* edited by Raymond B. Hames and William T. Vickers. San Francisco: Academic Press.

Erikson, Philippe

1986   Altérité, tatouage et anthropophagie chez les Pano: La belliqueuse quête du soi. *Journal de la Société des Américanistes* [Paris] 72:185–210.

Ernst, Thomas M.

1999   Onabasulu cannibalism and the moral agents of misfortune. Pp. 143–160 in *The Anthropology of Cannibalism,* edited by Lawrence R. Goldman. Westport, Conn.: Bergin & Garvey.

Everett, Daniel L., and Barbara Kern

1997   *Wari': The Pacaas Novos Language of Western Brazil.* New York: Routledge.

Fausto, Carlos

1999   Of enemies and pets: Warfare and shamanism in Amazonia. *American Ethnologist* 26(4):933–956.

Ferreira, Manoel Rodrigues

1981   *A ferrovia do diablo: História de uma estrada de ferro na Amazônia.* 2d edition (revised). [Originally published in 1962.] São Paulo: Edições Melhoramentos, Secretaria de Estado da Cultura, São Paulo.

Fernandes, Florestan

1963   *Organização social dos Tupinambá.* 2d edition. [Originally published in 1949.] São Paulo: Difusão Européia do Livro.

1970   *A função social da guerra na sociedade Tupinambá.* 2d edition. [Originally published in 1952.] São Paulo: Pioneira/Editôra da Universidade de São Paulo.

Fernando Carneiro, J.

1947   A anthropofagia entre os índios do brasil. *Acta Americana* 5(3):159–184.

Folha de São Paulo

1962   Sertanista não conseguiu impedir que os índios devorassem a menina morta. 13 January, pp. 188–191.

Forsyth, D. W.

1983   The beginnings of Brazilian anthropology: The Jesuits and Tupinamba cannibalism. *Journal of Anthropological Research* 39(2):147–178.

Freud, Sigmund

1981a   Mourning and melancholia. [Originally published in 1917.] Pp. 243–258 in *The Stan-*

dard Edition of the Complete Psychological Works of Sigmund Freud, vol. 14, edited by James Strachey. London: The Hogarth Press and The Institute of Psychoanalysis.

1981b   Totem and taboo. [Originally published in 1913.] Pp. 100–155 in *The Standard Edition of the Complete Psychological Works of Sigmund Freud,* vol. 13, edited by James Strachey. London: The Hogarth Press and The Institute of Psychoanalysis.

Gardner, Don

1999   Anthropophagy, myth, and the subtle ways of ethnocentrism. Pp. 27–50 in *The Anthropology of Cannibalism,* edited by Lawrence R. Goldman. Westport, Conn.: Bergin & Garvey.

Garn, Stanley, and Walter D. Block

1970   The limited nutritional value of cannibalism. *American Anthropologist* 72:106.

Gillison, Gillian

1993   *Between Culture and Fantasy: A New Guinea Highlands Mythology.* Chicago: University of Chicago Press.

Globo, O

1961   Levou os índios a devorar a cadáver de uma criança para vender as fotografias. 27 December.

Goldman, Lawrence R.

1999   From pot to polemic: Uses and abuses of cannibalism. Pp. 1–26 in *The Anthropology of Cannibalism,* edited by Lawrence R. Goldman. Westport, Conn.: Bergin & Garvey.

Gomez de Arruda, Roberto

1985   Entrevista de Dom Roberto, Bispo de Guajará-Mirim, a Egon. 22 March. Transcript in archives of CIMI (Conselho Missionário Indigenista), Brasília, Brazil.

n.d.   Rápidas anotações sobre a expedição Gov. Máfra—Pacificação dos índios "Pacaas Novos." Ms. in archives of CIMI (Conselho Missionário Indigenista), Brasília, Brazil.

Gordon-Grube, Karen

1988   Anthropophagy in post-Renaissance Europe: The tradition of medicinal cannibalism. *American Anthropologist* 90(2):405–409.

1993   Evidence of medicinal cannibalism in Puritan New England: "Mummy" and related remedies in Edward Taylor's "Dispensatory." *Early American Literature* 28(3):185–221.

Gorer, Geoffrey

1965   *Death, Grief, and Mourning.* Garden City, New York: Doubleday.

Gottlieb, Richard

1991   The European vampire: Applied psychoanalysis and applied legend. *Folklore Forum* 24(2):39–61.

1993   Rethinking cannibalism: Some considerations of the roles of cannibalistic fantasy in psychoanalysis. Proposal for paper to be presented at the 1993 meetings of the American Psychoanalytic Association, New York City.

Gow, Peter

1991   *Of Mixed Blood: Kinship and History in Peruvian Amazonia.* New York: Clarendon Press, Oxford.

Graham, Laura

1995   *Performing Dreams: Discourses of Immortality Among the Xavante of Central Brazil.* Austin: University of Texas Press.

Gregor, Thomas

1977   *Mehinaku: The Drama of Daily Life in a Brazilian Village.* Chicago: University of Chicago Press.

1985   *Anxious Pleasures: The Sexual Lives of an Amazonian People.* Chicago: University of Chicago Press.

Gross, Daniel R.

1975   Protein capture and cultural development in the Amazon Basin. *American Anthropologist* 77:526–549.

Hand, Wayland D.

1980   *Magical Medicine: The Folkloric Component of Medicine in the Folk Belief, Custom, and Ritual of the Peoples of Europe and America.* Berkeley: University of California Press.

Harner, Michael

1977   The ecological basis for Aztec sacrifice. *American Ethnologist* 4:117–35.

Harris, Marvin

1977   *Cannibalism and Kings: The Origins of Cultures.* New York: Random House.

1985   *The Sacred Cow and the Abominable Pig.* New York: Random House.

Hertz, Robert

1960   *Death and the Right Hand.* [Originally published in 1907.] Translated by Rodney Needham and C. Needham. Glencoe, Ill.: Free Press.

Himmelman, P. Kenneth

1997   The medicinal body: An analysis of medicinal cannibalism in Europe, 1300–1700. *Dialectical Anthropology* 22:183–203.

Hogg, Garry

1958   *Cannibalism and Human Sacrifice.* New York: Citadel Press.

Irion, Paul E.

1968   *Cremation.* Philadelphia: Fortress Press.

Jackson, Michael, and Ivan Karp

1990   Introduction to *Personhood and Agency: The Experience of Self and Other in African Cultures,* edited by Michael Jackson and Ivan Karp. Washington, D.C.: Smithsonian Institution Press.

Kantner, John

1999   Anasazi mutilation and cannibalism in the American Southwest. Pp. 75–104 in *The Anthropology of Cannibalism,* edited by Lawrence R. Goldman. Westport, Conn.: Bergin & Garvey.

Kelly, Raymond

1977   *Etoro Social Structure.* Ann Arbor, Mich.: University of Michigan Press.

Kensinger, Kenneth M.

1981   Food taboos as markers of age categories in Cashinahua. Pp. 157–171 in *Food Taboos in Lowland South America,* edited by Kenneth M. Kensinger and Waud H. Kracke. Working papers, South American Indians 3. Bennington, Vt.: Bennington College.

1985   An emic model of Cashinahua marriage. Pp. 221–251 in *Marriage Practices in Lowland South America,* edited by Kenneth M. Kensinger. Urbana, Ill.: University of Illinois Press.

1991   A body of knowledge, or, The body knows. *Expedition* 33(3):37–45.

1995   Disposing of the dead. Pp. 231–236 in *How Real People Ought to Live: The Cashinahua of Eastern Peru.* Prospect Heights, Ill.: Waveland.

Kiltie, Richard A.

1980   More on Amazon cultural ecology. *Current Anthropology* 21:541–544.

Knauft, Bruce M.

1993   *South Coast New Guinea Cultures: History, Comparison, Dialectic.* New York: Cambridge University Press.

Kracke, Waud

1978   *Force and Persuasion: Leadership in an Amazonian Society.* Chicago: University of Chicago Press.

1981   Kagwahiv mourning: Dreams of a bereaved father. *Ethos* 9:258–275.

1988   Kagwahiv mourning II: Ghosts, grief, and reminiscences. *Ethos* 16:209–222.

1993   Discussion: Visions of death in Amazonian lives. *Latin American Anthropology Review* 5(2):79–80.

Lathrap, Donald

1968   The "hunting" economies of the tropical forest zone of South America: An attempt at historical perspective. Pp. 23–29 in *Man the Hunter,* edited by R. B. Lee and I. DeVore. Chicago: Aldine.

Léry, Jean de

1990   *History of a Voyage to the Land of Brazil.* Translated by Janet Whatley. Berkeley: University of California Press.

Lestringant, Frank

1997   *Cannibals: The Discovery and Representation of the Cannibal from Columbus to Jules Verne.* Translated by Rosemary Morris. Berkeley: University of California Press.

Lévi-Strauss, Claude

1969   *The Raw and the Cooked.* New York: Harper & Row.

1973   *Tristes Tropiques.* [Originally published in 1955.] Translated by John Weightman and Doreen Weightman. New York: Washington Square Press.

1977   *Structural Anthropology.* Vol. 2. New York: Basic Books.

1984   *Paroles Données.* Paris: Plon.

Lewis, I. M.

1986   *Religion in Context: Cults and Charisma.* New York: Cambridge University Press.

Lifton, Robert J.

1979   *The Broken Connection: On Death and the Continuity of Life.* New York: Simon and Schuster.

Lindenbaum, Shirley

1979   *Kuru Sorcery.* Palo Alto, Calif.: Mayfield Publishing Company.

1982   Review of *The Man-Eating Myth,* by W. Arens. *Ethnohistory* 29(1):58–60.

1983   Cannibalism: Symbolic production and consumption. Pp. 94–106 in *The Ethnography of Cannibalism,* edited by Paula Brown and Donald Tuzin. Washington, D.C.: Society for Psychological Anthropology.

Mason, Alan

1976   Oronao social structure. Ph.D. dissertation, Anthropology Department, University of California at Davis.

Mather, Cotton

1972   *The Angel of Bethesda.* [Originally published in 1722.] Edited by Gordon W. Jones. Barre, Mass.: American Antiquarian Society and Barre Publications.

Mauss, Marcel

1985   A category of the human mind: The notion of person; the notion of self. Translated by W. D. Halls. Pp. 1–25 in *The Category of the Person,* edited by Michael Carrithers, Steven Collins and Steven Luks. New York: Cambridge University Press.

Maybury-Lewis, David

1974   *Akwe-Shavante Society.* New York: Oxford University Press.

Maybury-Lewis, David, ed.

1979   *Dialectical Societies: The Gê and Bororo of Central Brazil.* Cambridge, Mass.: Harvard University Press.

McCallum, Cecilia

1996a   The body that knows: From Cashinahua epistemology to a medical anthropology of lowland South America. *Medical Anthropology Quarterly* 10(3):347–372.

1996b   Morte e pessoa entre os Kaxinawá. *Mana: Estudos de Antropologia Social* [Rio de Janeiro] 2(2):49–84.

McHugh, Ernestine L.

1989   Concepts of the person among the Gurungs of Nepal. *American Ethnologist* 16:75–86.

Meggers, Betty J.

1985   Aboriginal adaptation to Amazonia. Pp. 307–327 in *Amazonia,* edited by Ghillean T. Prance and Thomas E. Lovejoy. New York: Pergamon Press.

Meigs, Anna

1984   *Food, Sex and Pollution: A New Guinea Religion.* New Brunswick, N.J.: Rutgers University Press.

Meireles, Denise Maldi

1986   Os Pakaas-Novos. Master's dissertation, Departamento de Antropologia, Universidade de Brasília.

Melatti, Júlio Cezar

1976   Nominadores e genitores: Um aspecto fundamental do dualismo krahó. In *Leituras de Etnologia Brasileira,* edited by Egon Schaden. São Paulo: Companhia Editora Nacional.

1979   The relationship system of the Krahó. Pp. 46–79 in *Dialectical Societies: The Gê and Bororo of Central Brazil,* edited by David Maybury-Lewis. Cambridge, Mass.: Harvard University Press.

Metcalf, Peter, and Richard Huntington

1991   *Celebrations of Death: The Anthropology of Mortuary Ritual.* 2d edition. New York: Cambridge University Press.

Métraux, Alfred

1947   Mourning rites and burial forms of the South American Indians. *América Indígena* 7(1):7–44.

1949   Warfare, cannibalism, and human trophies. *Handbook of South American Indians* 5:383–409.

Migliazza, Ernest C.

1982   Linguistic prehistory and the refuge model in Amazonia. Pp. 497–519 in *Biological Diversification in the Tropics,* edited by Ghillean Prance. Proceedings of the Fifth International Symposium of the Association for Tropical Biology, 8–13 February 1979, at Macuto Beach, Caracas, Venezuela. New York: Columbia University Press.

Millikan, Brent Hayes

1988   The dialectics of devastation: Tropical deforestation, land degradation, and society in Rondônia, Brazil. Master's thesis, Department of Geography, University of California at Berkeley.

Milton, Katharine

1984   Protein and carbohydrate resources of the Makú Indians of northwestern Amazonia. *American Anthropologist* 86:7-27.

Montaigne, Michel de

1991   On the cannibals. Pp. 228-241 in *The Essays of Michel de Montaigne,* translated and edited by M. A. Screech. London: Penguin.

Murphy, Robert

1960   *Headhunter's Heritage.* Berkeley: University of California Press.

NOVA

1996   *Warriors of the Amazon.* NOVA Adventures in Science Series. Boston: WGBH Educational Foundation. Videocassette.

Ortiz de Montellano, Bernard R.

1978   Aztec cannibalism: An ecological necessity? *Science* 200:511-617.

Osborne, Lawrence

1997   Does man eat man? Inside the great cannibalism controversy. *Lingua Franca* 7(3):28-38.

Overing, Joanna

1986   Images of cannibalism, death and domination in a "non-violent" society. *Journal de la Société des Américanistes* [Paris] 72:133-156.

Paré, Ambroise

1841   Discours de la mumie. [Originally published in 1575.] Pp. 474-490 in *Oeuvres Complètes d'Ambroise Paré,* vol. 3, edited by J. F. Malgaigne. Paris: J. B. Ballière.

Peacock, Mabel

1896   Executed criminals and folk medicine. *Folklore* [London Folklore Society] 7:268-283.

Pickering, Michael

1999   Consuming doubts: What some people ate? Or what some people swallowed? Pp. 51-74 in *The Anthropology of Cannibalism,* edited by Lawrence R. Goldman. Westport, Conn.: Bergin & Garvey.

Pollock, Donald

1993   Death and the afterdeath among the Kulina. *Latin American Anthropology Review* 5(2):61-64.

1996   Personhood and illness among the Kulina. *Medical Anthropology Quarterly* 10(3):319-341.

Pouchelle, Marie-Christine

1990   *The Body and Surgery in the Middle Ages.* Translated by Rosemary Morris. Oxford: Polity Press.

Preston, Douglas

1998   Cannibals of the canyon. *The New Yorker* 30 November, 76-89.

Ramos, Alcida Rita

1990   *Memórias Sanumá: Espaço e Tempo em uma Sociedade Yanomami.* São Paulo: Editora Marco Zero.

Rawson, Claude
1997   The horror, the holy horror: Revulsion, accusation and the Eucharist in the history of cannibalism. *Times Literary Supplement* [London], 31 October, 3–5.

Reichel-Dolmatoff, Gerardo
1971   *Amazonian Cosmos.* Chicago: University of Chicago Press.

Rivière, P. G.
1980   Review of *The Man-Eating Myth,* by W. Arens. *Man* 15(1):203–205.

Rosenblatt, Paul C., R. Patricia Walsh, and Douglas A. Jackson
1976   *Grief and Mourning in Cross-Cultural Perspective.* New Haven, Conn.: HRAF Press.

Ross, Eric Barry
1978   Food taboos, diet and hunting strategy: The adaptation to animals in Amazon cultural ecology. *Current Anthropology* 19:1–16.

Rumsey, Alan
1999   The white man as cannibal in the New Guinea highlands. Pp. 105–122 in *The Anthropology of Cannibalism,* edited by Lawrence R. Goldman. Westport, Conn.: Bergin & Garvey.

Ryden, Stig
1942   Notes on the Moré Indians, Rio Guaporé, Bolivia. *Ethnos* 7(2–3):84–124.

Sagan, Eli
1974   *Cannibalism: Human Aggression and Cultural Form.* San Francisco: Harper & Row.

Sahlins, Marshall
1978   Culture as protein and profit. *New York Review of Books* 25(18):45–53.
1979   Cannibalism: An exchange. *New York Review of Books* 26(4):45–47.

Salas, Julio C.
1920   Los índios caribes. In *Estudio Sobre el Origen del Mito de la Antropofagia.* Madrid: Editorial America.

Sanday, Peggy Reeves
1986   *Divine Hunger: Cannibalism as a Cultural System.* New York: Cambridge University Press.

Schroeder, Johann
1963   *D. Johann Schröders Trefflich Versehene Medicin-Chymische Apotheke, Oder: Höchstkostbarer Arzeney Schatz,* vol. 2. [Originally published in 1641 as *Pharmacopoeia Medica-Chymica.* Translated by Friedrich Hoffmann in 1685.] Munich: Konrad Kölbl.

Seeger, Anthony
1981   *Nature and Society in Central Brazil: The Suyá Indians of Mato Grosso.* Cambridge, Mass.: Harvard University Press.
1987   *Why Suyá Sing: A Musical Anthropology of an Amazonian People.* New York: Cambridge University Press.

Seeger, Anthony, Roberto da Matta, and E. B. Viveiros de Castro
1979   A construção da pessoa nas sociedades indígenas brasileiras. *Boletim do Museu Nacional* [Rio de Janeiro], Antropologia, n.s., 32:2–19.

Shapiro, Judith
1985   The sibling relationship in lowland South America: General considerations. Pp. 1–7 in *The Sibling Relationship in Lowland South America,* edited by Kenneth M. Kensinger. Working papers, South American Indians 7. Bennington, Vt.: Bennington College.

Shepard, Glenn

n.d.   Three days for weeping: Dreams, emotions, and death in the Peruvian Amazon. Un-
         published ms.

Siegel, James T.

1983   Images and odors in Javanese practices surrounding death. *Indonesia* 36:1-14.

Sowls, Lyle K.

1984   *The Peccaries.* Tucson: The University of Arizona Press.

Staden, Hans

1928   *Hans Staden: The True History of His Captivity.* [Originally published in 1557.] Edited
         by Malcolm Letts. London: George Routledge & Sons.

Steadman, Lyle B., and Charles F. Merbs

1982   Kuru and cannibalism? *American Anthropologist* 84:611-627.

Stephen, Michele

1998   Devouring the mother: A Kleinian perspective on necrophagia and corpse abuse in
         mortuary ritual. *Ethos* 26(4):387-409.

Stern, Steve J., ed.

1987   *Resistance, Rebellion and Consciousness in the Andean Peasant World.* Madison, Wis.:
         University of Wisconsin Press.

Strathern, Andrew

1982   Witchcraft, greed, cannibalism and death. Pp. 111-133 in *Death and the Regeneration of
         Life,* edited by Maurice Bloch and Jonathan Parry. New York: Cambridge University
         Press.

Strathern, Marilyn

1988   *The Gender of the Gift: Problems With Women and Problems With Society in Melanesia.*
         Berkeley, Calif.: University of California Press.

1992   *After Nature: English Kinship in the Late Twentieth Century.* New York: Cambridge
         University Press.

Sullivan, Lawrence E.

1988   *Icanchu's Drum: An Orientation to Meaning in South American Religions.* New York:
         Macmillan Publishing Company.

Taussig, Michael

1987   *Shamanism, Colonialism, and the Wild Man: A Study in Terror and Healing.* Chicago:
         University of Chicago Press.

Taylor, Anne Christine

1993   Remembering to forget: Identity, mourning and memory among the Jívaro. *Man,* n.s.,
         28(4):653-678.

Temkin, Owsei

1971   *The Falling Sickness: A History of Epilepsy from the Greeks to the Beginnings of Modern
         Neurology.* 2d edition. Baltimore: Johns Hopkins University Press.

Torok, Maria

1994   The illness of mourning and the fantasy of the exquisite corpse. [Originally published
         in 1968.] Pp. 107-124 in *The Shell and the Kernel 1: Renewals of Psychoanalysis. Writings
         of Nicholas Abraham and Maria Torok,* edited by Nicholas T. Rand. Chicago: Univer-
         sity of Chicago Press.

Turner, Christy G. II, and J. A. Turner
1999   *Man Corn: Cannibalism and Violence in the American Southwest and Mexico.* Salt Lake City, Utah: University of Utah Press.

Turner, Terence S.
1980   The social skin. Pp. 112-140 in *Not By Work Alone,* edited by Jeremy Cherfas and Roger Lewin. Beverly Hills, Calif.: Sage Publications.

1995   Social body and embodied subject: Bodiliness, subjectivity, and sociality among the Kayapo. *Cultural Anthropology* 10(2):143-170.

Ultima Hora
1961   Bispo afirma: Pacaás novos comem gente. 27 December.

Vayda, Andrew P.
1970   On the nutritional value of cannibalism. *American Anthropologist* 72:1462-63.

Vidal, Lux B.
1977   *Morte e vida de uma sociedade indígena brasileira.* São Paulo: Editora Hucitec.

Viertler, Renate Brigitte
1991   *A refeição das almas: Umas interpretação etnológica do funeral dos indios Bororo—Mato Grosso.* São Paulo: Hucitec.

Vilaça, Aparecida
1989   Comendo como gente: Formas do canibalismo Wari' (Pakaa Nova). Master's dissertation, Programa de Antropologia, Museu Nacional, Universidade Federal do Rio de Janeiro.

1992   *Comendo como gente: Formas do canibalismo Wari'.* Rio de Janeiro: Editora UFRJ (Universidade Federal do Rio de Janeiro).

1996   Quem somos nós: Questões da alteridade no encontro dos Wari' com os brancos. Ph.D. Dissertation, Programa de Antropologia Social, Museu Nacional, Universidade Federal do Rio de Janeiro.

2000   Relations between funerary cannibalism and warfare cannibalism: The question of predation. *Ethnos* 65(1):83-106.

Viveiros de Castro, Eduardo B.
1979   A fabricação do corpo na sociedade xinguana. *Boletim do Museu Nacional* [Rio de Janeiro], Antropologia, n.s., 32:40-49.

1992   *From the Enemy's Point of View.* Chicago: University of Chicago Press.

1995   Os pronomes cosmológicos e o perspectivismo ameríndio. *Mana: Estudos de Antropologia Social* [Rio de Janeiro] 2(2):115-144.

1998   Cosmological deixis and Amerindian perspectivism. *Journal of the Royal Anthropological Institute* 4(3):469-488.

von Graeve, Bernard
1989   *The Pacaa Nova: Clash of Cultures on the Brazilian Frontier.* Peterborough, Ontario: Broadview Press.

Walens, Stanley, and Roy Wagner
1971   Pigs, proteins, and people-eaters. *American Anthropologist* 73:269-70.

Wallace, Alfred Russel
1889   *A Narrative of Travels on the Amazon and Rio Negro.* 2d edition. London: Ward, Lock, & Company.

Weismantel, Mary
1997   White cannibals: Fantasies of racial violence in the Andes. *Identities* 4(1):9–43.
Whatley, Janet
1984   Food and the limits of civility: The testimony of Jean de Léry. *The Sixteenth Century Journal* 15(4):387–400.
White, Timothy
1992   *Prehistoric Cannibalism at Mancos 5MTUMR-2346.* Princeton, N.J.: Princeton University Press.
Whitehead, Neil L.
1984   Carib cannibalism: The historical evidence. *Journal de la Société des Américanistes* 70:69–88.
Zerries, Otto
1954   Wild-und buschgeister in Südamerika. *Studien zur Kulturkunde 11.* Wiesbaden: F. Steiner.
1960   Endocanibalismo en la América del Sur. *Revista do Museu Paulista* [São Paulo], n.s., 12:125–175.
Zubrinich, Kerry M.
1999   Asmat cosmology and the practice of cannibalism. Pp. 123–142 in *The Anthropology of Cannibalism,* edited by Lawrence R. Goldman. Westport, Conn.: Bergin & Garvey.

INDEX

affines, 38–41, 45, 94, 98–100, 229, 230–
231, 235; in afterlife, 196, 261n9; conflicts among, 40–41, 99; and pollution,
124–125; roles in funerals, xvi–xvii,
41, 45, 69–72, 76–83, 201, 234–235,
255n2(Ch.4); roles in illness, 66, 96,
99–100, 127; and spider monkeys, 195
afterlife: absence of animals in, 196–197;
parties, 41, 44–45, 183, 195; sensory
misperception in, 102; society, 195–202,
205–207, 229–230; spirit's revival in,
165–166; as utopia, 196, 199–200
agency: and bodily transformation, 146,
202–203; and fire, 185, 203; and ontological predation, 154; and predator-
prey relations, 201–204, 214; and
relationality, 146, 149, 151, 152–153, 203,
233–234
aging, 61, 155, 200, 222
aggression, xxix, 94–99, 105, 130, 238; and
cannibalism, 32–33
agriculture. *See* farming
Amahuaca, 13, 253n6
ambivalence, 97–102, 192–193, 199
Anasazi, 7, 254n7(Ch.1)
ancestors, 45, 195–201, 211; as cannibals,
enemies, or predators, xxvi, 196, 214;
as peccaries, xxi, 163–165, 183, 198,
205–208, 217, 219–223, 225–230, 259n2

animals: absence in afterlife, 196–197;
edible species, 193–194, 260n3, 261n7;
kinship with shaman, 121, 192–193,
257n5(Ch.6); origin myth, 243–244;
relations to humans, 181–183, 204, 230,
232–233. *See also* animal spirits; carnivores; hunting; peccaries, white-lipped
animal spirits: attacks on people, 154–155,
190–192, 219–220; change of identity, 190; cooking of, 163–164; fear of,
212; as human spirits, 188–190; jaguar
archetype, 188–189; offenses against,
96, 97, 164; and reciprocal predation,
45, 182, 186; and shamanic initiation,
120–122; as shamans' helpers, 192–
193. *See also jami karawa;* peccaries,
white-lipped; shamans; water spirits
annatto: and animal spirits, 188, 190, 257n4;
at end of mourning, 232; marker of
humanity, 120, 155, 188; in menstruation,
123; painting of corpse, 201; repelling
jaguars, 125; in shamanic curing, 155
anthropology and cannibalism, xxii–xxiii,
xxviii–xxix, 3, 6–8, 13–14, 87, 88, 90,
93–95, 238–239; in Wari' contact, 53,
56
Araweté, xxvi, 153, 260n8
Arens, William, 6–7, 11, 22, 253n6(Ch.1)
ascites, 191

277